A WORD IN SEASON

A Word in Season

PERSPECTIVES ON CHRISTIAN WORLD MISSIONS

Lesslie Newbigin

WILLIAM B. EERDMANS PUBLISHING COMPANY
GRAND RAPIDS, MICHIGAN

SAINT ANDREW PRESS
EDINBURGH

© 1994 Wm. B. Eerdmans Publishing Co.

255 Jefferson Ave. S.E., Grand Rapids, Michigan 49503

Published jointly 1994 in the United States by
Wm. B. Eerdmans Publishing Co.
and in the U.K. by
Saint Andrew Press
121 George Street, Edinburgh EH2 4YN, Scotland

Printed in the United States of America

00 99 98 97 96 95 94   7 6 5 4 3 2 1

Library of Congress Cataloging-in-Publication Data

Newbigin, Lesslie.
A word in season / Lesslie Newbigin.
p.   cm.
Includes bibliographical references.
ISBN 0-8028-0730-5 (paper)
1. Mission — Theory.   I. Title.
BV2063.N43   1994
266 — dc20   94-19013
                                             CIP

Saint Andrew Press ISBN 0 7152 0704 0

Contents

Editor's Introduction

The genesis of this book is rather unusual and so needs to be explained, if only to account for the fact that someone who is a church historian and former archivist is called upon to edit a book of which the major theme is mission. Normally collections like this appear when someone is dead, and not only is Bishop Lesslie Newbigin (at 84) very much alive, but his ideas have moved even further along the road he is traveling since the "canon" of this volume was closed. Indeed, it was with great reluctance that I had to say that the latest paper he has given ("Religious Pluralism, a Missiological Approach," in *Studia Missionalia*, vol. 42, 1993) could not be included, even though the final four pages are a magnificent "Credo." Many other significant pieces also had to be rejected in order to focus on the theme of mission.

Following the success of Bishop Newbigin's previous publications, Mr. William Eerdmans wrote to him to ask if he had anything unpublished that ought to be published, or any project in hand. This was just as Bishop Newbigin was preparing to leave Selly Oak in August 1992. He had unearthed five folders of talks, lectures, and articles either unpublished or published previously only in German or Dutch. I first got to know Bishop Newbigin in 1975 when I was pursuing my research into the life of Dr. William Paton and was setting up an ecumenical archives center in the Selly Oak Colleges. Bishop Newbigin decided to deposit his papers in that center and to allow me to extract a selection for publication. The papers span the period 1960–1992, but papers directly linked to the Gospel as Public Truth project were omitted, for obvious reasons.

These chapters include formal sermons, lectures, articles composed for publication in another language, and transcripts of more informal taped conversation. As with the second edition of *Unfinished Agenda,* care has been taken not to alter basic speech patterns unless the transcription has produced something ungrammatical or incomprehensible. It is hoped that those who have heard Bishop Newbigin talk or deliver a paper will have no difficulty hearing those distinctive tones again. It seems important to do this for one who is so aware of language constricting meaning or molding philosophy. Although the papers are addressed to widely diverse audiences in America and Europe, ranging across the whole spectrum of "liberals," "evangelicals," and "pietists" to the subscribers of the *Ecumenical Review,* the *Expository Times,* the *International Bulletin of Missions,* and *Kerk en Theologie,* they show a remarkable consistency. While the proponents of Thatcherism may not appreciate this (privatization is a dirty word in this book), Bishop Newbigin has a remarkably broad appeal. This is so rare in these times of the polarization and fragmentation of church and society that for that reason alone it would be worth publishing these papers.

Meanwhile I had moved to Lancaster to take up a post at St. Martin's College, where I found that *The Other Side of 1984* was a prescribed text for the course on Christian doctrine and that other Newbigin writings formed an invaluable part of the "Dialogue and Mission" course. In other institutions also Bishop Newbigin's books form an essential part of a variety of courses. This provides a second reason for producing this book. Also for this reason the book has been provided with copious footnotes. The plain fact of the matter is that despite the efforts of ecumenical historians like myself, many of the people mentioned by Bishop Newbigin have been forgotten, or never had a very high public profile. The most obvious example is J. H. Oldham, with whom Newbigin shares more than a Scottish connection. Myths need to be laid to rest — for example, what the "great new fact of our time" (in 1942) really is. But more important, it is earnestly to be hoped that the student or layperson reading this book, or even just dipping into one article, will want to go further and read either Newbigin's sources or his own further writings on the subject. For this purpose a bibliography has also been provided. Since Newbigin's theology is highly contextual, arising from his yearning to address a word from his context to that of his audience, it is most opportune that a second edition of his fascinating autobiography, *Unfinished Agenda,* with a provocative new final chapter, has just appeared (St. Andrew Press, 1993). There is more than a little autobiographical material in this present volume as well. Finally, it should be noted that because much of this book was originally spoken rather than written, it is more accessible than some of his books. Given the high quality of Eerdmans' covers, one may confidently say that it can be read in the bath as well as the study.

However, this book is not published simply to provide a handy work of reference or a help to students. While it could have been called "Newbigin in a nutshell" because it represents the quintessence of his thought, it is primarily a statement of a message he still feels bound to proclaim. "Not that I have already obtained this or am already perfect; but I press on to make it my own, because Christ Jesus has made me his own . . . forgetting what lies behind and straining forward to what lies ahead, I press on toward the goal for the prize of the upward call of God in Christ Jesus" (Phil. 3:12–14). This book is an invitation to share that quest.

Inevitably in a work of this kind, there is much repetition of material both within the work and overlapping with works already published. General Simatoupong's appearances have been kept to a minimum, but his question "Can the West be converted?" will not go away and its repetition in this book demonstrates its importance. In fact, the book is to be seen in a similar way to Brahms' Variations on the Saint Antony Chorale. The theme is always there as an undercurrent in the rhapsody as the pilgrims press on to their goal, singing. So it is with Newbigin here, and the equally compelling theme is mission.

This book begins with a sermon preached at the Riverside Church in New York when Bishop Newbigin was traveling in America to explain the principles behind the integration of the International Missionary Council (IMC) and the World Council of Churches (WCC). It provides a baseline of the principles that inspire unity in mission. This is expanded in two further talks in the series given at the time to explain the changes in the structure and pattern of the missionary enterprise and the changes appearing in the theology of mission. Unfortunately, the middle lecture in the series, on mission in relation to the demand for social justice, has been lost. In attacking the paternalism and dependency relationships of modern mission structures, by harking back to Roland Allen's ideas (c. 1904), Newbigin not only makes many practical suggestions that have since been realized, but points the way forward to a new ecclesiology based on the "all in each place" formula. It is a question of doing things not so much in the *right* spirit as in *the* Spirit, and trusting to the power of the Spirit. One realizes that if these talks are interesting because so much has changed since 1960, they are also a challenge because so much has not changed.

The next three articles address specific "front-line" situations: mission in a modern city, which is Madras in 1974, though the questions raised have a wider relevance; the pastor's role in the inner city (Winson Green, Birmingham); and the future of the parish church. In all three articles there is a wide vision of mission as the work of the whole Christian community, and strong criticism of any whiff of clerical monopolies or denominationalism.

Bishop Newbigin then moves to the more difficult frontier created by the resistance of modern society to the gospel and addresses the problems of evangelism that face us when we are so conditioned by our culture that we mistake customs and conventions of modern philosophy for eternal truth. In the manner of Luther describing the "Babylonian Captivity of the Church," Newbigin describes the cultural captivity of the Church (in Stuttgart, 1984). His diagnosis of the wrong turns taken in Western thought since 1648 is well known, but bears reexamination, not only because he touched a raw nerve, somewhat in the way that J. A. T. Robinson's *Honest to God* did, but also because so few theologians have taken seriously the challenge of the philosophy of modern science. Newbigin devotes as much care to this as he ever did to the claims of Vedantism. Nothing less than a reconstruction of the premises of systematic theology is required in response to this. Thus Newbigin asks, "By what authority" do we operate? If it was the burning question for Jesus' audience in the temple, it is no less so today.

Secularization and the other symptoms of Western society are then addressed in this book as well as the consequences of witness in a world of religious and ideological pluralism. Finally Newbigin sets the agenda for mission for friends in the Netherlands, students in Edinburgh, missionaries in Dublin, and indeed all concerned with obedience in faith today. Invited to "dream dreams" by the editor of the *Ecumenical Review,* he does just that, and is no less challenging in 1991 than in 1960. Perhaps the most significant pages come in the final chapter, "Learning to Live in the Spirit in Our European Home" (Hannover, 1992), where he reveals the sources of his strength for meeting this challenge. There is no easy solution for any of the problems he exposes, but by breaking down the old parameters of thought, he makes it possible for us to appreciate the "enduring validity of cross-cultural mission."

Consistent with his approach to our cultural limitations, Bishop Newbigin has adopted "inclusive" language in his most recent works. However, pronouns have not been changed in earlier papers because that would be anachronistic.

I cannot close this introduction without a word of thanks to my colleagues Dr. Brian Gates and Dr. Francesca Murphy for encouraging this project; to my long-suffering husband, Klaus-Dieter Stoll, for domestic support; to my young sons for putting up with deferred holidays and trips to the park; and above all to Christine Armstrong for deciphering not only my scrawl but also that of Bishop Newbigin, and for producing a high-quality manuscript and disk. Thanks also are due to Bishop Newbigin himself for so patiently answering my constant questions. Hopefully this book does justice to the fullness of Bishop Newbigin's vision and forms a tiny part of the Good News in Christ.

Carey Day, August 1993   ELEANOR JACKSON

1

A Riverside Sermon

The great new fact of our time, which the Edinburgh Conference saw and hailed with joy, is the fact that the Church of the Lord Jesus Christ is now for the first time a universal family present in almost every nation. We rejoice in that fact. But we grievously misrepresent this fact if we forget that the church is present everywhere *as the home base for a world missionary task:* rejoicing in the existence of the younger churches and helping them in their tasks must not become a substitute for missionary commitment. Interchurch relations are not a substitute for foreign missions. Global ecclesiastical introversion does not cease to be introversion by being global. It is necessary to say this rather sharply in order to separate a false from a true understanding of the new situation we are in. The Church is in the world for the sake of the world, and its concern is with the whole world. The specifically missionary concern is with the world that is outside the Church and does not acknowledge Jesus as Lord. God has brought us — through the faithfulness of his servants — to the point where the Church is present now in almost every land. But we do not stop there; we press on to the ends of the earth. This perspective of the ends of the earth is essential to the integrity of the Church's confession that

---

Extract from a sermon delivered 25 May 1960 at Riverside Church in New York, at the observance of the fiftieth anniversary of the World Missionary Conference held in Edinburgh in 1910.

Jesus Christ is Lord — essential anywhere, whether the Church is old or young, strong or weak. The Church, wherever it is, is not only Christ's witness to its own people and nation, but also the home base for a mission to the ends of the earth. It is not enough to say of the younger churches, "They and we are brethren — they being Christ's witnesses there in Asia and Africa, and we here in America." On the contrary, both they and we can only confess Christ truly where we go with him to the ends of the earth. So on the one hand we can rejoice as we see the churches of Asia sending out two hundred missionaries beyond their own borders and planning missions to some of the big cities of Europe and North America. On the other hand *we* must recognize that our obligation to take the gospel to the ends of the earth is as urgent and compelling in 1960 as it was in 1910. Our witness must be in some recognizable sense a joint witness, so that men may see not us but God, who has made us partners and brothers who were once strangers and foreigners to each other. I am not asking for large organizations, for the wholesale pooling of funds and resources. I do not believe that this would be helpful. I am asking for a variety of specific arrangements in particular cases, in which Christians of different nations and denominations pool their efforts in such a way that men will recognize in our mission not the remnants of colonialism and the cultural expansion of the West, but the going forth into all the world of him who is the Savior of the World.

The forms and patterns of the missionary task are changing and will change as the consequence of the fact that the Church is now worldwide. But the missionary task is still fundamentally the same — to go forth outside the frontiers of Christendom and make Christ known among all the nations. That colossal task is still largely ahead of us. The meeting of the gospel with the great non-Christian religions has hardly yet begun. There is no possible ground for any

1. This statement became the famous "All in Each Place" declaration on Christian unity of the World Council of Churches World Assembly held in New Delhi in 1961, to be found in W. A. Visser 't Hooft, ed., *The New Delhi Report* (London: SCM, 1962), p. 116. Lukas Vischer, ed., *A Documentary History of the Faith and Order Movement 1927–63* (St. Louis: Bethany Press, 1963), 144f. gives the full report.

slackening of the foreign missionary concern. We must press on together as partners in obedience towards the goal, to the prize of the high calling of God in Jesus Christ.

The Edinburgh Conference, after speaking of comity, conference, and joint action, went on to speak of unity. It was precluded by its terms of reference from discussing questions of faith and order on which the churches disagreed; but whatever its terms of reference, it could not avoid recognizing the fact that the question of unity was involved in faithfulness to the missionary task. In fact, its Committee on Unity and Cooperation unanimously endorsed the judgment of the Missionary Conference of Shanghai three years earlier that "the purpose of foreign mission is the creation in every country of a single united church." That was fifty years ago. It was a passion for the evangelization of the world that produced that sentence. Men who had stood up in the streets of great Asian cities to preach the gospel knew that the issue could not be avoided. You have to answer the question, "What is the fellowship into which the evangelist is inviting the convert?" Is it a body that represents one cultural and religious segment of mankind, or is it a fellowship that represents in principle simply mankind as a whole, redeemed and recreated in its true image through Jesus Christ? If we define the task of the Christian world mission as offering the whole gospel to the whole world, then it cannot be other than the whole Church, the whole healed and reconciled fellowship of men in Jesus Christ, that offers this invitation. The question of the unity of the Church is thus not a question of the size or number of our churches. It is a question of the meaning of our churchmanship. It is not a question of taking the existing denominational structures and riveting them together on a wider frame to form one structure of the same kind. That picture of reunion rightly frightens many who have a true understanding of the nature of the Church. The task of reunion can never be severed from the task of renewal. The search for unity is in principle a penitent return to the Lord of the Church himself with the prayer that he may show us where we have gone astray, and may give us again that unity in him that will enable men to recognize in the Church the lineaments of the household of God. The proper bearer of a universal gospel is a universal fellowship.

We cannot, with any hope of being believed, preach to men the word of our Lord that he, when he is lifted up from the earth, will draw all men to himself, if we continue stubbornly to say that even his love is not enough to draw us close to one another and enable us to live together as brethren in one family. The task of Christian reunion must begin with penitent and believing prayer to the Lord of the Church himself that he may so cleanse and renew the Church that men everywhere may be able to recognize in the Church of Christ their own true home. Then men who see us under whatever sky and from whatever tribe may be constrained to say: This is not a strange or foreign thing, this is my Father's house, this is home.

The Edinburgh Conference spoke of the unity of the Church as a vision very far off, but they were not ashamed to confess that it was the goal towards which they must move. I believe that we have reached the point in the story of the ecumenical movement when we must ask ourselves whether we still agree about the goal, and whether, having traveled this road together for fifty years, we have come near enough to define our goal with greater accuracy. That is the question being put to the World Council of Churches by its Faith and Order Commission in the report that is to come before the meetings in Scotland this summer. The council, and through it the member churches, will be asked whether they are willing to accept a more precise statement of the nature of the unity that we seek than has been possible up till now. I believe this discussion will be of vital significance to the future of the ecumenical movement. It will show whether the movement can still move; whether our present forms of cooperation are to be recognized as a stage on the way to a full recovery of the proper form of the Church or fixed as a permanent substitute for it; whether we are willing to be a pilgrim people ever ready to forget what lies behind and press on towards the goal. Every movement that gathers to itself great reserves in men, in experience, and in money runs the risk of becoming chiefly interested in its own existence and development. The ecumenical movement is not immune from these dangers. It behooves us to remember that we are called to be dwellers in tents, not in houses, that we are never to be content with what has been done, but always to press on towards the goal, to the prize of the high calling of God in Christ Jesus. The true fulfillment of the ecumenical movement will come when its organizational structures are no longer necessary because the Church itself has been led — through whatever sufferings and humiliations — to the recovery of its true unity, its true form as the one household of God in which the redeemed of every nation are at home.

I have been speaking of the ecumenical movement, of churches, of councils. But of course in the end it is not to these that the Word of God is addressed: it is addressed to men and women. Tonight this word is spoken to us. We have been thinking of the great soldiers and servants of Christ who went before us in this work, men who spent themselves to the uttermost in his service and have now gone from our sight. This work is now put in our hands. Let us — as men and women who are on our way to the judgment seat of God — listen again to the words of the great apostle (Phil. 3:8–14):

> For his sake I have suffered the loss of all things, and count them as refuse, in order that I may gain Christ and be found in him, not having a righteousness of my own, based on law, but that which is through faith in Christ, the righteousness from God that depends on faith; that I may know him and the power of his resurrection, and may share his sufferings, becoming like him in his death, that if possible I may attain the resurrection from the dead.

> Not that I have already obtained this or am already perfect; but I press on to make it my own, because Jesus Christ has made me his own. Brethren, I do not consider that I have made it my own; but one thing I do, forgetting what lies behind and straining forward to what lies ahead, I press on toward the goal for the prize of the upward call of God in Christ Jesus.

Does that describe you and me, brethren? Is that the impression that people get when they look at us in this ecumenical movement? Do we count everything rubbish for Christ's sake — power, position, security, a good reputation? Do we count it a privilege if we have some share in his sufferings? And do we know the power of his resurrection? Is our life and work marked by that supernatural quality for which there is no name except holiness, and no explanation except the presence of the Holy Spirit himself? Are we pressing forward with that goal before us — to be holy as he is holy? Let us not deceive ourselves. Everything we say about unity and mission, about drawing all nations into the one household of God, about being Christ's witnesses and servants to the ends of the earth, remains mere clap-trap — except on one condition: that there is at the heart of it all a supernatural life lived here in this twentieth century in the form of the Holy Spirit, a life that has its roots deep down in a discipline of secret prayer and self-denial, and its fruit in a strong and cleansing charity. Here also it is always a matter of pressing on towards the goal. If you stand still you slide back. We are on pilgrimage, not in permanent quarters. We serve a Lord who for the joy set before him went forward to the Cross, despising the shame. If we would follow him, we must press on, not slacking, not accepting any concordat with the world, not looking for ease or security, but seeking only to offer him new obedience day by day until he comes.

2

The Pattern of the Christian World Mission

In these three talks I want to say something about the changes both in the pattern or structure of the missionary enterprise and in the theological understanding of the missionary enterprise that are necessitated by the profound changes in the world situation and in the situation of missions.

It is not necessary to speak at great length concerning the changes in the situation of missions. I will very briefly speak of three — first, what one might call the reversal of the tides of world power. The missionary movement as we know it today, the modern missionary movement, took its rise and acquired its characteristic pattern and psychology in a period when the tides of political power, of economic and cultural expansion, were flowing out from western Europe and North America into the other parts of the world. It was assumed both in the Western world and in most of the rest of the world that it was the white races who determined the general direction and speed of the events throughout the world. The missionary effort of the churches of

---

The first of a series of three talks given in New York in late 1960 as part of a program to assist the integration of the International Missionary Council (IMC) and World Council of Churches (WCC). The manuscript of the second lecture has unfortunately been lost. It was probably on mission in relation to secular events. The third lecture forms the next chapter of this book.

western Europe and North America was just flowing down the current, down the stream of world power, and its pattern of thought and action was profoundly shaped by that fact. For vast multitudes in Asia and Africa, the great fact of our time is not the so-called East-West conflict; it is not the conquest of interplanetary space by man. It is the ending of the era of the dominance of the white races. Missions, which have been accustomed to flowing down the current of world power, are now faced with the necessity of learning for the first time to swim against the current. (If you want bibliography for that, read K. M. Panikkar, *Asia and Western Dominance,* especially the last chapter.)[1]

The second closely related fact is the renaissance of the non-Christian religions. In the great period of missionary expansion, in the past two hundred years, the non-Christian faiths were to a large extent passive in relation to missionary advance. Their resistance to it was a conservative resistance. Today the situation is wholly different. These non-Christian faiths have passed over to the offensive. They are mounting an increasingly effective counterattack. Their ablest representatives are confident that they have taken the measure of Christianity and have nothing further to fear from it. They are convinced that they have learned what they need to learn from Christianity, that they have rediscovered the forgotten depths of their own faiths, and that they are now in a position to offer to twentieth-century man a more satisfactory answer to the problems of existence than Christianity can. They see the age that has ended as an age in which the white races, the so-called Christian countries, had an opportunity for world leadership and threw it away. I think it is difficult for those who have not lived outside of Europe or North America to appreciate the extent to which our Western civilization has discredited itself before the rest of the world. Our frightful wars, our atomic bombs, and our lamentable moral standards are together quite sufficient to convince most of the non-Christian world that any claim that we may make for moral leadership in the world can be laughed out of court. The educated Hindu — if I may speak of what I know best — the

1. K. M. Panikkar, *Asia and Western Dominance: A Survey of the Vasco da Gama Era of Asian History, 1498–1945* (London: George Allen & Unwin, 1953); see also his *Foundations of New India* (London: George Allen & Unwin, 1963).

educated Hindu of today feels no sense whatsoever of inferiority in the face of our Western civilization with regard to technical and scientific aspects. He feels quite competent to master them, and plunges freely into the stream of modern technological advance without any sense that he is thereby losing his moorings in the ancient faith of his fathers. As for its religious aspect, he is completely confident that he has in the Vedanta a standpoint from which he can both appreciate what is good and useful in Christianity, and also see it as merely one of the local and temporary relative attempts to express in human terms the inexpressible truth that is finally embodied in the mystical and metaphysical tradition of the Vedanta.[2] Naturally he regards Christian missions as a deplorable attempt to present a relative approximation of the truth as absolute truth, and as in fact simply a survival or a hangover from the colonial era that can be tolerated simply because it is totally ineffective.

The third new fact is the rise of "younger churches"[3] to positions

2. Vedantism ("The end of the Vedas"), also called Uttara Mimamsa ("further inquiry"), is based on the Brahma Sutras of Badarayana, written in the first century A.D. Its most important exponent was Sankara (788?–820), but since leading modern thinkers such as Vivekananda, Aurobindo, and Radhakrishnan took up the system, it has been of enormous influence in the twentieth century. In it the only reality is Brahman, the world soul, with whom both the human soul and God are identified. Compared with this higher truth, the world with its multiplicity of forms, shapes, and feelings is an illusion. Realization of truth brings liberation. Originally devised to refute the claims of Buddhism, the system is monist. The Ramakrishna order has popularized the system and anchored it firmly to social and religious reform. See A. L. Basham, *The Wonder That Was India* (New York: Collins, 1961); N. K. Devarajah, *Hinduism and the Modern Age* (New Delhi, 1975).

3. The term *younger churches* became popular in the ecumenical movement as their representatives found a voice at the Jerusalem 1928 IMC Conference, partly because indigenous church leaders had stepped into the breach when European missionaries were withdrawn or interned in 1915, partly because the YMCA, YWCA, and SCM had raised up independent-minded, well-educated third world leaders, and partly because of patriotic demand for change. The term referred to the fact that most of the churches concerned were founded after 1800, and replaced the now offensive term *native churches* that was used at Edinburgh in 1910. However, it was redolent of paternalism, if not of racism, and since the IMC/WCC integration it has been rejected in turn. See H. R. Weber, *Asia and the Ecumenical Movement* (London: SCM, 1963); E. M. Jackson, *Red Tape and the Gospel* (Selly Oak, 1980), chaps. 7–8.

of maturity and authority. The existence of a great family of churches in all parts of Asia and Africa and the islands of the sea as the fruit of the missionary effort of the past two hundred years is one of the great facts of our time. The Christian mission from the Western world has been slow to recognize all the implications of this fact, but theological seriousness has required us to acknowledge that the existence of the younger churches invalidates much of the traditional pattern of the nineteenth-century Western missionary operation. If, as we must do, we acknowledge that the "younger church" is simply the body of Christ in the place where it is set, that it is the Church of God, the temple of the Holy Spirit, then it is no longer possible to conceive of the missionary task as something directed from a home base here in Europe and carried on from this base over the head of the younger church in the territory beyond. The center of the operation is there, with the church that God has placed there. This means that there is, as Dr. Walter Freytag said at the Ghana Assembly in 1957, a certain "lost directness" in the missionary task.[4] It is no longer in quite the old sense a matter of going straight out from Christendom to heathendom. The missionary must place himself at the disposal of the body that is there, that God has placed there in the midst of heathendom as his appointed agent and witness. At once the question arises: Is the missionary today an asset or a liability for that church? He may bring with him very valuable gifts. But his foreignness, his imperfect understanding of the language and the culture of the people, and his obvious connection with the former colonial power may make him in many situations a liability. He may fail to detect the aroma of colonialism that still tends to hang about a mission station even in countries where the colonial era has ended in the political sphere. Who then can be surprised if many young missionaries, including precisely the most able and alert and spiritually sensitive among them, are uncertain as to whether they are in the right place?

These three changes, these three facts — the reversal of the tides of world power, the renaissance of the non-Christian faiths, and the rise of the younger churches — add up to a change in the whole situation

4. Ronald Orchard, *Report of the Meeting of the IMC Held in Accra, Ghana, 1957* (London, 1958).

so profound that it is understandable if on one hand the missionary enterprise appears to many in both East and West as an anachronism, and on the other hand the missionary administrator or director is pulled out of his office chair into his study chair, being compelled to rethink the basis of both the pattern and the motive of the missionary task.

The first and fundamental thing that needs to be said about the pattern of the Christian missionary enterprise is that we must recover the sense that it is the enterprise of the whole Church of God in every land, directed towards the whole world in which it is put. We have to recover a sense of the Christian mission based upon such fundamental scriptural texts as the word of our Lord in John 12:32 — "I, when I am lifted up from the earth, will draw all men to myself." This gives a picture of the Church as the body that is drawn together by the risen and exalted Christ and that exists in the world everywhere as the agent of his gathering grace. We need to think of it in terms of the great power of John 17:18, 21: "As thou didst send me into the world, so I have sent them into the world. [I pray for them] that they may all be one . . . that the world may believe." We need to think of it in terms of the whole argument of the Ephesian letter, as the working of God to break down the middle wall of partition, and to provide the place of reconciliation where all races and peoples are brought together in a single body through the cross (Eph. 4:15–16).

In other words, the immediate task of the missionary enterprise today can be formulated in the following terms: to recognize and to draw the practical conclusions from the fact that the home base of missions is now worldwide. The necessity of this task arises from two facts. Firstly, there is the simple fact that the Christian Church is no longer confined to a small part of the world, but is, though in many places a small minority, to be found in almost every country. This is the "great new fact of our time," as Archbishop Temple called it in 1942.[5] The second fact is the rediscovery of the biblical truth that the missionary responsibility belongs to the Church as such wherever it is, that the Church — as Emil Brunner puts it in a much-quoted phrase — "exists by mission as fire exists by burning."

---

5. F. A. Iremonger, *William Temple, Archbishop of Canterbury: His Life and Letters* (London, 1948), p. 387.

These two facts — one, that the Church is now no longer restricted to one part of the earth's surface, but is global in its extension, and two, the rediscovery of the theological truth that the mission is not a detachable part of the Church's being, but is the central meaning of the Church's being — these two facts require that we place as the number one priority in the missionary enterprise today the recognition of the fact that the whole base of missions is now in every country, and draw the consequence of this. This means we must move the Christian missionary enterprise out of the colonial era into a radically new situation. This is easy to say, but difficult to do. The pattern of the modern missionary movement, its attitudes and methods, were shaped by the fact that missionaries of the modern era (I am not speaking of course about missionaries of the early centuries) were also representatives of the expanding and colonizing races of the West. In this respect the modern missionary movement has been totally different from what we find in the New Testament. The modern missionary movement has depended, in a manner unparalleled in the New Testament, upon the continuing guidance, support, and direction of the "daughter" church by the "mother" church. There is no parallel to that in the Acts of the Apostles. The young churches of the modern missionary movement have been from the beginning placed in a position of dependence that is not only financial and administrative but also spiritual. The struggle of both the older and the younger churches to break out of this false situation and to recover a true relationship of spiritual equality has been at the center of the missionary movement for the past two or three decades. The ending of the colonial era in most parts of the world has hastened analogous developments in the church, but it is very unfortunate if the changes are accepted merely as a necessary consequence of the pressure of political events instead of being accepted as a theological imperative. What is needed is the widespread and deep recovery throughout the churches, old and young alike, of the truth that to be a Christian is to be part of a universal fellowship in which all are committed to participation in Christ's reconciling work for the whole world. The traditional picture of the missionary enterprise has been of the lonely pioneer going out from the secure citadel of Christendom into the world of heathendom. Today the picture must be redrawn. It must be the picture of one universal family present in almost every land, possessing the secret of reconciliation to God through Jesus Christ and offering that secret to all nations and peoples.

As one of the practical consequences of that picture, I suggest, first, that every church, however small and weak, ought to have some share in the task of taking the gospel to the ends of the earth. Every church ought to be engaged in foreign mission. This is part of the integrity of the gospel. We do not adequately confess Christ as the Lord of all men if we seek to be his witnesses only among our neighbors. We must seek at the same time to confess him to the ends of the earth. The foreign missionary enterprise belongs to the integrity of our confession. This confession is brought into living relationship with the other faiths by which men seek to guide their lives only if it remains a living confession. Without this actual meeting it becomes a mere slogan. And the dimension of the ends of the earth must be part of our acting, not merely of our speaking, if we will truly confess his Lordship. It is a very encouraging fact that the young churches of Asia are now accepting the responsibility to take the gospel to the lands beyond their own borders. At the Assembly of the East Asia Christian Conference at Kuala Lumpur in Malaya last year, it was important that there were already some two hundred missionaries of the Asian churches working in lands beyond their own borders, and plans were developed at Kuala Lumpur for extending this work, the foreign mission of the Asian churches, to some of the big cities of Europe and North America, especially where there are large non-Christian Asian populations. An increase in the foreign missionary activity of the younger churches will help to put the whole missionary enterprise into a more biblical perspective.

Second, there must be such a measure of internationalization of missions as will help to remove the taint of colonialism and meet the real needs of the rapidly changing situations in many countries. When, for instance, the National Christian Council of India pleads with the Indian government to permit the entry of foreign missionaries on the ground that the presence of these foreign missionaries is a symbol of the international character of the Church, the false impression is given that this is merely giving a new name to an old commodity, and that in fact missionaries simply represent the continuance in the ecclesiastical sphere of the colonial relationship that has been ended in the political sphere. It is necessary to be able to show that something more has happened than a mere change of terminology. It is necessary for the integrity of our preaching of the gospel that this gospel should come to all nations in the name of a body that is truly ecumenical, that represents in some recognizable way not merely the religion of the West, but the Savior of the world.

There are many situations that cannot effectively be tackled by one mission or even by the missions of one country working together. In most of the territories of Asia and Africa, missions from more than one country have worked. If they work in isolation from each other, following different methods, and with different kinds of resources, only confusion will result. Intimate and constant collaboration is necessary. A few examples will indicate this point. The first is the problem of penetration of the great non-Christian cultures by the gospel. It has long been recognized that Christianity has won its converts only from the outer fringes of Asian society, and that in general the great non-Christian cultures of Asia remain almost entirely opaque to the gospel. In fact there is less real contact between the gospel and these non-Christian faiths than there was fifty years ago. The situation calls for the mobilization of the able minds of the Church to assist the process of contact and dialogue between Christians and non-Christians. This is something that cannot be achieved by the efforts of any individual mission; it can only be achieved on an ecumenical basis. The recognition of this has led the International Missionary Council over the past three or four years to sponsor the creation of a series of centers for the study of the non-Christian faiths[6] in the Near East, in Pakistan, at Bangalor in India, in Ceylon, in Burma, in Hong Kong, and now this year for the first time in Japan. These study centers are on an international and ecumenical basis. They represent a concerted

---

6. About these centers for the study of non-Christian faiths, see "Mission to Six Continents," in *The Ecumenical Advance: A History of the Ecumenical Movement,* vol. 2, *1948–68,* ed. Harold Fey (London: SPCK, 1970), 171–197; "Developments during 1962: An Editorial Survey," *International Review of Missions (IRM)* 52:3–14, 242–246, 369–373, 508–512; Stanley Samartha, *Living Faiths and the Ecumenical Movement* (Geneva: WCC, 1971).

ecumenical effort to bring the gospel into living touch with the great non-Christian faiths.

A second example is what we call the Islam-in-Africa project. For a long time it has been a matter of serious concern that Islam is spreading in large areas of Africa south of the Sahara, but that the churches and missions in those areas have little knowledge of Islam, little experience of it, and little idea of how to bring about a creative encounter between the gospel and Islam. Again it is a problem that cannot be tackled by any one mission, or even by the missions of one nation. So what is now underway is the development of a very simple piece of ecumenical organization by which specialists — theologians who are also scholars in the field of Islamic studies — are sent from many different churches or mission boards to key centers in different parts of tropical Africa, there to work as the center of all churches and missions in that area, providing training, teaching, and leadership in respect to the Church's contact with Islam. It is an ecumenical effort in which churches of different confessions and different nations are collaborating. It involves no elaborate machinery, it is very simple, but it is sufficient to indicate that we are speaking not on behalf of one culture or one power or one part of the world, but in the name of the ecumenical fellowship in Christ.

A third example that may well occur in the near future is an analogous effort to meet the spiritual problems arising from the rapid urbanization in Africa. Ecumenical teams could be stationed in key centers where urbanization is proceeding at a tremendous rate. It will be seen from these examples that what is contemplated is not the creation of an international missionary bureaucracy, a sort of super mission board. What is needed, and experience shows that it is possible, is a series of simple and flexible organs of cooperation by which the missionary work of the Church at these vital points will be both strong enough to meet the real situation and also recognizable as the mission of the universal fellowship that is as wide as mankind.

There must be a genuine partnership between older and younger churches for making decisions about the great issues of missionary enterprise. The present structure of relationships inherited from the missionary methods of the nineteenth century does not allow for this genuine partnership. It sounds like a very simple idea to say that the whole Christian Church throughout the world should be regarded as one fellowship in which the stronger will help the weaker. But it is much less simple than it appears, because we are facing the problem of the selfhood of the "younger churches." This problem arises from the fact that under the spiritual and financial dominance of the older churches, it has been exceedingly difficult for the younger churches to achieve spiritual freedom, a sense of responsibility to God, a sense of genuine selfhood.

We are familiar with the fact that the cutting off of all foreign missionary help to the church in China, rather than being regarded as a disaster by the Christians in China, was held by them as a deliverance that made them feel for the first time free to be themselves. We cannot reflect too long or too deeply upon the significance of that fact. And I have to confess that as a missionary in India, I have sometimes been tempted to pray that all foreign money and all foreign personnel might somehow or other be cut off from the church in India, because it seemed as though there were no other way the church in India could achieve a real spiritual freedom.

The place where I first worked as a missionary — a town called Kanchipuram — had nearby a small village called Muthupettu where some fifty years previously two men had been converted and baptized and then had become the foundation for the Christian church. My predecessor,[7] out of a generous desire to protect these two converts from the troubles of this world, had bought a piece of land for them, divided it in two, and presented it to them. The result of this charitable action is that there has never been another convert in that village, and it is possible to conceive that there never will be another convert short of the second coming, because if there were another convert that piece of land would have to be divided into three. That is a small symbol of a spiritual situation that profoundly affects the life of the younger churches. The financial and administrative power of the Western

7. This was the great J. H. MacLean, who claimed to be the first British SVMU volunteer, and was popularly believed to have rain-making powers. He retired from India in 1942, having been one of the architects of the CSI. See Lesslie Newbigin, *Unfinished Agenda*, 2nd ed. (Edinburgh: St. Andrew Press, 1993), 49f., 52f., 68f. For Newbigin's ministry in Kanchipuram, see ibid., chaps. 6–8.

missions — a power, remember, that St. Paul never had — has created a situation in which it is possible for the Church to be a sort of vested interest for the original Christian families, and in which it is exceedingly difficult for the Church to be quite simply the people of God responsible for the whole village.

Therefore, like other missionaries, I have been tempted to pray that somehow or other all foreign support might be cut off from the church in India. And yet, that is only half of the dilemma, for the other half is this: I had been sent to India as a missionary to preach the gospel, to make Christ known to the whole people of India. Can I return to the church that sent me and say I am no longer needed, my mission is finished, I am returning home — when only 3 percent of the people of India have accepted the gospel, and probably 90 percent of the people of India have never heard of the gospel? Will not my own church that sent me reply, this is not mission completed, it is mission abandoned? There may be a case in certain situations for a temporary withdrawal of missionary support for the sake of the younger church. But it cannot be that the Christian mission as a whole can speak in terms of withdrawal when the unfinished evangelistic task is so stupendous in certain respects, so much greater than it was when the first missionary pioneers of the modern missionary movement set out. Is there a way out of this dilemma? Is there a way that the strength of the older churches can be used for the task of world evangelization without spiritually weakening the younger churches? I believe that there is.

First we must look at the reason for the present weakness. Each of the younger churches is at present locked into a relationship with a single mission board in the West. This one-way relationship between one body that is always the donor and the other body that is always the recipient does not provide the circumstances in which genuine partnership in freedom can be achieved. The older churches and mission boards feel themselves under an obligation to limit their financial support for the sake of the spiritual independence of the younger churches. But this means that fewer resources are available for the task of world evangelization. In the effort to escape from the relationship of paternalism on the one hand and dependence on the other, mission boards have taken as their goal the famous trinity:

self-supporting, self-governing, and self-propagating churches.[8] This has been for many decades the target that mission boards have set before themselves, but increasingly it is being recognized that this is a wrong statement of the goal. The true position of the church is neither dependence nor independence, but interdependence, a mutual interdependence of the different members of the one body that rests upon the absolute dependence of each upon God.

True interrelationships cannot evolve within the old pattern of one track between a single younger church and a single mission board. One of the very thrilling things we experienced at Kuala Lumpur at the inaugural assembly of the East Asia Christian Conference was to see the development of something new, a real sense of interdependence among the churches of Asia, based upon a sense of common responsibility to God for the witness of Christ. The peoples I lived among knew a great deal about the Church of Scotland, which was the church this mission had come from, but they did not know anything about the church in Indonesia, or the church in the Philippines, or the church in Sian, Thailand. They did not even know that there was a church there. This was the situation even twenty-five years ago. Today one can see the churches of Asia — of the Philippines, Thailand, Bangkok, Indonesia, Burma, Pakistan, Japan — coming together as one family, and accepting that "we are God's people in Asia, and we are responsible to God for the evangelization of Asia, and we therefore depend much upon one another for this task."

8. Best known in the form it took in China, where the "Three Selfs Movement" in the 1920s became the prewar demand for independence from European control, and then the postwar National Patriotic Committee coordinating the Protestant churches' relationships to the state. The idea is found *in nuce* in the writings of the Serampore Mission c. 1810, but being one of the few missions to achieve Newbigin's desiderata, they found themselves at odds with the BMS and could not maintain their independence after the Calcutta bank crash of 1832. Missionary administration professed these aims throughout the nineteenth century but only took effective devolution measures in the 1920s, when the "younger churches" were justifiably skeptical, suspecting the recession rather than theology as the motivating force. By then mission plant was impossible to sustain without overseas aid. See the discussion in Gordon Hewitt, *The Problems of Success: A History of the Church Missionary Society, 1910–42*, vol. 2 (London: SCM, 1977), 78–93, 211f.; David Paton, *Christian Missions and the Judgement of God* (London: SCM, 1952).

A growth of similar regional fellowships in Africa, and the first steps in the same direction in Latin America and in the South Pacific, are among the most encouraging developments of modern times. I believe that it is along this line that we shall break out of the dilemma I spoke of. One of the proposals that has been launched from the Kuala Lumpur conference is that in each area, in each territory, there shall be a periodic strategic conference at which all representatives of the churches and the representatives of the mission boards that cooperate with the churches can sit together around the table as equals, all potentially givers and all potentially receivers, to consider together the unfinished evangelistic task around them, and to agree together as to the deployment of the resources available for meeting that task. I believe that it is only in this multilateral pattern of relationships that we can achieve a genuine spiritual partnership between the older and younger churches, in which the resources of both can be used to the full for the completion of the unfinished evangelistic task.

Fourth and finally, there is need to bring members of the younger churches into more intimate contact with the life of the older churches, and especially with the tasks of missionary promotion and education in the whole churches of the West. I stress the importance of this for the following reasons.

Dr. Hendrik Kraemer has often said to us that the real meeting between the gospel and non-Christian faiths is still ahead of us. I believe that is true. And I think that the churches of the West are very illprepared for that meeting. The conception of missions, the conception of the heathen, the non-Christian people, that the Western churches are on the whole still working with and on the basis of which many of them continue to support foreign missions, is a picture that does not correspond with the reality. Unless I am much mistaken, the picture that is still projected on the screen when foreign missions are spoken about is largely a picture of the backward, the underprivileged, the underdeveloped, the sick, the blind, the uneducated, the ignorant. Consequently missions are able to appeal to the powerful motive of pity. This was possible in a day when the contacts between the Western churches and the great lands of Asia and Africa were very, very limited. Today the situation is different. Great numbers of not only students but also businessmen and government servants and people of all kinds move back and forth between the different parts of the earth. Ordinary church members in the West have the opportunity to meet the mature and cultured and highly competent representatives of the non-Christian religions, and the experience is something of a shock to them. The picture of the heathen that was in their minds is found to be invalidated, and the missionary appeal is therefore discredited. This means that precisely what Hendrik Kraemer has said is true, that there has not yet been a meeting between the gospel and the non-Christian world as it really is. We have been dealing with a picture of the non-Christian world that does not represent reality.

Now the ordinary Christian in the West is having the opportunity to meet a really spiritually mature representative of a non-Christian faith, and is having to ask himself seriously, perhaps for the first time: Is Jesus Christ the truth? Or is he only the name we give in the West, a symbol we have in the West, for that ultimate and universal experience of religion that is the general property of mankind? There is therefore no more important question before the churches in the West today than this: Will our methods of missionary promotion and education continue to work along the traditional lines, or can they become the means by which the ordinary church member in Europe or America is prepared for a real meeting of the gospel with the non-Christian faiths? I believe that one of the most practical ways of securing the right answer to this question would be to bring some of the ablest representatives of the younger churches for limited periods into the home organization desks of the great sending organizations of the Western churches.

The purpose of these few suggestions in the field of missionary practice is to ensure that the world mission of the Church is recognized as truly being not part of the cultural expansion of the Western world but simply the embassy of God's people on earth, the continuation of the mission of him who said, "I, when I am lifted up from the earth, will draw all men to myself" (John 12:32).

3

Missions and the Work of the Holy Spirit

In my talks yesterday morning I suggested that we have to think of the mission of the Church as the mission of the whole body of Christ on earth in every land, directed to the whole world, and that we must understand the home base of the foreign mission to be in every place that the Church is.

This morning I wish to complete this statement of the missionary task by saying that it is not enough for us to think in these terms if we neglect the very central teaching of the New Testament, that properly speaking the mission is the mission of the Holy Spirit. It is not necessary, I think, to remind you of the many places in the New Testament where this fact is emphasized. In Mark 13:11 it is said with regard to the witness of the Church to all the nations: "It is not you who speak, but the Holy Spirit." And the same thing can be illustrated at many different points. When he promises the coming of the comforter, our Lord says, "When the Counselor comes, whom I shall send to you from the Father . . . he will bear witness to me; and you also are witnesses" (John 15:26–27). The witness of man is secondary to the witness of the Holy Spirit. When the risen Lord sends forth his

This is the third and final talk of a series of lectures given in New York in late 1960 as part of a program to assist the integration of the International Missionary Council and the World Council of Churches.

disciples and says, "As the Father has sent me, even so I send you," he immediately adds, "Receive the Holy Spirit" (John 20:21–22). So also in Acts 1:8 when he says to them, "you shall be my witnesses in Jerusalem and in all Judea and Samaria and to the ends of the earth," he says in the same breath, "You shall receive power when the Holy Spirit has come upon you." Over and over again we find that it is taken for granted that witness is essentially a witness borne to Jesus by the Holy Spirit, and that the part that the Church plays is a secondary instrumental part.

I tried to suggest in my previous talk that during the past missionary period of two hundred years when, in the providence of God, the expansion of mission has coincided with the political and cultural expansion of the Western world, we have been tempted to forget this truth. We have been tempted to look at the missionary task too much in terms of our responsibility to undertake a program of teaching and training and guiding. And there is here a sharp contrast with the missionary situation of the first apostles. St. Paul came with no superior financial or cultural authority and did not establish the kind of links between the church of Antioch and the churches of Galatia, for instance, that we have established between the churches of Europe and America and the younger churches. On the contrary, St. Paul appeared to base his entire faith on the power of the Holy Spirit to create new forms of churchmanship very different from the forms that had existed in Judea in the old church of Jerusalem. And I believe that in this time that lies immediately ahead of us, in which as I say the missionary enterprise has to learn to swim against the stream of world events, we may be forced to take much more seriously the pattern of the New Testament in this matter, rather than the pattern of the previous one and a half or two centuries.[1]

I can best explain what I have to say in an autobiographical form. For I do not believe that I am any exception to the general rule when I say that I have come to this position not through pure theological

---

1. See further Roland Allen, *Missionary Methods, St. Paul's or Ours?* with a foreword by Lesslie Newbigin (Grand Rapids, Mich.: Eerdmans, 1962); Lesslie Newbigin, "Bringing Our Missionary Methods under the Word of God," *Occasional Bulletin from the Missionary Research Library* 13 (1962): 1–9; *Mission in Christ's Way: Bible Studies* (Geneva: World Council of Churches, 1987).

reflection in a state of abstraction from the world, but rather by facing concrete and ordinary practical missionary experiences.

When I went as a young missionary to India, I came into a situation that was typical of large parts of the so-called mission field. It was assumed that the method of evangelization was to have paid catechists or evangelists who preached the gospel to various villages, and if the people of a village wished to become Christians, then someone was employed to live in this village and teach the people what Christianity is. Later they were baptized, and they continued to live under the guidance and control of this agent, this evangelist. So the missionary was a man who sat at a desk in a large bungalow, and he controlled a large army of agents who were the fingers, so to speak, of his hands and whom he sent and withdrew and transferred and dismissed in accordance with his own good pleasure. Now, I came at a time when, owing to various events in Wall Street and other places, the mission was running short of money. We were under instructions not to expand our budgets. It was therefore necessary that no more people should wish to be baptized. It was therefore necessary that we should not preach the gospel. It was therefore necessary to correct Mark 16:15 to read: "Go into all the world and preach the gospel, budgetary conditions permitting." I was sufficiently obstinate to believe that there must be a mistake somewhere in this logic, and that one must therefore reexamine this structure and ask whether this is really the only possible understanding of the missionary task.

If one reexamines that structure, one comes back again to a debate that took place at the very beginning of modern Protestant missions, a debate that was conducted by correspondence between Ziegenbalg and Plütschau on the one hand, and the Pietist supporters of the mission in Halle, Germany, on the other: namely, whether it is proper for the mission to employ paid agents for its work. The missionaries plausibly contended that one could for a small amount of money hire a very large number of agents and that thereby the capacity of the gospel to spread could be greatly multiplied. And it appeared to be a reasonable argument.[2]

2. Arno Lehmann, *It Began in Tranquebar* (Madras: CLS, 1956); J. F. Fenger, *The History of the Tranquebar Mission* (Madras: Leipzig Mission Press, 1906).

The result of that argument was that this became the standard method, not only in India but in most parts of the world.[3] Then the question was, How do you go from the mission agent to the ministry? What is the relationship between this army of agents and the ministry of bishops, priests, and deacons or pastors or whatever you call them? In a large part of the mission field this problem was solved in the following way. After the basic work has been done by the paid mission agents, one then begins to develop a ministry. With regard to the ministry there are three axioms we have to accept: (1) that the ministry is a paid profession, a full-time profession; (2) that it is composed of people who have an academic education comparable to that of the ministry in Britain or Germany; and (3) that the ministry should be supported by the giving of the people. None of these axioms is derived from the New Testament. If one adopts these as axioms, the result is that in developing countries one must ask not what is the fundamental theological relationship between the minister and the congregation, and not how many people one pastor can effectively shepherd, or for how many sheep one shepherd is necessary, but how many people with this particular income are needed to pay the salary of a pastor. The resulting situation is (and this is typical of large areas of the world) that you have ministers, pastors, presbyters, priests — whatever you call them — who are responsible for ten, twenty, thirty, or even fifty and sixty village congregations. There are areas in India where one ordained minister is responsible for sixty village congregations. You thus have a very peculiar ecclesiastical situation — a double tier

3. The situation was actually rather more complicated than this, with Carey giving a number of reasons for adopting the system in his reports to the BMS, such as the very high death rate among Europeans, and the difficulty they had in learning proper Bengali idiom and living simply among the homes of poor people. The first converts were poor craftsmen and women, and were paid because they could not afford to lose their earnings when they traveled with missionaries on preaching tours. Their wages were kept low so that they could not adopt the alien European lifestyle or be said to have converted for money. However, the system became institutionalized. In the 1830s to 1850s a number of highly intelligent high-caste students converted and were ordained to minister to the emerging Anglican and Congregationalist/Presbyterian congregations. They were outcasted by their families, and dependency relationships were inevitable. Strangely, ordination seemed to provide some protection from kidnap and assault.

of ministries. You have the basic layer of mission agents, who are a pragmatically developed phenomenon unrelated to any doctrine of the ministry. It makes no difference whether you are Episcopalians or Presbyterians or Congregationalists or Baptists — you have this basic layer of paid agents. And then over it you have a ministry that is constructed in accordance with your particular church doctrine. But this means that the following weaknesses result.

First, the people who are actually trained for the task of teaching and preaching, namely the ministers or pastors, have no time for that because they are engaged in administering a small diocese; they are principally employed as the peripatetic dispensers of sacraments. Second, the person who is actually pastorally in charge of the congregation, namely the village agent, is precisely the man who has not had the training for that task. Third — and this is most fundamental — these village congregations are not congregations in the biblical sense of the word. They are outstations of the mission. They are not the *ecclesia Theou* in that place, with the dignity that belongs to the Church of God in any place. The relationship between the congregations and the man who lives among them is not the relation of a congregation to the minister. They are the outstations of an organization that is controlled from a center away from the congregations. And finally, as I have already said, under this situation no real evangelistic advance is possible except when there happens to be a surplus in the mission budget, which is rare.

Now, on finding this pattern unsatisfactory, I at least, like others, was compelled to look back again at the New Testament and ask whether it can show us a different pattern of missionary advance that delivers us from the kind of dilemma that I have described. And when you look at the Acts and the Epistles, even though there is very much that we cannot know about the methods of St. Paul, and even though we have to be careful about trying to copy the details of a missionary method applied to a different situation from our own, at least these three things are clear about the missionary method of St. Paul. First, there is nothing corresponding to the mission organization with which we are familiar. He does not establish in Philippi or in Derbe or in Lystra two organizations, one called the church and the other called the Antioch mission, Lystra branch. There is only one body in that place, which is at the same time both the church and the mission.

In the second place, this church is treated from the moment of its beginning as simply the Church of God. It is the *ecclesia Theou* that is in Philippi, Thessalonica, or what have you. There is only the body of Christ. However weak, however backward, however erring, however sinful, as the church in Corinth certainly was, it is still simply the body of Christ, to which St. Paul addressed himself as to the body of Christ. He may have rebuked them, he may have warned them, he may have chastised them with his tongue and his pen, but he never treated them as a class of pupils who were being trained up to *become* the Church. This phrase, which we have become so accustomed to in missionary language — the idea of "handing over responsibility" to the young church — appears nowhere in St. Paul's writings. On the contrary, according to the theology of St. Paul, responsibility, freedom, liberty are not commodities in his possession to hand over to the church when he thinks they have reached maturity. Rather, they are given *with* the gospel. To receive the gospel means to be given freedom, to be given responsibility. It means to be put from that moment in the position of freedom under grace before God.

Third, therefore, it is taken for granted that from the very beginning the church is equipped with a ministry. There are bishops (superintendents) and deacons, there are elders, and there is a multitude of other ministries, various and flexible according to the needs of the situation. Now, we know that this whole approach of St. Paul came under severe attack. We know that there came out after him from Jerusalem and from the church in Judea those who said that the church must be circumcised and must be taught to keep the whole law of Moses, that it must be, in other words, trained up in accordance with the pattern of the mother church. And only in this way could it be regarded as in the way of salvation. St. Paul on the other hand appears to have been convinced that once the gospel had been handed over, once the church was established in the faith in Jesus Christ, then they were responsible to God and were equipped by his Holy Spirit with all the gifts and all the ministries needed for growth in Christ. When one looks at this picture, it seems to me impossible to avoid the conclusion that in our missionary methods we have been nearer to the Judaizers than to St. Paul.[4]

Well, these kinds of theological reflections led on, as far as I was concerned, to an attempt at experimenting in new patterns. As a very modest first beginning in the area where I was, faced with this budgetary barrier I have spoken of, we began to draw together the ordinary village elders, the farmers or coolies or artisans or whatever they were, who were regarded by the village congregations as their natural leaders. We began to gather them together for conference and Bible study, and to develop in them a sense of responsibility to the Church of God in their area. Then it happened that I was transferred and made a bishop in an area where the shortage of funds had caused such a drastic cutting down of budgets that a large number of village schools had been closed, the evangelists had been withdrawn, and more than half of the village congregations were without any kind of regular pastoral oversight. I took this as a God-given opportunity to experiment in the other understanding of the Church's missionary advance, and we were able to completely turn over the seminary that we had for the training of evangelists and catechists to the training of lay voluntary leaders of the congregations. We got the seminary out of its building, put it on wheels, and sent it around the diocese so that the staff of the seminary would be available in all parts of the diocese to give practical biblical and pastoral training to the natural leaders of the congregations. We very quickly began to discover that those congregations under a voluntary local ministry of this kind were far more spiritually alive than those under the oversight of the paid agents of the mission. We had a God-given opportunity to extend this experiment still further when a mass movement of the village people

4. Following the conflict between Paul and those who felt that the provisions of the old covenant with Israel had been fulfilled, not destroyed (see Acts and the Letter to the Galatians), Judaizing has become synonymous with a legalistic approach to religion. It is obvious that a religion that offers salvation if one simply sticks to the rules has more appeal than one involving total open-ended commitment in love. However, recent scholarship has shown that much New Testament scholarship is based on mistranslation and misunderstanding, with the conditions of later Judaism being read back into the first century A.D. See E. P. Sanders, *Paul and Palestinian Judaism* (London: SCM, 1977).

of a certain area began to develop. This was an extension of a move-ment that had taken place in the adjacent area under the Methodist mission. In that area they have developed this movement in accord-ance with the old pattern by putting a paid agent into every new village as the people turned to Christ and asked for baptism.

We decided that we would experiment in the exactly opposite direction on our side of the boundary, and that from the very beginning we would put each new congregation under the charge of one, two, or three of its own leaders. When any new group of people came, we would not offer to send them a paid agent to teach and train them, but we would first of all ask: Who are the men and women here whom the Holy Spirit has touched? Let them be the God-ordained pastors and leaders for this new congregation. And my own experience has always been that when such a turning to the gospel takes place, when a new group or village comes asking for baptism, there is in that group at least one man whose life has been actually touched by the Holy Spirit, who has had some genuine experience of the supernatural power of Christ. And that man, I believe, is the man whom God has chosen to be the elder, the presbyter, the pastor of this new group. It is absolutely vital that we begin by building upon what God has already done. The older pattern meant that we put that man aside and put in his place a young man whom *we* had trained in our seminary, who was under *our* control, and whom *we* could rely upon to guide the congregation in the way that *we* believed to be right. But the "new" method means that we begin by accepting as the starting point what God has done, and that we build upon that. We make it clear from the first day that the responsibility for further growth in Christ rests upon them, and that God will provide for them the ministries and the spiritual gifts they need for their growth in grace. When that is the starting point, we then go on to say: But you will need to learn much that you cannot learn for yourselves, and therefore we will send for a limited period, for six or nine months, one or two Christian people to live in your village and to give you everything that we can give concerning the gospel, the sacraments, the faith of the Church.

In this way I have seen the gospel spreading from village to village, so that in this particular area where there were only thirteen congrega-tions ten years ago, there are now nearly sixty entirely as the result of this kind of voluntary spontaneous expansion of the Church, and without requiring the addition of further burdens to any kind of mission budget. I have been able to watch the development of some of these village men as genuine pastors with the authentic lineaments of the good shepherd, even though they were very simple and in some cases uneducated men. I think of two of such men, one of them a coolie who was baptized ten years ago, who has continued to devote his spare time to evangelistic work and has won three villages for Christ and prepared them for baptism. He continues to act as a pastor for his people even though he also earns his own living as a laborer. I think of another man who was a member of a congregation that was baptized about twenty years ago and that backslid, went away from the gospel, and was abandoned by the mission. The little prayer-house that had been built was closed and locked, and the whole thing was abandoned. This one man, who was illiterate, an ordinary village laborer, every evening when he came back from his work would kneel down in front of the closed door of this prayer-house and pray that the gospel might come back to his village. He continued in this way for about five years. At the end of this five-year period, a new movement began to flow in to the village, and a new group of people in the village came asking for baptism. When we discovered the history, it was clear to us that this man was the God-ordained pastor for that village; there could be no other man who had the same spiritual right to be their pastor. But he was illiterate, and therefore it was necessary for him to begin, even though he was forty years of age, to learn to read so that he could read the Scripture and explain it to his people. He did make that tremendous effort, and he is now able to read the Scriptures intelligibly and to conduct the worship of his congregation. And, what is more important, he has shown himself to be a real pastor. We have had a young American missionary living in that village for some years, and she has told me that in her times of spiritual difficulty, without her telling him this village coolie has understood that she was having some spiritual difficulty, and has come to her home and prayed with her, and put her back again into a right relationship with God. He is, as I say, an ordinary village laborer who has simply learned to read in order that he may fulfill this ministry. But I cannot possibly doubt that he is the man God had chosen to be the pastor of this little flock.

The result of this experiment was that after about five years of intense debate the church authorities gave permission that some of these men should actually be ordained to the ministry of the Word and sacraments. And there followed a four-year period in which they were given a theological training, not in a theological college but in their own village, along with their own work, a sort of apprenticeship in the gospel, as the result of which the first group of them has now been ordained to the ministry of the Church in their village.[5]

Now, I have given these personal experiences to illustrate a thesis that I want to put before you: that we have been tempted by our possession of wealth and culture and influence to think of the missionary task too much as a program of teaching and training and uplifting in which *we* were doing the guiding and the directing, in which *we* determined the syllabus and set the exams. And we have thereby created this relationship of paternalism on the one hand and dependence on the other, which is such a perplexing difficulty in the whole missionary enterprise. And this relationship of paternalism and dependence reproduces itself even where there is no racial difference between the two sides. I have found in India, for instance, that even where we have Indian missionary societies like the National Missionary Society of India and some of the other ones, under the word *mission* the same kind of paternalism develops, and the same kind of infantile dependent attitude develops on the other side. And surely the root of this error lies in our failure to take seriously enough the fact that the mission of the Church is not a program of teaching and training analogous to a cultural program of expansion; that while there is a teaching ministry involved in it, the fundamental witness to Christ is a witness borne by the Holy Spirit himself. He is able to create under totally different conditions the forms of the Church in such a way that they belong to that place and people, instead of being mere pale reproductions of the form of the Church with which we have

5. Newbigin, *Unfinished Agenda,* 2nd ed., 139, 157. Andrew Wingate's research in the 1980s following up the results of the scheme showed that lack of support from Newbigin's successors had undermined the scheme. See Andrew Wingate, "An Experiment in Local Non-Stipendiary Ordained Ministry: A Case Study from Tamil Nadu," *Religion and Society* 30:2 (June 1983): 45-59.

been familiar so that they have their own authentic roots within the life and experience of the people themselves.

Please forgive me for telling, in conclusion, a story that you may think rather shocking and rather frivolous, but that I think is nevertheless relevant to what I have tried to say. The malaise, the weakness of the missionary enterprise nowhere becomes so clear as when the board secretary, the Missionsinspektor,[6] of a home society engages in his travels around the Church. When this happens, one has the sad experience that even a church that has developed real selfhood and responsibility will throw its adult status to the winds and will become — I won't say a collection of children, but wherever the Missionsinspektor goes, there the church gathers, and they say, "You are our father and our mother, you are the body we depend on. We cannot live by ourselves, you must give us a school, you must give us a hospital, you much give us a catechist, you must support us, otherwise we cannot live." A friend of mine who is the Missionsinspektor of one of the big American societies was traveling around India for three months. For the whole three months he had nothing other than this experience, and he was getting very tired of it. At the end of his journey he visited a village near Bombay where as usual the people, after putting a garland round his neck and offering him a tray of fruit, said, "You are our father and mother, we have no catechist in this village, without a catechist we cannot be Christians, the mission must send us a catechist immediately." And my friend, with a kind of inspired desperation, said to them, "Kneel down, all of you," and they

---

6. The Missionsinspektor system was originally devised by the Basel Mission. The Basel Mission was established in 1815 by pious members of the quasi-aristocratic merchant classes in Basel, who formed the directorate. Missionary candidates were generally drawn from the farms and workshops of Baden Wurtemburg and educated in the Missionshaus, Basel and/or the CMS training school in Islington. University graduates were usually too much influenced by the Enlightenment to volunteer. The Missionsinspektoren were an intermediate middle-class group of mission administrators, the clerks of the enterprise, who took over when the administration became too great for businessmen to do in their spare time, and who did not have direct field experience. Only in the 1860s did high-caliber returned serving missionaries such as Joseph Mullens (LMS) and Alexander Duff (FCSM) join the administration in Britain. Thus the home administration structures were as hierarchical and class based as the relationships between missionary and mission agent.

all knelt down. And then he went to the end of the row, and he said, "I appoint you a catechist. I appoint you a catechist. I appoint you a catechist . . ." right down to the end of the row, and then he went to Bombay and boarded his ship for America. Well, these were simple people, they believed in God, they believed that this was a man of God, and they believed that this man of God had come and appointed them catechists, and so they *were* catechists, and so they began to behave like catechists. The result was that when he came back again two years later, he found, instead of a drooping and weak and infantile church, a church that was itself expanding and preaching the gospel to other people.

Now, this may perhaps be too frivolous a story. I know that everything is not so simple as that. Yet I believe there is a truth in it that is essential for us to learn in the missionary movement today, that in the last analysis the witness to Christ is the witness borne by the Holy Spirit himself, who is able to use as his instruments not only the educated and the able and the powerful, but also — and even much more — the simple and the uneducated. I believe that the glory of the Christian mission is that in every place God uses the Holy Spirit in his own way to create his own witness to Christ, and that it does not all depend on us. What does depend on us is that in each situation, whoever we are and wherever we are, we should be the faithful witnesses of him who is the Savior of the world.

4

Mission in a Modern City

I have been working for the past nine years in the city of Madras, India. Like most of the world's cities, it is growing fast — nearly three million now, and adding one hundred thousand each year. It includes the whole range of human situations, from the very rich and powerful to the families who cook and sleep on the pavements.

Seven percent of these three million people are Christians, and they also cover the whole spectrum, from people holding key positions in government, business, and the professions to the pavement dwellers.

The business of this 7 percent is to be an effective sign, instrument, and firstfruit of God's purpose for the whole city. Each of those three words is important. They are to be a *sign*, pointing men to something that is beyond their present horizon but can give guidance and hope now; an *instrument* (not the only one) that God can use for his work of healing, liberating, and blessing; and a *firstfruit* — a place where men and women can have a real taste now of the joy and freedom God intends for us all.

The 7 percent are there for the sake of the whole city. That is what God called them for. But churches in Madras — as everywhere — forget this. They think that if numbers keep on growing and budgets keep on swelling and fine new churches and halls are being built (and all that is happening in Madras), then they are pleasing to God. It is an old illusion.

A talk given while on furlough in Scotland, summer 1974.

The other day I was visiting a parish in the city. After the service I was talking with the elders. I asked them, "What function does this church perform?" They were a bit embarrassed. Then one of them said, "It caters to the needs of its members." I said, "Then it should be disbanded."

Churches find it hard to accept that, especially when things are going well and numbers are increasing. But being a united Church does help you to get the right perspective. Thirty years ago I worked in these same Madras congregations when they were divided into competing denominations, each trying to do its own thing separately. I can feel the difference now. It is much easier as a united Church to think of what God wants for the city as a whole, and not just of our own separate ambitions.

How do we function as a sign, instrument, and firstfruit of God's purpose for the city? In the old days we used to do a lot of street preaching. I have done a lot of it myself, and I believe in it. I cannot accept the view that would seek to downgrade evangelism. Anyone who has a faith that he really believes — whether he is a Marxist or a Muslim or a disciple of the Maharishi — wants to persuade others to believe it too. If you do not want to share it with others, it is not your real faith.

But — and this is a big "but" — no one is going to listen to your evangelism unless he sees that it comes out of a fellowship that cares. Too much of our evangelism has not met that test. I must confess that as I look back on my younger days as a missionary, there have been too many times when I have gone with a band of friends to preach in the streets of some town or village, perhaps made some contacts, but then gone home to a good supper and a comfortable bed without being really involved with these people to whom I had preached, without sharing the burden of their hunger and their despair.

The churches in Madras are slowly learning that the precondition for preaching is caring. But how do two hundred fairly comfortable congregations set about caring for a city of three million? Obviously — in the first place — it means working together with the other agencies that God has ordained for man's welfare, including particularly the manifold agencies of national and local government. This has meant we have had to overcome the fear that has affected the Indian churches so much — the fear of working in full and open partnership with Hindus, Muslims, and Marxists.

We began by making a map of the city and marking on it the six hundred or so slum areas where people are living in huddled clusters of mud-and-thatch huts without water or sanitation, and the two hundred or so Christian congregations. We divided the first among the second, and in the name of the Christian Council, the Roman Catholic Archbishop and I wrote to every congregation in the city asking them to take into their care the three or four slums named in the letter. We followed this up with training programs for church members (especially young people) in how to act promptly and effectively to help slum people in times of flood and fire. It has been a joy to find, after some years of this training, that when these disasters strike the poorer parts of our city, as they so often do, the young people of our churches are on the spot within a few hours with relevant and effective action.[1]

The next step was a plan to equip thirty-six of these slums with modern sanitation; this was to be a pilot project that would give a lead to the city authorities. With the help of funds from Christian Aid, mainly from Scotland, we started out. In the course of the next two years I learned more about what can go wrong with a latrine than I thought possible. When we were about one-third of the way to our target, the government announced a big plan to rehouse the slum people of Madras in modern flats that would have their own water and sanitation. The dynamic political leader who was in charge of the program readily accepted the suggestion of the Council of Churches that it was essential to the success of the plan to tackle the human side of the problem along with the physical. As he himself put it in a meeting a few days ago, "You cannot help the man in the slum unless you deal with the slum in the man." We set up a joint body representing the government, the churches, and private citizens to recruit and deploy highly trained community workers as resident welfare officers in each of the new housing projects. Under their leadership it has proved possible to mobilize the residents of the new blocks of

1. Lesslie Newbigin, *Unfinished Agenda*, 1st ed. (London: SPCK, 1985), 220; 2nd ed. (Edinburgh: St. Andrew Press, 1993), 208.

flats as active agents in creating a healthy community life. An experienced social worker from England who visited Madras last year remarked that the kind of young people who would be classified as juvenile delinquents in an English city were here going about proudly bearing their badges as members of the volunteer health and cleanliness squads. Our own church's Community Service Centre has played an important part in providing courses of training for all sections of the new communities.

The latest development is a plan for a massive program of community health care and education in which young people of the local congregations join with young people in the new housing projects to train under expert guidance as community health workers.

I would like to say that very much of what has been accomplished has been due to the presence of one of our own Church of Scotland missionaries, Murdoch Mackenzie.[2] He has been the creator and inspirer of a remarkable group — the 77 Society — that draws together men in leading positions in the city and focuses attention on vital issues so that action by government or private bodies follows. The 77 Society has given a lead to the city on pollution, on housing, on the care of the victims of leprosy, and other matters. As the minister of one of the most influential congregations in the city, Mackenzie has also been able to give a lead to the other congregations in these matters.

For in all these things, the essential thing is that the congregation as such should be involved. People should be able to see that being a member of a Christian congregation means caring for your neighbors as surely as it means sharing in worship and in the ministry of the Word and sacraments — indeed that the Word and sacraments of the gospel are emptied of their meaning if they are not part of the life of a caring congregation.

This is hard to take. It has been hard for congregations in Madras to throw open their buildings to provide day care centers for children whose parents are both working, to provide places where poor students can find light and space for study at night, to provide shelter for slum families whose huts have been destroyed by flood or fire.

---

2. Newbigin, *Unfinished Agenda*, 1st ed., 221; 2nd ed., 209. Murdoch Mackenzie is now minister of Carrs Lane Church (URC), Birmingham.

There are angry elders who ask why our beautiful buildings should be spoiled by all these people from the slums. And there is always the temptation to allow these two things to fall apart — to let the so-called "social work" be a program on its own, and let the congregation keep the Word and sacraments of the gospel as a private solace fenced off from this dirty and noisy world. But that is fatal to both. The Word and sacraments of the gospel are denatured when they are domesticated within the walls of a congregation that lives only for itself. And social work becomes a futile exercise in self-righteousness unless it is part of a movement that seeks to enlist men's total commitment to radical change in the ordering of personal and public life.

This call for total commitment is the very center of our mission. But what are we asking men to be committed to? While we were engaged in the public sanitation program one of our workers was asked, "What are you doing this for? Are you trying to convert us?" It would have been easy for him to answer, "Oh no, we are just trying to help you." To say that would have meant that we were not taking the people seriously. He answered, "Of course we are trying to convert you; do you think we want to leave you as you are?"

The point is: what do we mean by conversion? This is the crucial question for our mission. Conversion does not mean — as it is so often understood to mean in India — merely the transfer from one self-centered religious community to another. Nor does it mean only finding one's own personal peace with God. It means being so changed that you become an agent of change. It means being so turned around in your tracks that you begin to share in God's saving work for all mankind. It means becoming so related to Jesus Christ that you begin to learn to follow him, in the fellowship of his people, in bearing the sin and sorrow of the world — begin therefore to taste the powers of the new world, the world to come, and so begin to have hope. And I am talking about hope in the biblical sense of the word, not the way we use it when we say that we hope it will be a fine day tomorrow, but the way that St. Peter uses it when he says that we are begotten again to a living hope by the resurrection of Jesus from the dead. I am talking about hope that is an eager pressing forward to what God has promised us, to what we have already begun to possess through the Spirit of the risen Jesus.

One of the things we are doing in Madras is what is called Community Organization. This is a semitechnical term used to describe a method of arousing a group of deprived and exploited people to act effectively together to solve their own problems. The aim is that the exploited group should become itself the agent of change, and the method is to help them to identify the source of their problem and to bring pressure to bear on those responsible for the needed change. We sent two men for training in the Philippines, and for the past two years they have been at work in one of the most depressed and congested areas of the city. By getting all the political parties to work together, they have been able to get things done in the way of better water supply, street lighting, and public transportation. The other day the people in the area asked me to come for a public meeting and to see what had been accomplished. They had gotten hold of an old lorry for a platform. There was a big crowd jamming the street. All the local political leaders were on the platform and they all spoke. The last to speak before my turn came said something like this: "To live a human life we need three things: food for our bellies, clothes for our bodies, and a roof over our heads." The crowd responded with a shout of agreement. When it was my turn I said, "I agree that we need hope." I was myself surprised at the response that came from the crowd. But I ought not to have been. Whether in the unbelievably affluent world of Scotland or in the slums of Madras, you cannot live without hope. You cannot live in an ideological vacuum. That was the illusion of the 1960s. The myth of the Secular City has been dissolved. Men cannot live without some shape, some meaning for their lives. And in the long run, when you have been all over the world and tasted something of the ideologies that men live by, you come back to this: there is no other place in human history where the ultimate issues of man's life — his interior personal life and his public political and social life — are finally exposed and settled, except in the living and dying and rising again of Jesus Christ. There is no other in all the human story who could possibly be the King and Head of the human race. And when men see a company of men and women who live by that faith and who are not afraid to take it out into all the political and social life of a great modern city, then they begin to have hope. Perhaps one good way to describe the mission of the

Church is just to say that it is "hope in action." But hope need not be mute. We owe it to our neighbors to learn in each new situation to give an account of our hope, to point them to Jesus Christ.

Not long ago I was visiting one of the many new congregations in the newly developing industrial belt west of Madras. This church was built only seven years ago, and from the beginning the minister and congregation have been deeply involved in industrial mission. As I talked with the young people, I was struck by the number of new converts. I found that in the previous eighteen months there had been about forty adult baptisms. I asked the minister to ask each of these forty people to write down a statement of what had drawn him to Christ. Every one of them had come by a different road. For one it was friendship with the man at the next bench in the Dunlop factory; for another a visit in the hospital when he was ill; for another the word of a street preacher; for another the reading of a Gospel; for another the personal ministry of the pastor; for another a dream; for another an answered prayer in the name of Jesus.

My point in telling this is just to remind you that the real missionary is God's own Spirit who, in his own way and time, uses as he will our faltering witness. What matters is the presence of congregations living the life — the daily dying life — of the crucified and risen Jesus, in worship, Word, and sacrament, and in the life of the city, the factory, the trade union, the school; the life of hope in action, a hope that knows how and when to speak.

When that is there, God can be trusted to carry on his mission.

5

*The Pastor's Opportunities:
Evangelism in the City*

The small congregation with which I now minister worships in a
Victorian building situated immediately opposite the Winson
Green Prison in Birmingham.[1] In an early document the area served
was defined by the following boundaries: "HM Prison, the Lunatic
Asylum, the railway, and James Watt's famous factory." It is now an
area of very high unemployment, an exceptionally high proportion
of single-parent families, and a rich ethnic mix in which native Anglo-
Saxons form a minority. In comparison to the nation as a whole it
would be described as an area of relative deprivation. In terms of
absolute poverty, or — for example — in comparison with the Indian
villages where most of my ministry has been exercised, its people
have considerable material resources. Every home has a television,
and this provides, for most of the time, the visible center of life in the
home. The commodity in shortest supply is hope.

The older inhabitants speak much of earlier times when there

---

1. For Newbigin's Winson Green ministry from 1979 to 1988, see Newbigin,
Unfinished Agenda, 2nd ed., pp. 235-246.

An article written at the invitation of the editor of the *Expository Times,* in which
periodical it first appeared in 1986 and is now reproduced by kind permission
of the same.

was a closely packed community in which neighbors knew and helped each other. Much of this was destroyed in the name of "improvement." The terrace houses were pulled down and their inhabitants forced to move to the suburbs. One 18-story tower-block was built, and those who inhabit it have one main ambition: namely, to escape. Older people comfort themselves with nostalgic memories of the past and are fearful of the present. For young people, especially for those of the Afro-Caribbean community, there is little reason for hope about the future. There is a famine of hope.

We have good news to tell. Before we begin to think about how it is communicated, it is well that we begin with a negative point. It is *not* communicated if the question uppermost in our minds is about the survival of the Church in the inner city. Because our society is a pagan society, and because Christians have — in general — failed to realize how radical the contradiction is between the Christian vision of what is real and the assumptions that we breathe in from every part of our shared existence, we allow ourselves to be deceived into thinking of the Church as one of the many "good causes" that need our support and that will collapse if they are not adequately supported. If our "evangelism" is at bottom an effort to shore up the tottering edifice of the Church (and it sometimes looks like that), then it will not be heard as good news. The Church is in God's keeping. We do not have the right to be anxious about it. We have our Lord's word that the gates of hell shall not prevail against it. The crux of the matter is that we have been chosen to be the bearers of good news for the whole world, and the question is simply whether we are faithful in communicating it.

But how to communicate? In my experience the hardest part is trying to communicate to the native Anglo-Saxons. The others are, in general, people who know that God is the great reality, even if we may think that their knowledge of him is imperfect. To the Muslim the gospel is shocking but at least it is significant. To Hindus and Sikhs it is something really worth listening to — even if they finally decides that it is just another version of the "religion" that is common to us all. Many of the Afro-Caribbean people in our inner cities are devout Christians whose faith, hope, and love put most of us to shame. But for the majority of the natives, the Christian story is an old fairy

41

tale that they have put behind them. It is not even worth listening to. One shuts the door and turns back to the TV screen, where endless images of the "good life" are on tap at all hours.

How can this strange story of God made man, of a crucified savior, of resurrection and new creation become credible for those whose entire mental training has conditioned them to believe that the real world is the world that can be satisfactorily explained and managed without the hypothesis of God? I know of only one clue to the answering of that question, only one real hermeneutic of the gospel: congregations that believe it.

Does that sound too simplistic? I don't believe it is. Evangelism is not some kind of technique we use to persuade people to change their minds and think like us. Evangelism is the telling of good news, but what changes people's minds and converts their wills is always a mysterious work of the sovereign Holy Spirit, and we are not permitted to know more than a little of his secret working. But—and this is the point—the Holy Spirit, is present in the believing congregation gathered for praise and the offering up of spiritual sacrifice, scattered throughout the community to bear the love of God into every secular happening and meeting. It is they who scatter the seeds of hope around, and even if the greater part falls on barren ground, there will be a few that begin to germinate, to create at least a questioning and a seeking, and perhaps to lead someone to inquire about where these germs of hope came from. Although it may seem simplistic, I most deeply believe it is fundamental to recognize that what brings men and women and children to know Jesus as Lord and Savior is always the mysterious work of the Holy Spirit, always beyond our understanding or control, always the result of a presence, a reality that both draws and challenges—the reality who is in fact the living God himself. And his presence is promised and granted in the midst of the believing, worshiping, celebrating, caring congregations. There is no hermeneutic for the gospel but that.

The first priority, therefore, is the cherishing and nourishing of such a congregation in a life of worship, of teaching and mutual pastoral care, so that the new life in Christ becomes more and more for them the great and controlling reality. That life will necessarily be different from the life of the neighborhood, but the important thing is that it be different in the right way and not in the wrong way. It is different in the wrong way if it reflects cultural norms and assumptions that belong to another time or place; its language and style must be that of the neighborhood. But if it is *not* different from the life around it, it is salt that has lost the saltiness. We ought to recognize, perhaps more sharply than we often do, that there *must* be a profound difference between a community that adores God as the great reality, and one where it is assumed that he can be ignored.

But here a problem arises that is perhaps especially pressing in deprived areas. It happens over and over again, and it has happened throughout history, that the effect of conversion and Christian nurture is that an individual acquires new energies, a new hope, and a new sense of dignity. And it can follow that his next step is to leave the area where he sees only depression and despair, and to seek a better place. He leaves the inner city and moves to the leafy suburb. The congregation that bears the Good News is weakened by its very success.

This means, surely, that in all our preaching and teaching about the hope that the gospel makes possible, we have to keep steadily in view the fact that what the gospel offers is not just hope for the individual but hope for the world. Concretely I think this means that the congregation must be so deeply and intimately involved in the secular concerns of the neighborhood that it becomes clear to all that no one and nothing is outside the range of God's love in Jesus. Christ's message, the original gospel, was about the coming of the kingdom of God, that is to say, God's kingly rule over the whole of his creation and the whole of humankind. That is the only authentic gospel. And that means that every part of human life is within the range of the gospel message; in respect of everything the gospel brings the necessity for choice between the rule of God and the negation of his rule. If the Good News is to be authentically communicated it must be clear that the Church is concerned about the rule of God and not about itself. It must be clear, that is, that the local congregation cares for the well-being of the whole community and not just for itself. This will — in the contemporary situation of such areas as Winson Green — lead to much involvement in local issues of all kinds.

But, and this reminder is very necessary, this involvement must not become something that muffles the distinctive note of the gospel. The Church ought not to fit so comfortably into the situation that it is simply welcomed as one of the well-meaning agencies of philanthropy. I think this warning is necessary because of the frequency with which I hear Kingdom set against Church in discussions about our role in society. I have insisted that the Church's message is about the kingdom. The Church is called to be a sign, foretaste, and instrument of God's kingly rule. But it is the *Church* to which the calling is given. We have too often heard Kingdom issues set against Church issues in a way that conceals the fact that Kingdom issues are being conceived not in terms of the crucified and risen Jesus, but in terms of contemporary ideology. In the heyday of progressive liberal capitalism, advancing the Kingdom meant enabling more and more people to share in its blessings. Today the ideas are more generally colored by Marxist ideas about the oppressed as the bearers of liberation. One has much sympathy with this in view of the contemporary attempt to persuade us that the way to maximize public good is to give free rein to private greed. We live in a society that is being ideologically polarized by this attempt as never before. It is not easy to keep one's head. But it is essential to keep all our thinking centered in the fact that the Kingdom of God is present in Jesus — incarnate, crucified, risen, and coming in judgment. The life of the Church in the midst of the world is to be a sign and foretaste of the Kingdom only in so far as its whole being is centered in that reality. Every other concept of the Kingdom belongs to the category of false messiahs, about which the Gospels have much to say.

To put it even more sharply: the hope of which the Church is called to be the bearer in the midst of a famine of hope is a radically otherworldly hope. Knowing that Jesus *is* King and that he *will* come to reign, it fashions its life and invites the whole community to fashion its life in the light of this reality because every other way of living is based on illusion. It thus creates signs, parables, foretastes, appetizers of the Kingdom in the midst of the hopelessness of the world. It makes it possible to act both hopefully and realistically in a world without hope, a world that deals in illusions. If this radically otherworldly dimension of the Church's witness is missing, then all its efforts in the life of the community are merely a series of minor eddies in a current that sweeps relentlessly in the opposite direction.

But if one insists, as I am doing, upon the radically otherworldly nature of the Christian hope, it is necessary at the same time to protect this against a misunderstanding that has brought this aspect of the Christian message into disrepute. A recognition of this otherworldly element has often been linked with a privatization of religion characteristic of our post-Enlightenment culture. When this happens, the Church is seen not as a bearer of hope for the whole community, but as a group of people concerned about their own ultimate safety. It is thus seen as something essentially antisocial. And, especially in a religiously plural society, this attracts justifiable censure. "Evangelism" is then easily identified as "proselytism" — the natural attempt of every human community to add to its own strength at the expense of others. From the point of view of people concerned with the total welfare of a human community, "evangelism" is seen as something at best irrelevant, and at worst destructive of human unity.

Is there a valid distinction between "evangelism" and "proselytism"? It must be admitted that in many discussions of the subject I have sensed that the distinction was very simple: evangelism is what we do, and proselytism is what the others do. But I think it is possible to get beyond this obvious illusion. Everything depends on the point I made at the beginning: namely, that the conversion of a human mind and will to acknowledge Jesus as Lord and Savior is strictly a work of the sovereign Holy Spirit of God, a mystery always beyond our full comprehension, for which our words and deeds may be — by the grace of God — the occasions but never the sufficient causes. Anything in the nature of manipulation, any exploiting of weakness, any use of coercion, anything other than "the manifestation of the truth in the sight of God" (2 Cor. 4:2) has no place in true evangelism. Of course anyone who knows Jesus as Lord and Savior will rejoice when the company of those who love him grows. But he will also know that Jesus is much greater than any of our understandings of him, and that it therefore behooves us to make no final judgments until the Judge himself comes. It is he alone who decides whom he will summon to be with us in the company of witnesses.

If we are clear about the distinctions between evangelism and proselytism, we shall be in a position to say something constructive about the matter of evangelism among people of other faiths. I have mentioned the fact that in the area of my present pastoral charge there is a large proportion of families of Muslim, Hindu, or Sikh faith. I have said that I find it much easier to talk with them on matters of religious faith than with most of the natives. But I am also frequently told, sometimes by Christian clergymen, that evangelism among my neighbors of other faiths is an improper activity and that I ought to confine myself to "dialogue." I find this exceedingly odd. We live in one neighborhood. For good or ill we share the same life. We wrestle with the same problems. It is, surely, a very peculiar form of racism that would affirm that the Good News entrusted to us is strictly for Anglo-Saxons! After the last annual Assembly of the United Reformed Church, which had given much attention to evangelism, one of the participants wrote to the church's monthly paper to ask why this word was reserved for our relations with unchurched Anglo-Saxons, while in respect of our relations with people of other faiths we spoke only of "dialogue." The question was not answered.

How has it happened that "evangelism" and "dialogue" are presented as opposed alternatives? Surely because both have been misunderstood. "Evangelism" has been misunderstood as proselytism. There is reason for this, and all of us who seek to be true bearers of the gospel need to take note. If "evangelism" is the attempt of a religious group to enlarge itself by cajoling or manipulating those unable to resist, then it is rightly suspect. But a believing, celebrating, loving Christian fellowship, fully involved in the life of the wider community and sharing its burdens and sorrows, cannot withhold from others the secret of its hope, and certainly cannot commit the monstrous absurdity of supposing that the hope it lives by applies only to those of a particular ethnic origin.

And the word *dialogue* too needs to be examined. The sharing of the Good News takes place in the context of a shared human life, and that means in part the context of shared conversation. In such conversation we talk about real things, and we try both to communicate what we know and to learn what we do not know. The sharing of the Good News about the kingdom is part of that conversation and cannot happen without it. But why do we have to substitute the high-sounding word *dialogue* at this point? Is it because we fail in the simple business of ordinary human conversation? I confess that in the Winson Green neighborhood we have not established any "dialogue" between representatives of the different faiths, but we do have quite a lot of conversation. It is the kind of conversation that is not an alternative to but the occasion for sharing our hope. And it leads some people to ask the sort of questions that lead further.

Some, but not many. I certainly cannot tell any story of "success" in terms of numbers. I guess that this is the experience of many working in such areas. The church remains small and vulnerable. I do not find ground for much discouragement in this. The kingdom is not ours. The times and seasons are not in our management. It is enough to know that Jesus reigns and shall reign, to be privileged to share this assurance with our neighbors, and to be able to do and say the small deeds and words that make it possible for others to believe.

6

Does Society Still Need
the Parish Church?

W ell, sisters and brothers, I feel that I am really the most incompetent person to lead this discussion because I am now only at the end of my life learning the basic things that I ought to have learned at the beginning about how to be the pastor of a local congregation.

I was ordained in the Church of Scotland for foreign missionary service, and went out, with about eleven years of the old British Raj still to go, as an old-fashioned district missionary, monarch of all I surveyed and telling everybody else what to do, but not yet having learned really to do it myself. And then I became a bishop of a diocese, with twelve years of very exciting experience in seeking to knit together two very different traditions, Anglican and Congregationalist —they put a Presbyterian in to keep the peace between the two! Then I became what I suppose one would call an ecumenical bureaucrat and went back to India to the very different kind of role of being Bishop in Madras, an enormously expanding city.

Now at the very end, as I said, I am beginning to learn what I ought to have learned at the beginning, because I am the minister of a little URC congregation. If you want to visit me, you ask for Winson

Transcript of a tape of a talk given by Bishop Lesslie Newbigin at a seminar held by the Centre for Explorations in Social Concern, 5 November 1985.

Green Prison and then look for the building just opposite, which Hitler unfortunately missed, and that is where I try to minister. It is one of these typical inner-city areas where a demolition order was put on the church thirty-five years ago that has neither been withdrawn nor carried out. All the shops and houses around have been knocked down. My congregation points to a field of thistles and says, "That's where I was born and brought up," and the folks who have gradually been brought in are, as the local beat policeman said to me, "all OHMS." I thought he was saying something about the prison and I said, "What exactly do you mean?" And he answered, "Only Hindus, Muslims, and Sikhs." So we have this situation of a very, very loyal congregation of aging white people who, not of their own will, have been banished to the suburbs and do not have cars to travel in, trying to minister to a local area where it is not just thistles and tin cans but mostly Hindus, Muslims, and Sikhs. So that's the sort of background out of which I have to try to speak.

I do have a very special interest in this problem, partly because in the days when I worked in Scotland as an SCM Secretary, I was in very close contact with George MacLeod, who was the one who recalled the Church of Scotland to the parish principle. The Church of Scotland has a much more dominant position in Scotland than the Church of England does in England, and so the concept of the parish has been able to exercise a much more dominant influence in Scotland than in England. And then when I was Bishop in Madras, where we had about 120 congregations in this exploding city of three million people, I was constantly facing the fact that although these congregations were growing very rapidly (I often used to point out that while our Lord promised to be present where two or three are gathered, he never made that promise for two or three thousand), they were associational congregations. They were not congregations of people who were born in that place; they were not congregations who felt that, intrinsically, they were responsible for that bit of the city. Therefore I spent a lot of my ten years as Bishop in Madras trying to hammer the parish principle into congregations that were very largely shaped by the associational principle. So perhaps that gives me a little bit of title to talk.[1]

1. See Newbigin, Unfinished Agenda, 1st ed., 220, 221; 2nd ed., 208, 209.

Second, I see the need for clarity about the criteria. Obviously, changing sociological conditions, changing cultural conditions, the enormous and rapid changes that are taking place in our society are relevant to the way that we understand our task. But I do most deeply believe (and I have tried to act on that belief in many different situations) that when we are looking for guidance and renewal, fundamentally we have to go to the Scriptures. We do so not in a sort of unintelligent and stupid way, just picking up odd texts, but with the faith that the Church lives by — that the character and the purpose of God are rendered apparent for us in the Scriptures, and are understood as we read them in the power of the Holy Spirit and in the fellowship of the whole Christian Church in all ages. I think it's important to say this because all of our society, all of our thinking in the last two hundred years, has been dominated by the inductive principle: in trying to find our way we assemble all the facts and then, on the basis of the facts, make some kind of theory about how we ought to go. And the inductive principle, which has been so enormously creative in producing what we call a modern scientific worldview, is a method with strict limited application. The inductive principle is not applicable to the question of our ultimate destiny because we will not have the data about our ultimate destiny until the universe comes to a conclusion. We have to depend upon another kind of reasoning. The Church exists because God has revealed himself in the story of Israel, in the ministry and death and resurrection of Jesus Christ, and we are in the world as the bearers of a revelation of God's purpose for creation. That is the only criterion, ultimately, by which we have to be guided. Obviously we have to have an enormous amount of discussion among ourselves about how we interpret the Scriptures, about how we relate what is given to us in the Scriptures to the new experiences that come to us as the world goes on its way. But we have to be, I think, quite unembarrassed and unambiguous about the fact that we are finding our ultimate criteria in what has been given to us in revelation, which is not available by a process of observation and induction from the human situation as we see it.

Third, I start with the very elementary point that in the New Testament the Church is always and only designated by reference to two realities: one, God in Christ, and the other, the place where the Church is. And when, as we know from the Corinthian letters, the believers are forming themselves into groups involving another name (I belong to Cephas, I belong to Paul, I belong to Apollos), Paul is exceedingly tough in his dealing with them. He says, "You are carnal" — that's a very strong word but it is the appropriate word. (1 Cor. 3:4). Paul responds to their divisions by simply presenting to them again the cross of Christ in relation to which every other name is relativized. No other name can take the place that belongs alone to the name of Jesus Christ, and therefore when believers propose to identify themselves with another name than that of the Lord Jesus Christ, they are, as Paul said, "carnal." They are falling back upon the flesh, upon human wisdom, power, spirituality, whatever, and they are therefore falling away from the Spirit, which is simply the life lived through what God has done finally and decisively in Jesus Christ. This is not accidental; it is fundamental.

Here we have to look at the interesting word that the New Testament writers use for the Church: *ekklesia Theou*. There was an enormous number of words available in the contemporary vocabulary of that Hellenistic world to describe religious groups of people who were drawn together by a common quest for salvation under some kind of name and with some kind of discipline and tradition of learning. There were a lot of Greek words for this, like *heranos* and *thiasos* and so on, and opponents of Christianity like Celsus constantly used those words to describe the Church. But in the first five centuries in the Christian Church you never find those words used. The Church never defines itself in the language that was used by these various religious groups composed of people in the quest of salvation. They used only this word — *ekklesia*.

In the Greek Old Testament there are two words used to refer to the congregation of God — *synagogue* and *ekklesia*. The New Testament writers could have chosen either of those words. The word *synagogue* was already used by the Jews in the Diaspora. But they chose the word *ekklesia*, which is the secular word for the assembly to which every citizen is summoned and expected to attend, in which the business of the city is dealt with. Paul always uses the word, all the New Testament writers use the term *ekklesia Theou*, the assembly of God — the assembly, in other words, to which all are summoned without exception. And it is summoned not by the town clerk but by God — not by Peter, not by Apollos, not by Paul, but by God. And that is why you have this interesting fact that you can use the words *Church* and *churches* interchangeably. You can say "the churches in Asia" or "the Church in Asia" because, in a sense, it is one reality, it is one God who is summoning all people, and therefore, whether it is simply that group that meets in Thessalonica or whether it is the whole reality in the whole world, it is the same reality. It is the catholic Church: the local church is not a branch of something else. The local church is the catholic Church. It is the *ekklesia Theou*, and Paul uses the most realistic language about it. Even when he has to tell them that they are sinners in all kinds of respects, they are nevertheless the *ekklesia Theou*, defined simply by the place where they meet, and any other definition is ruled out. And this principle has been carried on in the subsequent history of the Church. The basic units of the Church — the parish, the diocese — were all determined by secular realities. And that is fundamental.[2]

I remember once a fascinating discussion among a group of bishops about the proper size for a diocese. Some said that the size of the diocese must be determined by the number of people with whom a bishop can have a real pastoral relationship. I remember hearing Ted Wickham[3] saying in passionate opposition to that, "No,

2. The organization of church congregations on a territorial basis with parishes grouped into dioceses, and dioceses into provinces, dates from the late fourth century A.D. colonial Roman administration, but the roots of the system in Britain go back to the responsibilities of the pagan landowner or chief to provide facilities for worship for his followers and to maintain the priesthood. After the Reformation, dissidents formed "free" churches composed of believers and independent of the legal and territorial restrictions of the "established" churches. In India churches were of necessity "associational," but under the "comity" agreements, missions undertook not to enter the geographical areas of other missions; see H. Richard Niebuhr, *The Social Sources of Denominationalism,* 11th ed. (New York: World Publisher Company, 1971).

3. E. R. "Ted" Wickham was chaplain at a munitions works in 1944 when he was "spotted" by Bishop Leslie Hunter of Sheffield and employed to develop the famous Sheffield Industrial Mission. He subsequently became Bishop of Middleton. A self-educated Cockney and alpinist, his best known book is *Church and People in an Industrial Society* (London: Collins, 1957). See also Newbigin, *Unfinished Agenda,* 2nd ed., 109, 112, 193, 214.

the size of the diocese must be determined by the size of the human community. The diocese must be that which represents the purpose of God for this human community, and for the pastoral care of its members you have got to make the proper arrangements. But you cannot determine the size of the diocese by the internal needs of the Church. It must be determined by the secular reality for which the Church is there." That has been fundamental right through the history of the Church, that the structural forms of the Church are determined by the secular reality, and not by the internal needs of the Church; and I think that is true to Scripture.

The relation between the Church in a "place" and the secular reality of that "place" is intrinsic, not extrinsic. It's not just that it happens to be located in that spot on the map. It is the Church of God *for that place,* and that is because the Church does not exist for itself but for God and for the world that Jesus came to save.

One possible definition of the Church that I think is worth thinking about is that the Church is the "provisional incorporation of humankind into Jesus Christ." All humankind is incorporated in Adam. We are all part of this natural human world. Jesus Christ is the last Adam, and the Church is the provisional incorporation of humankind into Christ. It is provisional in two senses: in the sense that not all humankind is so incorporated, and in the sense that those who are so incorporated are not yet fully conformed to the image of Christ. So the Church is a provisional body; it looks forward. It is its very nature to look forward, but it looks forward in two ways — and both must be equally stressed — one, to the full formation of Christ in all its members, to the growth of its members in holiness to the stature of Jesus Christ; and two, to the incorporation of all of humanity.

But in talking about the world you have to talk about that segment of the world in which you are placed, and the Church has to be recognizable as *for* that place. Now, I'll say later that the geographical definition of that segment may not be the only one that is relevant, although I think it is the fundamental one. There can be other possible definitions of the "place," but it is of the very essence of the Church that it is *for* that place, for that section of the world for which it has been made responsible. And the "for" has to be defined

53

christologically. In other words, the Church is *for* that place in a sense that is determined by the sense in which Christ is *for* the world. Now, one could go into a whole theology of the atonement if one were to develop this, but obviously Christ on his cross is in one sense totally identified with the world, but in another sense totally separated from the world. The cross is the total identification of Jesus with the world in all its sin, but in that identification the cross is the judgment of the world, that which shows the gulf between God and his world. We must always, it seems to me, in every situation, be wrestling with both sides of this reality: that the Church is for the world against the world. The Church is against the world for the world. The Church is for the human community in that place, that village, that city, that nation, in the sense that Christ is for the world. And that must be the determining criterion at every point.

And so I took as a basic text, and this is really the heart of what I want to say, the Johannine version of the Great Commission. I think that missionary thinking has often been a little distorted by the fact that when people say "the Great Commission," they always mean Matthew 28:18–20. "And Jesus came and said to them, 'All authority in heaven and on earth has been given to me. Go therefore and make disciples of all nations, baptizing them in the name of the Father and of the Son and of the Holy Spirit, teaching them to observe all that I have commanded you; and lo, I am with you always, to the close of the age.'" An interesting fact is that this text was never used as a basis for mission until William Carey (1791). There are three basic forms of the Great Commission given to us. This Matthaean form is one. There is the Lukan form in Acts 1:6–8, "You shall receive power when the Holy Spirit has come upon you; and you shall be my witnesses." Here the mission of the Church is seen as a kind of overflow of Pentecost, not as a command laid upon us but as a gift given to us. Then there is the Johannine version (John 20:19–23), which I would like to take as a basic paradigm for our understanding because we have got to understand the sense in which the Church is for the place christologically, spelled out here in the greatest detail. The disciples are huddled together in a room withdrawing themselves from the world in fear of the world, and then, as he had promised, Jesus is present in their midst ("Where two or three have gathered together there am I.") And immediately his command is "Open the doors, go out into the world. As the Father sent me, so I send you." And that is the launching of the Church. The Church is a movement launched into the world in the same way Jesus is sent into the world by the Father.

I have always been terribly grateful for the fact that in my first diocese, which was a largely rural diocese, about half of our congregations had no buildings whatsoever. And so for my first twelve years as a bishop I was normally conducting worship in the open street — all the services of the Church without exception. My picture of the Church formed in those years is deeply etched in my mind, the picture of a group of people sitting on the ground, with a larger crowd of Hindus and Muslims and others standing around listening, watching, discussing; and, thank God, when I would come back a few months later, some of those would be in the group in the front. So I got the sense of the Church not as something drawn out of the world into a building, but as something sent out into the world. And the operative word in our text is the word "as" in the sentence "As the Father sent me, so I send you."

Now that "as" contains the whole crux of our question for today, doesn't it? I honestly think the question is not "Does society need the parish church?" but "Does God need the parish church?" That's really the question we're wrestling with. And this "as" contains the heart of the matter. How did the Father send the Son? Well, one could go back to that basic text in Mark 1:14 where Jesus comes into Galilee preaching the gospel of God, the Good News of God, and saying, "The time is fulfilled, and the kingdom of God is at hand; repent, and believe in the gospel — believe the good news that I'm telling you." Now, that is the announcement of a fact. It is news in the strictest sense of the word.

I used to get awfully tired when I was working as a bishop in Madras. My house was halfway between the airport and the city, so it was a wonderful place for ecumenical travelers to stop off and have lunch. After lunch I always got the question, "Are you optimistic or pessimistic about the future of the church in India?" to which I developed the standard reply, "I believe that Jesus rose from the dead, and therefore the question doesn't arise." In regard to a fact,

55

one is not optimistic or pessimistic. One is believing or unbelieving. But in regard to a program, you can be optimistic or pessimistic. We are conned by the media, who constantly suggest to us that the Church is a kind of good cause we have to support, and if we don't support it, it's going to collapse. Yes, if it's a program, then one can be optimistic or pessimistic. But about a "fact," these are not the appropriate words. The question is "Do you believe or do you not?" Here is a fact, and of course it is not a religious fact. It doesn't belong to that little slot in *Time* magazine between drama and sports where religion is kept. It belongs to the opening section on world affairs. The Kingdom of God is at hand. The reign of God is at hand. In what sense is that news? It's not news to the Jews that God reigns. They've known that for generations. What is new is that the reign of God is now a present reality that they have to come to terms with. It is no longer a theological idea, no longer a vision in Heaven, no longer something in the distant future. It is a reality they have to come to terms with. But one can't see it when one is facing the wrong way, looking in the wrong direction. Hence the call to repent — literally to turn round.

I remember once an occasion when I had to visit a village in the Madras diocese that like many of the villages was miles from any road. In order to get to this village you had to cross a river, and you could cross either at the north end or at the south end. In their wisdom the congregation had decided that I was coming in at the south end. So they had a magnificent reception prepared such as only a village congregation in India can prepare, with trumpets and drums and fireworks and garlands and fruit and everything you can think of. I came in at the other end and found a totally deserted village, which created a great crisis. I had to withdraw into the jungle and the whole village had to reorganize itself and face the other way, and then I appeared. Well, that is what the word *repent* means. It's a total U-turn of the mind. You are expecting something quite different from the reality that is coming upon you, and so you cannot see it. There has got to be a total U-turn of the mind. When you have done the U-turn, it becomes possible to believe. And so there comes the call: "Follow me," and Jesus calls Peter and Andrew and James and John. But the Kingdom isn't obvious. There is the complaint: "We don't see it.

Where is it?" And so there are the parables and the "mighty words" — the miracles.

But finally, there is the final parable and the final miracle, which is the cross. Ultimately the reign of God is present in the cross. And only to those who have been called as witnesses is the secret given that the cross is in fact not defeat but victory, that it is the victory of God over all the powers of this world. And therefore when Jesus says to them, "As the Father sent me, so send I you," he shows them his hands and his side. In other words, the Church will be recognizable as the bearer of this mission on which the Father sent the Son and on which the Son sent the Church insofar as the scars of the Passion are recognizable in its body. So you have in St. Paul's letters that classic definition of mission, which has been so much ignored, as "bearing in the body the dying of the Lord Jesus, that the life of Jesus might be made manifest in our body" (2 Cor. 4:10).

I think we have often missed something by concentrating entirely on that Matthean version, which can produce a kind of triumphalist picture of the mission of the Church. Here, however, the Church is recognizable as the bearer of the Kingdom, the presence of the Kingdom, insofar as it is marked by the scars of the Passion. And the Passion of Jesus is not passive submission to evil but the price paid for an active challenge to evil. The Passion is what theologians call the Messianic tribulations. It is what occurs at the frontier where the reign of God challenges the rulers of this world. That frontier runs right through the whole of human life, and it is when the Church is at that frontier that it bears in its body both the marks of the Passion and the power of the risen life of the Lord. And so then Jesus immediately says, "Receive the Holy Spirit." He gives them the power of his risen life so that they may be the bearers of his reconciling work. "Whosoever's sins you remit they are remitted, whosoever's sins you retain, they are retained." The Church bears in its body the reconciling power of the atonement insofar as it is marked by the scars of the Passion, and it is therefore the bearer of the risen life. If you see the mission of the Church in that sense, then all the futile discussion between evangelism and social action disappears. It is an irrelevant discussion. It is meaningless when you see the mission of the Church in the terms that this Johannine passage offers.

I suggest that this Johannine version of the Great Commission rules out three wrong ways of looking at the local church.

The first is the one that takes church growth by itself as the criterion. Now, I don't want to be unfair to the Church Growth school, because I know that they have been self-critical. My old friend Donald McGavran, who is the guru of the school, is perhaps a little less self-critical than he might be, but I know that the Church Growth school does try to get away from a kind of crude statistical measuring rod as the one criterion by which the Church is to be judged. Nevertheless, the main thrust of the Church Growth school is that the Church is there simply to make converts.[4]

Now there, of course, you get the associational model neat. When you ask what is the purpose of making converts, the answer is, so they can make more converts, and when you ask what is the purpose of those further converts, it is so they can make more converts. There is, in other words, an infinite regress. And, as we know from the medical analogy, the multiplication of cells unrelated to the purpose of the body is what we call cancer. That's a very hard thing to say, and I don't want to suggest that the folks who are in the Church Growth school are blind to these points. But I do think that a very sharp criticism needs to be made against the idea that the Church exists simply to make more members, irrespective of the purpose for which the Father sent the Son into the world, which is that the presence of the reign of God might be a reality *now*.

Second, I think John's Great Commission also rules out seeing the local church as simply the religious aspect of the local community, providing a focus for folk religion but failing to confront people with the sharp word that calls for radical conversion. I think perhaps this is more a temptation for the established Church. Remember, my background is Scotland, and I think the established Church in Scotland is inclined to yield to that temptation even more than the established Church in England. But it is the temptation for the established

4. D. A. McGavran, *The Bridges of God: A Study in the Strategy of Missions* (New York: Friendship Press, 1955; enl. 2nd ed., 1981; W. R. Shenk, ed., *The Challenge of Church Growth: A Symposium* (Elkhart, Ind.: Institute of Mennonite Studies, 1973); C. P. Wagner, *Church Growth and the Whole Gospel: A Biblical Mandate* (N.p., 1981).

Church. And one understands the power of it, the tremendously deep attachment that people have to their parish church even though they would never under any circumstances go into it until the day of their funeral. This concept of folk religion is one the Grubb Institute has been interested in. But I think it needs a good deal of analysis. Having lived most of my life in India, I am bound to say that an awful lot of what passes for religion is what in an Indian village we would call heathenism. But I think it is also mixed up with a lot of vestigial remains of Christianity. It is a very complex mixture, this thing called folk religion. One should certainly never be contemptuous of it or despise it. One should always be on the lookout for the signals that it gives of realities beyond the visible world. But the New Testament is very clear that a radical repentance, a radical conversion, is required if one is to see the Kingdom of God.

Now, in saying that, I want to say very strongly that conversion is the work of the Holy Spirit. Conversion is not something that can be programmed or accomplished or manipulated, even by the most expert evangelist. If there is one thing I have learned as a missionary, it is that though I was in a situation where, thank God, a great many people were being brought to Christ and to conversion, baptism, and church membership, the more I investigated the ways that had happened, the less I seemed to have to do with it. I think God works in a mysterious way. I have talked with scores of people who have come to the Christian faith from Hindu or Muslim or Marxist or secular humanist background, and I am always impressed by the fact that the conversion of any person to Christ is a very mysterious thing in which there are many different elements, but the strategy is always in the hand of the Holy Spirit. The folk religion concept tends to side-step the need of radical conversion, but any sort of manipulative evangelism will not do either. I do believe that the Holy Spirit himself, and he alone, is the agent of conversion.

Third, I think the Johannine Great Commission rules out the conception of the Church in purely functional terms. In the kind of circles that I move in (probably very peculiar circles), I constantly hear people talking about Kingdom issues versus Church issues. "Forget about the Church, all this ecclesiastical stuff that has nothing to do with God's will. On the last day when the sheep and the goats are finally separated, they are not going to be asked what their view of episcopacy was. These are all irrelevant questions. The important things are the Kingdom issues of justice, peace, liberation." This has a certain element of truth in it. But if it is taken by itself, then the Church just becomes one of the less effective pressure groups in our society. The Church, instead of being a bearer of liberation, becomes a crusader for liberation, which is a very different thing. I want to say that the Church cannot fulfill the Kingdom purpose that is entrusted to it if it sees its role in merely functional terms. And that leads me on to my last point, where I want to think of the Church as a sign, instrument, and foretaste of God's reign for that place and that segment of the total fabric of humanity for which it is responsible — a sign, instrument, and foretaste for that place with its particular character.

And I start with foretaste — the great New Testament word *arrabon,* which is such a wonderful word if you think about it. I was once making an elaborate explanation of this word *arrabon* in a class in the Selly Oak colleges and explaining how scholars used to be puzzled by it because it is not a classical Greek word. Then they dug up a lot of parchments in the sands of Egypt and found that they were shopkeepers' accounts, and that *arrabon* was just the word that the shopkeepers all used for cash on deposit, a pledge for a bill that you would pay at the end. And an Egyptian student in my class got up and said, "Well, we still use the same word in Cairo" — apparently the Arabic word *arbon* is still the operative word. If you want to buy a suit in Cairo you dicker about the cloth and the style and all that, but before the tailor will start making it he'll ask you to put down some cash. This is spendable cash, not just an IOU — he can go and have a drink with it. But the point of that cash is that it is a pledge that the full bill is going to be paid. And this is the word that St. Paul uses over and over again for the Holy Spirit.

To use an analogy closer to home, think of one of these very posh dinner parties where you are kept standing for ages and ages and wonder whether there's ever going to be anything to drink. Then a trolley is brought out and there is a tinkle of glasses, and you are extremely glad to get a drink, not only because you're getting very thirsty but, more importantly, because that trolley is a sign that something is cooking in the kitchen. Now, the Holy Spirit is the aperitif for the messianic banquet. It is something you enjoy now, and that's the great thing in the charismatic movement. You enjoy it. There is something really to enjoy and celebrate now. It's not just an IOU, a promissory note. But the whole point of it is that it is a foretaste, that it assures you of a greater reality still to come. And in that sense the Church is a foretaste of the Kingdom.

And here I think the Orthodox have something to teach us. The Orthodox often criticize us in the Western Church for having a too functional view of the Church, and I think they are right. Maybe they need a bit of correction the other way. But the Orthodox have always stressed the point that the Church is first of all a communion in the Holy Spirit in the life of the triune God, so that you must define the Church in ontological terms and not just in functional terms. The Church is defined by what it is. It is already a sharing in the life of God. I think we do need to emphasize that point. I felt that tremendously on the occasions when I have participated in the Orthodox worship in Moscow, where the Church, in functional terms, is almost powerless; it's not allowed to do anything. It's not allowed to preach. It's not allowed to do social work, nor to publish anything. But the Church there continues to draw converts, and it's just because when you step out of a Moscow street into an Orthodox Church and find yourself in the middle of the Orthodox liturgy, you know that you have stepped out from under one jurisdiction into another jurisdiction. There is another reality there, which just by being what it is challenges the world outside and draws us because we are made for God and our hearts are restless until they rest in him. The Church is a foretaste, and that means it will be different from the world. If it isn't, it's no good. Let us not be afraid of the fact that the Church is different from the world, that the reality that we celebrate, that we share, that we rejoice in in our worship, is a reality that the world treats as an illusion. But that's the whole point. It is the foretaste of another reality. I think we need to not evade that or try to slide over it or make it seem less sharp.

But insofar as the Church is a foretaste, it can also be an instrument. It can be an instrument through which God's will for justice and peace and freedom is done in the world. And that takes the

61

Church out into the secular world with whatever is relevant to the real needs of that world. If that is not happening, how is the world going to know that the reality we talk about is true? I have recently been very struck by the fact that in what is often called the mission charge in Matthew 10, the beginning says nothing about preaching at all. It simply says that Jesus chose these disciples and gave them authority over unclean spirits to cast them out and to heal every disease and every infirmity. Nothing about preaching there. Then the names of the twelve disciples are given. And only then does he say, "As you go, preach. And say the Kingdom of Heaven is at hand." If you look at it that way, you can see that the preaching is the explanation of what is happening. If there is nothing happening there is nothing to explain. But the preaching is the explaining. Other people were healers also. Other people cast out devils in the time of Jesus. But if you asked why devils were being cast out, why people were being healed, the answer would be, the reign of God is upon you. The preaching explains the happenings.

I used to think about this often in my first charge. I was in a very, very sacred Hindu city (Kanchipuram, Tamil Nadu). It has almost less Western influence than any other city in India. It is the ancient capital of the Pallava Empire, with a thousand temples and hundreds of thousands of pilgrims who come there every year. And I used to do a lot of street preaching. I often thought to myself, "Now, does this do any good? Is this just words?" And I would reflect that the people there know that we who are standing up are also teaching their boys and girls in the schools, and are helping their village people to do something about their desperate poverty, and are involved in attempts to make a more just society. It is because they know this that the words will have some meaning.[5] In other words, the words without the deeds lack authority! The deeds without the words are mute, they lack meaning. The two go together. And the Church, insofar as it is a foretaste of the reign of God, can also be an instrument of the reign of God, an instrument by which its justice is done. Not the only instrument, of course. God has other instruments — the state is an instrument for God doing justice in the world. I think we have often

5. Newbigin, *Unfinished Agenda*, 1st ed., 55; 2nd ed., 53.

neglected to remember this, that God has other instruments for the doing of his will in the world. But only the Church can be the foretaste, the *arrabon* of the Kingdom.

And, third, the Church is a sign. A sign is supposed to point to something not yet visible. If you want to direct people to Winson Green you don't put a sign up in Winson Green; you have a sign in Handsworth or Edgbaston or somewhere that says "Winson Green." The point of a sign is to point to something that is real but not yet visible. The thing is invisible not because it doesn't exist but because it is over the horizon. Now the Church is a sign of the Kingdom insofar as it is a foretaste. The Church is a sign that points people to a reality beyond what we can see. And the necessary "otherworldliness" of the Church seems to me something that has to be absolutely held on to. We do not offer, nor do we compete with all the other agencies in the world that are offering, solutions to human problems here and now. We are not offering utopian illusions. We are pointing people to a reality that lies beyond history, beyond death. But we are erecting in this world, here and now, signs — credible signs — that make it possible for people to believe that that is the great reality and to join us in going that way. Now, in all this I've been stressing the parish model, and I believe the parish model is the right one. And I think that my last point may be raising a lot of big issues that we ought not perhaps to go into.

I have only recently, through doing a bit of reading among the sociologists of religion like Thomas Luckmann and Peter Berger and so on, as well as a little bit of American history, come to realize how much the "denomination" has become the model by which we think of the Church, and how very recent a thing the denomination is. We are all tending to think of the churches as various denominations. And the sociologists of religion point out that a denomination is something new in Church history. It is not a schism, it is not a sect, it doesn't regard itself as *the* Church in contrast to the false churches. Most of our denominations don't. But it regards itself as one optional form for the Church, which is in a sense invisible. It does not apply to itself the language that Paul applies to the church in Corinth, which is the Church of God, period. It's not an expression of it, or a version of it; these people in Corinth *are* the Church of God, sinners as they are.

And my impression is that through the enormous power of the American model, which tends to dominate the rest of the world, all of our churches are being drawn into this denominational pattern. And I fear that one of the results of Vatican II might be that the Roman Catholic church allows itself to be drawn into that model too.

The sociologists of religion have pointed out to us that the denomination is precisely the visible form that the Church takes when a secularized society privatizes religion. The most striking fact about our culture is that we have a dichotomy between the private and the public worlds, a dichotomy that doesn't exist in premodern society. We have a private world of what we call values, where everyone is free to choose his or her own values, and we do not say about them that they are true or false. We glory in our pluralism. We say that in the realm of values (and religious beliefs are included in that realm), everyone must be free to have his own faith or her own faith. Pluralism reigns. But we have a public world of what we call facts where pluralism does not reign, where things are either true or false; and religion does not belong to that field. It does not belong to the public world. The denomination is the visible form that the Church takes in a society that has accepted the secularization of public life and the privatization of religion, so that the variety of denominations corresponds, if you like, to the variety of brands available on the shelves of the supermarket. Everyone is free to take his or her choice.

Now, the denomination cannot be the bearer of the challenge of the gospel to our society, because it is itself the outward and visible form of an inward and spiritual surrender to the ideology of that society. If, therefore, we are to recover the sense that the local church is the holy catholic Church for that bit of the world in which God has set it (which is the parish principle), then we have to challenge this whole acceptance of the denominational principle as the normal form in which Church life is expressed. I find this both a necessary thought and a frightening thought. I cannot avoid it if I try to be faithful to the Scripture, but I find it terribly challenging.

I told you before about my own personal situation. I'm the minister of a very small URC congregation in Winson Green. How do I try to carry out these ideas there? We have the parish church, we have a Pentecostal church, we have another URC church, we have a black church called the Church of the Firstborn, and we, without being a formal local ecumenical project (because I don't think our higher authorities would allow it), simply act together as clergy. We meet together constantly. We pray together constantly. We plan together constantly. We try to ask what, in spite of our divisions, our unity in Christ has to mean for the life of this community in Winson Green. And it seems to me, as I understand our local situation, that the development of that kind of local accepting of one another in spite of our divisions and our misunderstandings is the catholic Church *in* that place seeking to erect the signs of the Kingdom *for* that place. These two things are mutually involved. I don't think we will recover the true form of the parish until we recover a truly missionary approach to our culture. I don't think we will achieve a truly missionary encounter with our culture without recovering the true form of the parish. These two tasks are reciprocally related to each other, and we have to work together on them both.

7

The Cultural Captivity of Western Christianity as a Challenge to a Missionary Church

Twelve years ago, at the Bangkok Conference on "Salvation Today,"[1] I was sitting in a plenary session next to General Simatoupong. Simatoupong was the general who commanded the Indonesian forces that threw the Dutch out of Indonesia, and when there was no more fighting to be done, he naturally took up theology. We were discussing the global missionary situation, and Simatoupong had just made an intervention in the debate. And as he returned to his seat beside me, I heard him say sotto voce, "Of course the number one question is: Can the West be converted?" I have often thought of

1. The Commission on World Mission and Evangelism (CWME) of the World Council of Churches held a conference on the theme "Salvation Today" in Bangkok in January 1973, with sections on Culture and Identity, Salvation and Social Justice, and Churches Renewed in Mission. See Philip Potter, ed., *Salvation Today: The End or the Beginning of World Mission*, documents on the World Conference on Mission (Geneva, 1973); W. J. Hollenweger, *Glaube, Geist und Geister: Professor Unrat zwischen Bangkok und Birmingham* (Frankfurt: Otto Lembeck, 1975).

A lecture given on 3 October 1994 to members of the Evangelische Missionswerke organisation in Stuttgart, Germany, in connection with the publication of his book *The Other Side of 1984: Questions for the Churches*.

that since. I am sure he was right. What we call the modern Western scientific worldview, the post-Enlightenment cultural world, is the most powerful and persuasive ideology in the world today. As we know, it operates in two forms, Eastern and Western, which are in many ways mirror images of each other. Everywhere in the world it penetrates and disrupts the ancient religious systems with "the acids of modernity." The Christian gospel continues to find new victories among the non-Western, premodern cultures of the world, but in the face of this modern Western culture the Church is everywhere in retreat. Can there be a more challenging frontier for the Church than this?

Simatoupong's question has reverberated in my mind ever since. Most of my life has been spent as a "foreign missionary," and my thinking has been shaped by this experience. Now I am a pastor, along with an Indian colleague, of an inner-city congregation in Birmingham, and I find myself, as my Indian colleague also finds himself, faced with a kind of paganism much more resistant to the gospel than anything that one can find in India. And so the question becomes a burning one: Can the West be converted?

Everyone with experience of cross-cultural mission knows that there are always two opposite dangers, the Scylla and Charybdis, between which one must steer. On the one side there is the danger that one finds no point of contact for the message as the missionary preaches it, to the people of the local culture the message appears irrelevant and meaningless. On the other side is the danger that the point of contact determines entirely the way that the message is received, and the result is syncretism. Every missionary path has to find the way between these two dangers: irrelevance and syncretism. And if one is more afraid of one danger than the other, one will certainly fall into its opposite.

Since I came to live in England after a lifetime as a foreign missionary, I have had the unhappy feeling that most English theology is falling into the second danger — syncretism. Ours is an advanced case of syncretism. In other words, instead of confronting our culture with the gospel, we are perpetually trying to fit the gospel into our culture. In our effort to communicate, we interpret the gospel by the categories of our culture. But how can we avoid this? How can we, who are part of this culture, find a standpoint from which we can address a word, the word of the gospel, to our culture? Archimedes said: Give me a point outside of the earth and with a lever I will move the earth. Where is the Archimedean point from which we can challenge the culture of which we are ourselves a part? Can the experience of cross-cultural mission help us in this task?

When I went as a young missionary to India, I could find the elements of syncretism in Indian Christianity. I saw how, inevitably, the meaning of sentences spoken by my Christian friends was shaped by the Hindu background of the language. The words used, the only available words for God, sin, salvation, and so on, are words that have received their entire content from the Hindu religious tradition. I thought that I was in a position to correct this syncretism. Only slowly did I come to see that my own Christianity was also profoundly syncretistic. Many times I sat with groups of Indian pastors and evangelists to study together a passage of Scripture. Over and over again their interpretation of the text, as it spoke to them in their language, called my interpretation into question. And it was not always clear that my interpretation was in fact more faithful to the text. Many times I had to confess that my reading of the text, which I had hitherto taken for granted, was wholly shaped by my own intellectual formation in what we call the modern scientific worldview. My Christianity was syncretistic, but so was theirs. Yet neither of us could discover that without the challenge of the other. Such is the situation in cross-cultural mission. The gospel comes to the Hindu embodied in the form given to it by the culture of the missionary. That form is both a way of thinking and a way of living. It challenges the traditional Hindu form. The first converts will naturally accept it in the form in which it came from the missionaries, and the form and content cannot be immediately distinguished. But as the second and third and later generations of Christians make their own explorations in Scripture, they will begin to test the Christianity of the missionaries in the light of their own reading of the Scripture. So the missionary, if he is at all awake, finds himself, as I did, in a new situation. He becomes, as a bearer of the gospel, a critic of his own culture. He finds there the Archimedean point. He sees his own culture with the Christian eyes of a foreigner, and the foreigner can see what the native cannot see.

We do not see the lenses of our spectacles; we see through them, and it is another who has to say to us, "Friend, you need a new pair of spectacles." The question therefore is this: How can the European churches, whose life and thought is shaped so completely by this post-Enlightenment culture, become bearers of a mission to that culture?

I know that we are all very enthusiastic about dialogue with people of other faiths and cultures. It is interesting that we use this word *dialogue*. When I talk with my non-Christian neighbor across the garden fence, I just have a conversation, but when I am really serious, then of course it is a dialogue. And that is good, but the problem is that all this dialogue is conducted exclusively in the languages of Europe — German, English, Spanish. No one is qualified to take part in this kind of dialogue without having a full education in a European language and therefore being fully coopted into the post-Enlightenment worldview. That becomes very explicit in a little aside in Hans Küng's book *Christsein,* where he says that we cannot have real deep-going dialogue with the great world religions until they develop "a scientific theology."[2] In other words, the dialogue is only possible within the parameters of the post-Enlightenment worldview. That view remains unchallenged. We do not see it as our ideology. It is just how things are when you are properly educated! The gospel, along with all other religions, is simply coopted as one equal partner within that ideology.

And that brings me to the crux of the matter. In the little pamphlet — a small blast not of the trumpet but of the tin whistle — called *The Other Side of 1984,*[3] I said that it seemed to me that while the Roman Catholic church had attempted to erect barriers against the Enlightenment, the Protestant churches had, in effect, surrendered the public field — politics, education, industry, economics — to the ideology of the Enlightenment and sought refuge in the private world of the home and the soul. This sharp dichotomy between the public and the private world is one of the distinctive features of our culture.

2. Hans Küng, *On Being a Christian* (London: E. T., 1977).
3. Lesslie Newbigin, *The Other Side of 1984,* Risk Book Series no. 18 (Geneva: World Council of Churches, 1983); Newbigin, *Unfinished Agenda,* 2nd ed., 252f.

Such a dichotomy is not found in traditional premodern cultures. It corresponds to the distinction we draw between "facts" and "values." The public world of our culture is the world of what we call "facts," which do not depend upon the beliefs of the individual; "values" on the other hand are personal beliefs, and in the world of values pluralism reigns. Each one must be free to cherish the values that he or she chooses. No one, no state or church or party, has the right to dictate common beliefs regarding values. Everyone has the right to the pursuit of happiness, and — what is more important — everyone has the right to define happiness as he will. It is to this world of personally chosen values that religion is thought to belong. And Christianity is one among the options offered for personal choice. It has freedom to compete with others, provided it makes no claim to absolute truth. In contrast to this is the public world of what we call facts. Here pluralism emphatically does not reign. Here all are expected to agree. Where there are apparent contradictions between statements of alleged facts, we do not celebrate this as a good example of pluralism. We argue and experiment and test until we arrive at a point where all agree; and for those who cannot agree we have, of course, our mental hospitals. In the school textbook these agreed-upon conclusions will be simply stated as facts without the use of the prefix "I believe" or "we believe." Thus every student will be expected to know that the development of the human person is governed by the program encoded in the DNA molecules. This is a fact. But that every human person is made to glorify God and enjoy him forever is not a fact — it is a belief, one among many possible beliefs. It is not part of the school curricula. And yet, clearly the question of truth is at stake as much in the second matter as in the first. It either is or is not true that every human being must finally appear before the judgment seat of Christ. If it is true, it is universally true, just as the statement about the DNA molecule is true; if it is true at all, it is true for everyone. It belongs to the public sector as much as to the private.

What is the source of this dichotomy between the public world of facts and the private world of beliefs? It is a complex story, and I am not an expert in the history of philosophy. Certain things can, I think, be said with confidence. Ever since Galileo turned his telescope on the heavens and showed that the universe is not what it seems to be, there has been a passionate search for a kind of certainty, a kind of knowledge that does not depend on fallible human beliefs. Descartes sought it in the certainty of his own thought; the new scientists sought it in the precise observation of the data of the senses without reliance on the traditional beliefs of religion and philosophy, and particularly without reliance on the traditional concept of purpose through which the Greeks and the medieval scholars had tried to interpret phenomena. This new observation of the phenomena was held to give knowledge of what Francis Bacon called the facts. And a fact in this sense has no value. A thing can only be called good or bad if it is or is not fitted for the purpose for which it was made. And this purpose is real in the mind of the one who purposes, but it is not yet fully realized in the world of objects. It can, in principle, only be grasped by an act of faith. That faith enables us to understand the world of objects, not as mere facts about which no value judgment can be made, but in relation to the purpose for which they exist. And that gives a different kind of certainty from the certainty our culture seeks. It is not a certainty that relieves me of personal responsibility for my beliefs. It is a personal trust. It relies on grace. It does not claim — in contrast to the search of our culture — the kind of knowledge only God can have. It is the certainty of faith, not of omniscience. John Locke — whose thinking, I suppose, has shaped the Anglo-Saxon world almost more than any other since the Enlightenment — John Locke defined belief as something we fall back on when certain knowledge is unattainable.[4] I say "I believe" only when I am not in a position to say "I know." As I heard a philosopher put it wittily the other day, "If I believe, then I don't know." So I *know* the facts in the physics textbook, but I only *believe* what the gospel promises. The public world is the world of what we know, and here pluralism is excluded. The private world is the world of what we believe, and here pluralism rules.

But of course, this is profoundly false. Scientists themselves know that science rests on a faith-commitment that cannot be demonstrated, on the faith that the universe is both rational and contingent. If the

---

4. John Locke, *An Essay on Human Understanding*, ed. Peter Nidditch (Oxford: Clarendon, 1975). Originally written 1690.

universe were not rational, science would be impossible. If the universe were not contingent, science would be unnecessary. Faith therefore is not a substitute for knowledge. It is the precondition of knowledge. And the kind of certainty that our post-Enlightenment culture has aspired to is an illusion. The idea that brute facts simply imprint themselves on our minds apart from our deliberate and fallible efforts to grasp them is an illusion. And so also the idea that there is a body of objective value-free facts against which the Christian claims and the claims of all other religions have to be tested is nonsense. The Christian faith in God as creator and sustainer of a world that is both rational and contingent made possible the rise of modern science. Today, if I am not mistaken, our great danger is a total skepticism about any possibility of knowing the truth. I find among young people, and I think I understand and sympathize with them, a profound skepticism about any claim to the truth. Our danger is of a new irrationalism and nihilism. It is the despair that doubts there is anything worth believing and preserving. And even Christians are encouraged to think of their faith as only one among a number of options available for personal choice. We may be convinced that it is a source of comfort, of hope, of inner peace. And when we try to commend it to others, we try to show that it is not incompatible with the modern scientific worldview that controls public life; but we commend it as a responsible and respectable option for the private sector. Am I wrong? Is this a caricature?

If I think of the English church scene, I do not think so. Like others who have returned to the West after a lifetime as a foreign missionary, I am moved to ask, Who will be the missionaries to this culture? Who will confront this culture of ours with the claim of absolute truth, the claim that Jesus Christ is the truth? Who will be bold enough to say, not that the Christian message can be explained in terms of the facts as we know them, but rather that *all* so-called knowledge must be tested against the supreme reality: God incarnate in Jesus Christ, present yesterday, today, until the end, in the power of the Spirit? What will it mean to call for a missionary confrontation with this culture?

I confess that as I ask these questions I am alarmed. I do not know where they will lead us. I say that in all honesty: I do not know where they will lead us. And yet I am bound to ask these questions. Certainly we cannot expect or desire to return to the Corpus Christianum. We cannot reconstruct the total synthesis of Christian belief and public order that finally broke down in the religious wars of the seventeenth century. But equally, I think, and this may be more unpopular, we cannot simply go back to the New Testament and the primitive church. We cannot aspire now, after these nineteen centuries, to a kind of pre-Constantinian innocence. That kind of nostalgia is dangerous. I hear too many Christians saying, in effect, that the Church can have nothing to do with power, that its only function is to protest and demonstrate against all the powers. We cannot do without a theologically grounded Christian doctrine of the state. We must not fall into the error of dividing physical force as bad from soul force *(satyagraha)* as good. That is the old Manichean heresy. There is no going back. We are in a new and unprecedented situation, a new missionary frontier. How do we approach this task? As I said, I am puzzled and even frightened. I do not know what this will involve. I see dangers on all sides. But so that I may not end with a set of unanswered questions, let me try to make five constructive points:

1. If what I have been saying is true, there is need for what I would call a declericalizing of theology. Theology has been largely the preserve of clergy and academics. What is needed is the cooperative work of Christian laymen and women in specific sectors of public life — industry, politics, medicine, education, local government, welfare, administration, the media, literature, drama, and the arts. In each of these and other sectors of public life there is a need to examine the accepted axioms and assumptions that underlie the contemporary practice, to examine them in the light of the gospel. That will not happen as long as theology is the preserve of the clergy or, what is equally dangerous, simply an enclave within a secular academic community. There is an immense intellectual and pastoral task in which the experience of the foreign missionary movement could, I believe, be of great help to the churches in making this move towards a more truly missionary relationship with our culture.

2. It is obvious that this can only be done by the churches acting together. It can only be done as the Church *in* each place becomes recognizable as the Church *for* that place. But what is a denomination? Perhaps I could refer to the somewhat uncomfortable question raised

by Ulrich Duchrow in his book *Conflict in the Ecumenical Movement*.[5] This is a question that will not go away. A denomination is not a church, it is not a sect, it does not make the claim to the allegiance of society as a whole. It has been defined by one of its apologists, the American sociologist Sidney Mead, in the following terms: "It is a voluntary association of like-minded and like-hearted individuals who are united on the basis of common beliefs for the purpose of accomplishing tangible and defined objectives. One of the primary objectives is the propagation of its point of view." In that description we recognize the American denominational model, but it is clearly a model that is tending to reproduce itself everywhere, especially through the increasingly powerful operation of the world confessional bodies. And, as the sociologists have pointed out, the denomination is simply the institutional form of privatized religion. It is a voluntary association of individuals. It is — to put it simply — the outward and visible form of an inward and spiritual surrender to the ideology of our culture. It follows that, in strict logic, neither the denomination alone nor denominations federated in what is now, I believe, called "reconciled diversity" can become the instrument of a missionary challenge to our culture, because they are themselves the institutional form of a surrender to our culture. They cannot confront our culture as Jesus confronted Pontius Pilate with the witness to the truth, since they do not claim to be more than associations of individuals who hold the same opinion. We do not see clearly what the form of a restored and reunited catholic Church would be. That is our great task in the ecumenical movement. But I believe that it is possible to act effectively in each local situation in such a way that the Christians together in each place begin even now to be recognizable as the Church for that place.

3. If we are to escape from the ideology of the Enlightenment without falling into the errors of the Corpus Christianum, we must recover a doctrine of freedom of thought and conscience that is founded not on the ideology of the Enlightenment but on the gospel. At this point I think I must admit that my use of the word *dogma* in

5. Ulrich Duchrow, *Conflict in the Ecumenical Movement* (Grand Rapids, Mich.: Eerdmans, 1983).

my little book was perhaps a tactical mistake. It was intended to shock people into recognizing the fact that we all operate with dogmas. The difference is whether we recognize that we do. The freedom of conscience, the freedom of thought that was won for us by the men and women of the Enlightenment against the resistance of the Church, is a gift we cannot surrender. We must remember penitently our past in that respect. But if we now ask that the Christian faith claim the whole public life of the nation, of society in the name of truth, how can we safeguard that freedom?

What we must seek for is a doctrine of freedom based on the gospel and not on the ideology of the Enlightenment. And we must begin by distinguishing tolerance from neutrality or indifference. There is a beautiful description of Roman society in Gibbon's *Decline and Fall of the Roman Empire* that I think exactly describes ours. He said that in Roman society all religions were to the people equally true, to the philosophers equally false, and to the government equally useful. It would be difficult to deny that that is a true account of some modern developed societies. But that kind of neutrality is evidence either of impending collapse or else of the fact that some other ideology has taken the place usually occupied by religion as the overarching "plausibility structure" within which public life is conducted. Since total skepticism about ultimate beliefs is impossible, in that no belief can be doubted except on the basis of some other belief, indifference is always in danger of collapsing into skepticism or fanaticism. Tolerance in respect of what is not important is easy. How is it possible to combine real commitment to the truth in matters of supreme importance with tolerance of falsehood?

Clearly, if we are to be consistent, the answer has to be given from within our commitment to the truth as it is in Jesus, not sought from outside of that truth. It can be given in the form of three statements.

First, let us recall the fact that the risen Jesus, whose kingship was defined as bearing witness to the truth, also warned his Church against the temptation to expect immediately the manifestation of the truth in coercive power. "Lord, will you at this time restore the kingdom of Israel?" The answer is: It is not for you to know the times and seasons that the Father has set in his own authority, but you will receive the

Spirit, the foretaste, the *arrabon* of the kingdom and you will be my witnesses (Acts 1:6–7). In other words, it is the will of the Father to provide a space and a time wherein men and women can give their allegiance to the kingship of God in the only way that it can be given, that is, in freedom. To use the God-given authority of the state to deny this freedom is therefore to violate the space that God himself has provided and that he has put into the care — if I understand the New Testament rightly — of earthly governors, of the powers that be.

Second, the Church, which is entrusted with the truth, is also a body of sinful men and women who falsely identify their grasp of truth with the truth itself. Here we have that paradox of grace that the Church is a body of forgiven sinners, which applies equally to the Church's understanding of the truth. That is brought out with brilliant clarity in that incident in the Gospel where Jesus has to say to Peter, "You are the rock and on this rock I will build my church," and in the next breath, "Get behind me, Satan" (Matt. 16:18, 23). This deep fundamental paradox of the Church is real because sin remains a reality in the life of the forgiven community. The Church can and does allow the truth that is entrusted to her to become an ideological justification of her own human interest. And God consequently has to use his other servants, and especially the state, to bring the Church to repentance and renewal.

Third, I return to the Johannine discourses in which our Lord tells his disciples that they have yet much to learn of the truth that cannot be told them immediately, and that it is the Spirit who will be given to them who will lead them into the truth. The context of that saying is of course the long account of the missionary experience that lies ahead of the Church, its rejection by the world, and the witness that the Spirit will give in speaking for the Church, in confusing the wisdom of the world, and in glorifying Jesus by taking what belongs to the Father and showing it to the Church (John 15:18–16:15). This promise is being fulfilled as the Church goes on its missionary journey to the ends of the earth and to the end of time, entering into dialogue with new cultures and being itself changed, as parts of the Father's world are brought through the Spirit into the Church's treasury of truth. In this missionary dialogue the Church both learns new things and provides the place where witness is borne to Christ as head of the human race — Christ, who is so much more than any of us can yet grasp or state, who is seen more and more through the missionary experience of the Church as he truly is, but who will only be seen in his fullness when every tongue confesses that he is Lord.

Thus, if I am right, a true understanding of the gospel itself ought to enable Christians both to be firm in their allegiance to Christ as the way, the truth, and the life, and also to be ready to hear and enter into dialogue with those who do not give that allegiance but from whom the Church has still to learn of all that belongs to the Father. The mind that is firmly anchored in Christ, knowing that Christ is much greater than the limited understanding that each of us has of him, is at the same time able to enter freely into the kind of missionary dialogue I have described. This is the foundation for a true tolerance, not indifference to the truth. True dialogue is as far as possible from neutrality or indifference. Its basis is the shared conviction that there is truth to be known and that we must both bear witness to the truth given to us and also listen to the witness of others.

4. I want to make a strictly theological point. There can be no missionary encounter with our culture without a biblically grounded eschatology, without a recovering of a true apocalyptic. The dichotomy that runs through our culture between the private and the public worlds is reflected in the dissolution of the biblical vision of the last things into two separate and unrelated forms of hope. One is the public hope for a better world in the future, the heavenly city of the eighteenth-century French philosophers, the utopia of the evolutionary social planners, or the classless society of the revolutionary sociologists. The other is the private hope for personal immortality in a blessed world beyond this one. This dissolution is tragic. It destroys the integrity of the human person. If I pin my hope to a perfect world that is to be prepared for some future generations, I know that I and my contemporaries will never live to see it, and therefore that those now living can be — and if necessary must be — sacrificed in the interests of those as yet unborn; and so the way is open for the ruthless logic of totalitarian planners and social engineers. If on the other hand I place all my hope in a personal future, I am tempted to wash my hands of responsibility for the public life of the world and to turn inwards towards a purely private spirituality.

That tragic split runs right through our lives and our society, and only the biblical understanding of the last things can heal that dichotomy. The apocalyptic teaching that forms such an important part of the New Testament has generally in our culture been pushed to the margins of Christian thought. It has been treasured, of course, by small oppressed groups on the margins of our society, but it has been generally silenced in the mainstream of our established Christianity. Essentially this says to us: If I ask what in all my active life is the horizon of my expectations, the thing to which I look forward, the answer, it seems to me, cannot be some social utopia in the future and cannot be some personal bliss for myself; it can only be, quite simply, the coming of Jesus to complete his Father's will. He shall come again. He is the horizon of my expectations. Everything from my side, whether prayer or action, private or public, is done to him and for him. It is simply offered for his use. In the words of Schweitzer, it is an "acted prayer for His coming." He will make of it what he will. My most vigorous and righteous actions do not build the holy city. They are too shot through with sin for that. But they are acted prayers that he will give the holy city. And that embraces both the public and the private world. The holy city, as its name indicates, is on the one hand the crown and perfection of all that we call civilization. Into it the kings of the nations bring their cultural treasures. But it is also the place where every tear is wiped from our eyes and we are the beloved children of God who see him face to face. Only in that vision and hope is the tragic dichotomy of our culture healed.

5. Finally, I want to argue the need for a certain boldness that was evidently a characteristic mark of the first apostles. Some time ago I happened to have the privilege of sitting next to Cardinal Suenens at a conference, and he asked me what I thought of contemporary English theology. I replied "timid syncretism." Perhaps that was unfair. I am sure it cannot be true of German theology. What I am pleading for is the courage to hold and proclaim a belief that cannot be proved to be true in terms of the accepted axioms of our society, that can be doubted by rational minds, but that we nevertheless hold as the truth. It may sound simplistic to say that. Our modern scientific culture has pursued the ideal of a completely impersonal knowledge of a world of so-called facts that are simply there and

cannot be doubted by rational minds, facts that constitute the real world as distinct from the opinions, desires, hopes, and beliefs of human beings. Now, this whole way of trying to understand the world rests upon beliefs that are simply not questioned. Every attempt to understand and cope with experience has to begin with some act of faith. Every such belief is of course open to critical question, but no criticism is possible except by relying on beliefs that in the act of criticism are not criticized. All understanding of reality involves a venture of faith. No belief system can be faulted by the fact that it rests upon unproved assumptions. What can and must be faulted is a blindness to the assumptions one is relying upon. The gospel is not a set of beliefs that arise or could arise from empirical observation of the whole human experience. It cannot be based upon inductive reasoning. It is the announcement of a name and a fact that offer the starting point for the whole lifelong enterprise of understanding and coping with experience. It is a new starting point. To accept it means a new beginning, a radical conversion. We cannot side-step that necessity. It has always been the case that to believe means to turn around and face in a different direction, to be a dissident, to swim against the stream. The Church, it seems to me, needs to be very humble in acknowledging that it is itself only a learner, needing to pay heed to all the variety of human experience in order to learn in practice what it means that Jesus is King and Head of the human race. But the Church also needs to be very bold, bold in bearing witness to him as the one who alone is that King and Head. For the demonstration of the truth we have to wait for the end. Till then we have to be bold and steadfast in our witness and patient in our home, for, to quote the letter to the Hebrews, we are partakers of Christ if we hold our first confidence firm to the end (Heb. 3:14).

8

By What Authority?

The program "The Gospel and Our Culture"[1] is concerned to bring the insights developed in the history of Christian missions to bear upon the culture of the societies from which Christian missionaries have gone out to other parts of the world during the past two hundred years. The foreign missionary brings with him a book — the Bible — and a tradition of thought and practice regarded as being authorized by the Bible and by the teaching of the Church that has been the bearer of this tradition. But can the Bible and the Christian tradition speak in the same way to this culture, which has been so largely influenced in its history by precisely this book and this tradition? A recent reviewer of my book *Foolishness to the Greeks*[2] said that this attempt to criticize our culture from the point of view of "the Bible" (his quotation marks) was like pretending to move a bus when you are sitting in it. It is a serious point. The Bible and the

1. The genesis of the "Gospel as Public Truth" program is described in Newbigin, *Unfinished Agenda*, 2nd ed., 254f. A quarterly newsletter is issued, obtainable from the Selly Oak Colleges, Birmingham B29 6LE. See also Hugh Montefiore, ed., *The Gospel and Contemporary Culture* (London: SPCK, 1992).

2. Lesslie Newbigin, *Foolishness to the Greeks: The Gospel and Western Culture* (Grand Rapids, Mich.: Eerdmans/SPCK, 1986).

This paper was a first attempt to grapple with problems discussed more fully in *The Gospel in a Pluralist Society* (London: SPCK, 1989) and now the basis of his forthcoming book *Proper Confidence*.

Christian tradition of thought and action are part of our culture and are subject to the same kind of analysis and criticism as is any other part. What grounds can be shown for according to them the privilege of speaking a word *to* our culture?

This question of authority has been a crucial one from the beginning of the Christian mission. The first apostles were asked by what authority they acted, and replied, "In Jesus's name."[3] Jesus himself was asked for this authority; he replied by asking his interlocutors whether the baptism of John was from heaven or from men, and when they were unable to answer his question he refused to answer theirs. They had shown themselves incapable of recognizing authority when it was present. On the other hand, it is reported of "the crowds" that they recognized Jesus as one who taught having authority, unlike their scribes (Acts 4:5–10; Matt. 21:23–27; 7:28f.).

These references may serve to make the fundamental and obvious point that ultimate authority can only be the authority of God, and that if this authority is not recognized, there is no way of demonstrating it by reference to something else. We shall have to return to this fundamental point at the end. But it is impossible to avoid the question, "How is the authority of God mediated to us?" In attempting to answer this question, Christians have used four words: Scripture, tradition, reason, and — more recently — experience. It will be helpful to look at these four words in turn.

Scripture

It is notorious that Christians are deeply divided on the question of the authority of Scripture. For many centuries the Bible (*the* book) held a place apart from all other literature. Its authority was universally unquestioned. It provided the framework for the study of the laws of the natural world, as well as for the understanding of the

---

3. Acts 4:10; 5:40. Apostolic authority was, according to 1 Cor. 15, based on a commission from the risen Christ, the word *apostle* being derived from the Greek for "one who has been sent, an envoy," and depended not only on one's having seen the risen Lord, but on one's having been commissioned by him.

human mind. In the course of the last three centuries it has been subjected to critical analysis with the tools of the modern scientific method. The result is the split with which we are familiar between those who wish to affirm biblical authority by defending the factual accuracy of everything it contains, and those who see the biblical material as symbolic of human religious experience, there being — of course — many other varieties of religious experience. In this situation it has become difficult or impossible to speak with intellectual coherence about the authority of Scripture vis-à-vis any particular aspect of our culture.

What is not often noticed is that this split is only one manifestation of a much deeper fissure in our culture as a whole. It might be described briefly as a breakdown of the unity between the subjective and the objective poles of human knowing. It is customary to trace this breakdown back to Descartes, with his search for indubitable knowledge set forth in forms of expression that have the clarity and exactitude of mathematics. For the centuries since then we have been dominated by the ideal of a kind of knowledge that is objective in the sense that it involves no personal commitment on the part of the knower. It is "factual," disinfected of anything that personal interest might introduce. What is claimed to be knowledge but cannot be expressed in such "objective" terms is a matter of personal opinion. It is belief rather than knowledge, and — as Locke has taught us — belief is what we fall back upon when knowledge is not available.[4] "Values," in this view, are a matter of personal choice; "facts" are not. No logical ties can bind the two together. "Values" cannot be derived from "facts." The split is visible to all in the separation between science and "the humanities" in the curriculum of the universities.

Given this situation, it is natural that the Bible has to be understood as belonging to one or the other of these two halves of our culture. On the one hand are those who can only affirm the authority of Scripture by regarding it as a collection of factually true statements. On the other are those who see in it material that expresses in symbolic and poetic form certain values, including various kinds of religious experience. If the first choice is made, one is on a collision course

4. Locke, *An Essay on Human Understanding.*

with the findings of science, in spite of the efforts of the "creationists." If the second choice is made, the Bible simply has to take its place among the many varieties of moral and religious experience. It is part of the history of religions. George Lindbeck in *The Nature of Christian Doctrine*[5] proposes, as an alternative to these two views, what he calls a "cultural-linguistic model" for the understanding of Scripture. I find this helpful only if it is related explicitly to the basic epistemological split of which the fundamentalist-liberal split is only a surface manifestation.

In his exposition of the "cultural-linguistic" model for understanding doctrine, Lindbeck uses such phrases as "myths or narratives . . . which structure human experience and understanding of self and world," "an idiom that makes possible the description of realities," "something like a Kantian *a priori*."[6] Doctrine, in other words, is not so much something we look *at* as something we look *through* in order to understand the world. Here we are raising the epistemological question. All knowing involves a knowing subject, and knowing is only possible for a subject who has been inducted into a tradition of knowing embodied in language, symbol, story. Most of what we know is — normally — not the subject of our attention. It is the framework we use to order our experience and make sense of it. It is, in Michael Polanyi's phrase, the tacit component in all knowing.[7] When Lindbeck uses the term *cultural-linguistic* to describe his model for doctrine, he is rightly drawing attention to the fact that knowledge requires the ability to use a language and an accepted framework of understanding about "how things are and how things behave" that enables us to make sense of experience. When we use language to communicate information or to share a vision, we do not attend to the words we are using; we attend *through* the words *to* the matter in hand. Only when the words fail to establish communication do we attend to the words

5. George Lindbeck, *The Nature of Christian Doctrine: Religion and Theology in a Postliberal Age* (London, 1984), 32–33.

6. Alain Finkielraut, *The Undoing of Thought* (N.p., 1989). Discussed in *The Gospel and Our Culture*, Newsletter 3.

7. Michael Polanyi, *Personal Knowledge: Towards a Post-Critical Philosophy* (Chicago: University of Chicago Press, 1958), 88.

in order to find better ones. And words are part of a culture, of a whole way of understanding and coping with the world that has been developed in a specific community. But this necessary subjective component in all knowing does not mean that it is robbed of its objective reference. It is saved from a false subjectivity by being published, made the object of public scrutiny and discussion, tested against new situations. Yet this scrutiny can only be undertaken by knowing subjects who are themselves depending on a culturally shaped tradition. Is "objective truth" unobtainable?

We seem to be nearing the end of a period in which it was believed that modern science could provide a body of universal truth that would be the possession of all human beings, whatever their cultural differences. The enormous impact of Newton's physics has lasted until the present day, with its vision of a self-contained cosmos of particles of matter moving according to a precisely determined mathematical world in which the human mind had no place. Paradoxically, this dehumanized model had enormous human appeal. It gave birth to the idea of a universal reason equally applicable in all human cultures and of the universal rights of man simply as man and apart from the accidents of a particular society. It created for Lessing the "wide ugly ditch" between the universal truths of reason and the accidental happenings of history. It provoked (most notably in Germany) the reaction in favor of the *Volksgeist* as the true bearer of truth. In spite of all that has happened in the recent developments of physics to call the Newtonian vision into question, we are still left with the "two cultures":[8] a culture of science, which is supposed to be universally valid for all peoples, and a multiculturalism, which brands as imperialistic any claim to discriminate between less and more valuable elements in culture — including the area of religious belief.

It is simply impossible to remain content with this bisection of human experience into two halves that have no rational connection with each other, and that means that it is also impossible to accept the terms of the fundamentalist-liberal debate about the authority of Scripture. To borrow Lindbeck's words, Scripture functions as "the cultural-linguistic framework within which the Christian life is lived

8. See C. P. Snow, "The Two Cultures and the Scientific Revolution."

and Christian doctrine developed." The Bible is (Lindbeck again) "a narrative which structures human experience and understanding." It is, however varied its texture, essentially a story that claims to be *the* story, the true story both of the cosmos and of human life within the cosmos. After one has done all the work that can be done and has to be done to analyze its structures and trace the origins of its different parts, it is in its total canonical structure a story that provides the clue to the meaning of cosmic and human story in the story of a particular people and of a particular man among that people. Like every telling of the human story, it is a selection of a minute fraction of the available records and memories on the basis of a particular belief about the meaning of the story. World history as it is normally taught in schools is the history of the development of civilization. We are, naturally, the civilized people, and we are the point of the story. The Bible tells the story from a different view of what is significant, from the belief that the point of the entire story has been made in the doings and sufferings and triumphs of the man Jesus. Plainly, the farther one travels from this center the less precise are the details, until we reach the periphery of the story, the beginning and the end of the cosmos, where everything has necessarily to be in symbol.

The question "Which is the real story?" must determine everything else in our understanding of what it is to be human and what it is to handle rightly the natural world within which human life is set. The Bible, I suggest, functions properly in the life of the Church when it functions in the way Lindbeck's language suggests. It functions as the true story of which our story is a part, and therefore we do not so much look *at* it as *through* it in order to understand and deal with the real world. If I may revert to Polanyi's language,[9] I would want to say that the Bible ought to function primarily as the *tacit* component in our endeavor to understand and deal with the world. We have to *indwell* the story, as we indwell the language we use and the culture of which we are a part. But since we also live within this other culture,

9. Polanyi, *Personal Knowledge,* 88, 95-100, 140-141, 251. See the discussion in Lesslie Newbigin, *Truth to Tell: The Gospel as Public Truth,* 28-38, where Newbigin says he is following Drusilla Scott, *Everyman Revived: The Commonsense of Michael Polanyi* (N.p., 1991).

there is necessarily an internal dialogue within us. By all our cultural formation from infancy onward, we are made part of the story of our nation and our civilization. There is something to be learned here from the experience of a foreign missionary. As one learns to enter deeply into the mental world of another people, into their story, as one is drawn by the coherence and rationality of that other story, dialogue is set up between this and the Christian story. That internal dialogue is the precondition for true external dialogue. But clearly the story functions effectively in providing the "structure of understanding" only insofar as one really lives the story. The Bible cannot function with any authority except through the lives of those whose story it is, those who "indwell" the story. We cannot speak of biblical authority without speaking of tradition.

Tradition

It is of crucial importance in any discussion of authority to consider the significance of the fact that Jesus did not write a book. The only example recorded of Jesus' writing is when he wrote in the dust.[10] He did not bequeath a book to his followers. He devoted his ministry (as far as we know) to the formation of a community that would represent him to those who would come after. He taught them in ways that would be remembered and passed on to others, but he did not provide a written text. It is, surely, very important that almost all the words of Jesus have come to us in versions that are not identical. To wish that it were otherwise would evidently be to go against the intention of Jesus. The fact that we have four Gospels and not one is cited by Muslims as evidence that the real Gospel *(Injil)* has been lost. But the Church refused to substitute one harmonized version for the four disparate ones. On the one hand the New Testament writers insist that what they teach is (unless otherwise stated — e.g., 1 Cor. 7) a faithful rendering of the intention of Jesus. They are not originators but messengers. But on the other hand the teachings of Jesus and the

10. John 8:1-11, a passage omitted from modern translations because it is not found in a number of fourth-century Greek uncials and is not in Luke's Gospel.

stories of his ministry are told in the words of the writers, shaped to meet different situations.

The story the Bible tells is tied to particular times, places, languages, and cultures. If it were not, it would be no part of human history. It is told as the clue to the entire story — human and cosmic, from creation to the end of time. It cannot function as the clue to the whole story if it is simply repeated in the same words. It has to be translated, and translation is (fallible) interpretation. The many-layered material of the Old Testament is witness to the repeated re-telling of the fundamental story in new terms of new occasions. And Jesus expressly tells the disciples (in the Johannine interpretation) that although they have received a true and full revelation of the Father, they have yet much to learn that they cannot learn until later. They are promised that the Holy Spirit will guide them "into all the truth." In view of the perennial temptation to identify the Holy Spirit with the *Zeitgeist,* it is important to note that the promise is that the Spirit will glorify Jesus, for the Spirit will show the Church how all things in the cosmos belong to him. Raymond Brown paraphrases the promise as "interpreting in relation to each coming generation the contemporary significance of what Jesus has said and done."[11] The Church is not tied to a text in such a way that nothing will ever be done for the first time. In new situations those who "indwell" the story of which Jesus is the center will have to make new and risky decisions about what faithfulness to the Author of the story requires. There can be no drawing of a straight line from a text of Scripture to a contemporary ethical decision; there will always be the requirement of a fresh decision in responsibility to the One whose story it is.

There can, therefore, be no appeal to Scripture that ignores the continuing tradition of Christian discipleship. That would be to detach Scripture from the story to which it is the clue. But it is a delicate matter to state exactly what the relation between Scripture and tradition is. The tendency of Protestants to isolate the Scriptures from the tradition is, of course, mistaken, since no one has access to a Bible unless someone hands it over *(tradition);* but it is understandable in view of the long

11. Raymond Brown, *The Gospel According to St. John,* vol. 2 (New York: Doubleday, 1970), 716.

experience of the Roman Catholic tendency to treat Scripture and tradition as though they were separate and parallel sources of authority. The first draft of the Vatican II document on revelation was entitled "The Two Sources of Revelation." This was rejected, and the final text, simply entitled "Divine Revelation," begins with two chapters called "Revelation Itself" and "The Transmission of Divine Revelation." The first, beginning from God's word incarnate in Jesus Christ, affirms that God "can be known with certainty from created reality and by the light of human reason" and that he has spoken through the prophets and, last of all, in his Son. The second chapter speaks of Christ's commission to the apostles to preach the gospel to all, and of bishops as the successors of the apostles to whom this responsibility was entrusted. This tradition "develops in the Church with the help of the Holy Spirit" so that "the Church constantly moves forward towards the fullness of divine truth." It follows that "both sacred tradition and sacred Scripture are to be accepted and venerated with the same sense of devotion and reverence."

How is one to define the relation of tradition to Scripture? On the one hand the New Testament is itself part of the tradition. It is obviously based on oral testimony given at different times under different circumstances. But it claims to be the authentic representation of what it describes. "I delivered to you . . . what I first received," says the Apostle (1 Cor. 15:3). On the other hand, the closing of the canon of Scripture implies that what is included in the canon has a higher authority than what is excluded. What is included has a normative role in relation to all further tradition. In this respect the language of Vatican II is surely too triumphalist. Not all of what has been handed on is to be accepted. The accusation that Jesus leveled against religious teachers of his time, that they had made void the Word of God by their traditions, has to be leveled against some forms of the Christian tradition.[12] Development in Christian teaching is not a process that has its norm immanent in itself. The promise of Jesus to his disciples that the Holy Spirit would lead them into the fullness of the truth is linked to the promise that in doing so, the Spirit will

12. Mark 7:13. Though Jesus criticizes the Pharisees, his methods of exegesis are similar.

glorify Jesus. What the Spirit will show the Church is what belongs to Jesus, and every alleged teaching of the Spirit has to be tested by that criterion (John 16:14f.). On the other hand, the authority of Scripture lies in the fact that it renders in narrative form the character of the One who is the Author of history and is therefore the clue to all history. Consequently we cannot follow this clue without taking account of the way that it has been followed in the past. The centuries after the incarnation of the Word have filled out with further content the universal and cosmic implications of the incarnation, but what has followed has to be judged by the criteria furnished by the events of the incarnation. The relation between Scripture and tradition is thus reciprocal, but Scripture is normative in relation to tradition. It is true that it often happens that someone who knows nothing of Jesus or of Christianity reads a Gospel for the first time and is so captured by the sheer power of what he reads that he turns to Christ in full submission. But it is also true that such a reader will not learn what submission to Christ means except in the fellowship of the Church. The book is the book of the community, and the community is the community of the story that the book tells. Neither can be understood without the other.

Tradition, therefore, is not a source of authority separate from Scripture. Rather it is only by "indwelling" the Scripture that one remains faithful to the tradition. By this "indwelling" ("abiding") we take our place and play our part in the story that is the true story of the whole human race and of the cosmos. Reading the Scriptures as our own story in a shared discipleship with all those — past and present — who acknowledge with us that this *is* the true story, we trust the promise that the Holy Spirit will lead us into the fullness of the truth. Neither Scripture nor tradition furnishes us with an authority that releases us from the risky business of making our own decision in every new situation. But we have the confidence that though we may make mistaken decisions, the community that lives by the true story will not be finally lost (Matt. 16:18).

Reason

There is a long tradition that speaks of Scripture, tradition, and reason as the threefold source of authority in regard to Christian doctrine. I have argued that it is a mistake to put tradition alongside of Scripture as though it were a separate and parallel source of authority. The fact that this is a mistake is now widely accepted. It would be equally mistaken to think of *reason* as a separate and parallel source of authority. No one grasps or makes sense of anything in Scripture or in the tradition of scriptural interpretation except by use of reason. And reason can only operate within a continuous tradition of speech, the speech of a community whose language embodies a shared way of understanding. Reason is a faculty we use to try to grasp the different elements in our experience in an orderly way, so that — as we say — "they make sense." It is not a separate source of information about reality. It can only function within a continuous linguistic and cultural tradition. We learn to reason as we learn, in childhood, to use words and concepts, those words and concepts that embody the way our society makes sense of the world. All rationality is socially and culturally embodied.

When we look back on the "age of reason," and especially at the arguments used in the eighteenth century to defend the "reasonableness" of Christianity, it is obvious that the word *reason* was used to denote conformity with a set of assumptions derived from the science and philosophy of the time. The sociologists of knowledge have taught us to use the term *plausibility structure* to denote the structure of beliefs and practices that, in any given society, determine what beliefs are plausible within that society. When "reason" is adduced as a third source of authority alongside Scripture and tradition, it is obvious that what is being appealed to is simply the contemporary plausibility structure. This becomes especially obvious when we look at the "self-evident truths" of which the eighteenth-century thinkers spoke. It is obvious to us now that these truths are not self-evident. They are the product of a specific tradition of rationality. There is a parallel here with mathematics. The mathematician John Puddefoot has written, "An Axiom is not the foundation of a system, but the product of generations of mathematical enquiry as it has eventually been formalised or axiomatised."[13] Reason operates within a specific tradition of rational discourse, a tradition that is carried by a specific human community. There is no supracultural "reason" that can stand in judgment over all particular human traditions of rationality. All reason operates within a total worldview that is embodied in the language, the concepts, and the models by which those who share them can reason together. Christian doctrine is a form of rational discourse, and it has been developed in communities that find the clue to the rationality of the cosmos in the events of the biblical narrative and in the subsequent experience of those who have done the same. The fact that it is rooted in one strand of the whole human story in no way invalidates its claim to universal relevance. Every other form of rationality is rooted thus as well.

Does this lead to a total relativism? No, because all human reasoning is subject to the test of adequacy. There are more and less adequate ways of making sense of human experience and of coping with the world in the light of what sense one can make of it. All forms of rationality are subject to this test. They are therefore (in vigorous societies) always being modified to take account of new experience. Sometimes the modifications are minor; sometimes they are cataclysmic. There is a parallel here with Thomas Kuhn's distinction between "normal" science and the experience of "paradigm shifts." A way of seeing things is proposed that "makes sense" in a more adequate way than the one previously accepted. As Kuhn shows, there is no over-arching logical system that can justify the switch from one vision to the other; it is a kind of conversion to a different way of seeing things that always needs new language. The only test is adequacy to the reality that has to be understood and coped with. The new paradigm cannot demonstrate its "reasonableness" on the terms of the old. But the success of the new paradigm will depend on the vigor and competence of those who have committed themselves to work with it.[14] In every culture the Christian

13. John Puddefoot, *Logic and Affirmation*, 16.
14. Thomas Kuhn, *The Structure of Scientific Revolutions* (Chicago: University of Chicago, 1970), discussed in Lesslie Newbigin, *The Gospel in a World of Religious Pluralism* (London: SPCK, 1989), 44, and Newbigin, *Foolishness to the Greeks*, 52.

vision of how things are calls for a conversion and for the use of new language — none of which can be shown to be deducible from the reigning plausibility structure. How much the Christian paradigm convinces people of its superior rationality depends on the intellectual vigor and practical courage that those who inhabit the new plausibility structure use to demonstrate its adequacy and exacting use of reason. Paradoxically, one of the main functions of the twenty-first-century Church may be to defend the power of rational thought against the onslaught of antirational movements such as the New Age people.

There is a more specific way in which "reason" has been invoked as a source of authority, namely in contradistinction to "revelation." Granted that the reigning traditions of rationality in our culture are rooted in the specific history of Europe, these traditions rest upon the discoveries of the great scientists and philosophers and historians — discoveries that can be appropriated by any student who is willing to make the necessary effort. On the other hand, the Christian tradition of rationality rests upon alleged revelations that cannot be experimentally checked but have to be accepted in faith. It is asked, therefore, whether the idea of revelation is compatible with the requirements of reason.

The answer must be found, I think, by looking at two kinds of normal human experience that Martin Buber made familiar in his distinction between "I and you" and "I and it." In the latter situations the autonomous reason is in full control. I analyze, classify, dissect. I decide what questions to ask, and force the material to answer my questions. Reason is in the service of my sovereign will. But in the other situations, the situations of interpersonal relationships, matters are different. I am not in full control. I cannot force the other person to answer the questions I ask. Of course it is possible to treat the other person as an object in the "it" world, and to use the tools of science, including eventually the tools of the neurosurgeon, to find out how the brain of the person functions. But none of this gives knowledge of the other person as person. For that I must surrender control. I must listen and expose myself to question. And it is obvious that in thus surrendering sovereignty and moving to the position of one who is questioned, I have not abandoned the use of reason. I am still a rational person making rational judgments and drawing rational conclusions from data. The difference is in the role that reason is called to play. Reason has become the servant of a listening and trusting openness instead of being the servant of masterful autonomy.

The question, therefore, is not whether reason is employed. It is whether the total reality we as human beings have to deal with is to be understood exclusively as lifeless matter, to be investigated by the autonomous human subject, or whether this reality is such that a proper knowing of it is more the fruit of mature personal relationships. The debate is not between "reason" and "revelation"; it is a question about what kind of reality we are dealing with. If that reality is amenable to being understood along the lines we follow in a personal relationship, then it is reasonable to believe that a tradition of rational discourse could develop from the particular experiences of those to whom the Author of the universe has spoken and who have been alert and humble enough to listen. To "indwell" such a tradition, to live with this paradigm, to endeavor to show in every new generation its adequacy to human experience, its power to "make sense" of new situations, will be a fully rational enterprise. The proposal to set "reason" against "revelation" only arises if one is indwelling another tradition of rationality, one that sees the whole of reality only as an object for investigation. Within this latter tradition, of course, "religion" is one of the matters for investigation. There are "religious experiences." In this tradition one says, not "God spoke to Moses," but "Moses had a religious experience." The latter formulation leaves the investigator in charge; the former does not. But the long tradition of rational discourse that has followed from accepting the former as valid is not less rational than the one developed from the latter. Reason operating within the Christian (or Judaic or Muslim) tradition is still reason.

Experience

The fourth word often used in discussion about the authority of the Christian message is *experience*. It is a newcomer to theology. Until at least the beginning of the nineteenth century the word had the meaning that we now convey by the word *experiment*. Apparently it has

93

become popular in English theology as a translation of the German *Erlebnis.* One has to ask why it has become so popular. Earlier theologians did not appear to need it. Scientists, at least in the natural sciences, do not seem to need it. Neither a scientist nor anyone else knows anything except by — in some sense — having an experience — seeing it, reading it, or hearing it. When a new star appears in the telescope of an astronomer, he does not describe it as a new astronomical experience; he talks about the star. Why is it otherwise in theology? Why say "Moses had a religious experience," rather than "God spoke to Moses"? Obviously because the existence of God cannot be "objectively" demonstrated, whereas there is plenty of evidence to show conclusively that people have religious experiences, and these can be the object of scientific exploration. But it seems certain that only a minority of people who have had definite "religious experiences" can be the subject of this kind of investigation. I suppose that the most important factor in bringing this word into the theological debate is the impact of Schleiermacher's monumental effort to find a place for Christian belief among its "cultured despisers" by finding the evidence for God in the "feeling of absolute dependence" that, he held, is common to all. If Christian faith must leave the exploration of nature and history to those who operate on other presuppositions, it must find a habitation in the world of inward feeling. Leaving aside such paranormal religious experiences as are investigated by scientists, a great deal of Christian writing (and singing) is about inward experiences of peace and joy and penitence, rather than about realities outside the self.

In what sense can "experience" function as a source of authority? For those who have had the kind of definable "religious experience" that can be dated and described, such experience will seem an adequate basis for belief, even though it is also true that similar experiences are produced by the use of drugs. But such experiences, it would seem, always have some continuity with what has gone before. They are not totally unrelated to the rest of the person's experience of life. And they can only continue to provide authority for believing insofar as they enable the person to "make sense" of the rest of experience. The great majority of Christians, it would seem, hold the faith on grounds other than "religious experience" in this narrower sense.

They will, for example, continue faithfully to pray in private and worship in public along with others, even though there are long periods in which these exercises produce no vivid experiences like those associated with the conversion of St. Paul or St. Augustine. They believe because they have been brought, perhaps from childhood, into the life of the community that believes the gospel, orders its life by it, and finds in so doing that its truth is confirmed in experience.

All experience is within a framework of interpretation. Even the primary experiences of sight and sound make sense only as the infant learns to relate the lights and noises that impinge on it to a real world that is there to be explored. The Christian gospel provides a framework within which all experience is interpreted in terms of the wise and loving purpose of God. Something that, in another framework, is experienced as disaster may, within the framework of Christian faith, be interpreted as part of God's loving provision. The crucifixion of Jesus is "folly" in one framework, "the wisdom of God" in another (1 Cor. 1:18).

It would therefore be misleading to treat "experience" as a distinct source of authority for Christian believing, because the character of our experience is shaped by the faith we hold. There is a long tradition of teaching in the Church that advises us not to depend too much on special religious experiences (precious and needful as they may be from time to time) but to accept the call to walk by faith, trusting that this is the path that leads to the vision of God, of which all religious experience can only be a faint glimpse.

By What Authority?

How well do these reflections enable me to answer the charge that to invoke the authority of "the Bible" over against our culture is like pretending to move a bus when you are sitting in it? I have affirmed that the way we experience the world depends on a framework of understanding that we receive as part of a living cultural tradition. This tradition always has a specific history in which there are events that have a special significance in shaping the framework. As a product of western European culture I am part of this tradition. But as a

Christian I am also part of another tradition that celebrates other events as decisive for shaping a true understanding of the world. Here the analogy of the bus becomes inadequate. One cannot be in two buses at the same time, but one can share in two traditions. That is my situation. I have referred to the internal dialogue. The power of the reigning tradition is very strong. All the language of public debate and most of the language of personal conversation is shaped by the tradition of modern west European culture. But as a member of the Christian Church I am constantly invited to find my mental and spiritual dwelling place within another tradition that celebrates other events as decisive for the understanding of the world and of the human situation within it. There are many points at which these two ways of understanding are in radical contradiction. What authority can this other tradition have? If I say, "In the name of Jesus," what authority can that name have in a multicultural and religiously plural world?

Jesus "spoke with authority." He quoted from the Torah, and then added, "But I say to you. . . ." But he renounced any kind of coercive authority, as the story of the threefold temptation in the wilderness testifies. According to the Johannine version he said, "No one can come to me unless the Father who sent me draws him" (John 6:44). In the end even those who had come to him left him. But the company of those to whom he had entrusted the secret of his mission was promised the gift of the Advocate, the active presence of God's Spirit, who would be his witness and who would convict the world in respect of its most fundamental "self-evident truths." The authority of Jesus is the authority of the Father who sent him, and it can only be known and acknowledged by those to whom the Spirit speaks. There is no way that God's authority can be captured and institutionalized. But the presence of the Spirit is promised to those who "abide" in Jesus. Here is where we have to speak of tradition. Tradition is a living reality insofar as those who are committed to Jesus meet together to remember and retell the mighty acts of God, to relive the biblical story and the words and deeds of Jesus, and to offer their praise and prayer to the Father through him. It is in the Church's liturgy that the biblical story becomes a living tradition, remembered again and again, and — in the preaching of the Word — reinterpreted and applied to contemporary situations so that the written word of

Scripture becomes the living word of God for today. Out of such liturgy there arises action in the life of the world that faithfully embodies the understanding of God's purpose for the world, which is revealed in the biblical narrative. And through the words and deeds of the members of the believing community there come occasions when the Holy Spirit bears witness in the heart and conscience of a man or woman that the secret of life is to be found in the company of Jesus. No other kind of authority is involved. It is always a mysterious matter, but it is the way in which the authority of Jesus is exercised, and the way men and women — whether in Indian cities and villages or in an English city — come to live by a story different from the one that operates in society. There can be no ultimate authority except the authority of the Spirit of God speaking in the heart and conscience of a man or woman. But the presence of that Holy Spirit is promised to the community that "indwells" the story of which the incarnation, ministry, death, and resurrection of Jesus is the central key.

9

Our Missionary Responsibility
in the Crisis of Western Culture

Let us recall again the question that General Simatoupong of Indonesia posed: "Can the West be converted?" Simatoupong was looking at the West from outside, from the vantage point of a more ancient civilization. His was, if you like, the viewpoint of a foreign missionary. And the foreign missionary does have certain advantages over the native people. He sees things that they do not see because they take them for granted. They are just "how things have always been." I remember that when I went as an English missionary to India fifty years ago, and tried to understand Indian life and thought, I slowly came to realize how important it was that the doctrines of *karma* and *samsura* have hardly been changed in all the great revolutions from the Buddha to Gandhi. They describe how things are and have always been. Human life, like all of nature, is a cyclical affair, a matter of endlessly repeated birth, life, decay, death, and rebirth. In a world so understood, there is no way a particular happening in history can decisively change the human situation. It can only illustrate and exemplify what is always the case.

And that, in general, is how Indian thought understands Jesus.

Presented at a conference held in Arnoldshain, FRG, in May 1988, this paper represents a stepping stone between *Foolishness to the Greeks* (1986) and *The Gospel in a World of Religious Pluralism* (1989).

As a young missionary I used to spend an evening each week in the premises of the Ramakrishna Mission, studying with the monks the Upanishada and the Gospels. The great hall of the monastery was lined with pictures of the great religious figures of history, among them Jesus. Each year, on Christmas Day, worship was offered before the picture of Jesus. It was obvious to me as an English Christian that this was an example of syncretism. Jesus had simply been coopted into the Hindu worldview; that view was in no way challenged.

It was only slowly that I began to see that my own Christianity had this syncretistic character, that I too had to some degree coopted Jesus into the worldview of my culture. I remember an incident that made me realize this. I was taking a group of village teachers through St. Mark's Gospel. My Tamil wasn't very good, but I was fairly confident about my theology, fresh as I was from theological college. All went well till we reached the first exorcism. Now, Westminster College had not taught me much about how to cast out demons. My exposition was not very impressive. These village teachers looked at me with growing perplexity, and then one of them said, "Why are you making such heavy weather of a perfectly simple matter?" and proceeded to rattle off half a dozen cases of exorcism in his own congregation during the past few months. Of course I could have said, "My dear brother, if you will kindly let me arrange for you to come to Cambridge and take a proper training in modern science and then a postgraduate qualification in psychology, you will be able to understand that Freud and Jung and company have explained everything." In other words, "If you will permit me to induct you into my culture, you will see things as they really are." But this was a Bible study, and Mark's Gospel was sitting there, saying what it does. Inwardly I had to admit that he was much nearer Mark than I was. Outwardly I kept quiet and went on to the next passage.

I am not saying that there is an easy answer to my problem. One could put it this way: Do you try to understand the gospel through the spectacles provided by your culture, or do you try to understand your culture through the spectacles provided by the gospel? There is no easy answer, but it is a real question.

During the twelve years since I came back to England, and especially since I had a pastoral charge in Birmingham, I have come more and more to feel that England is as much a foreign mission field as India was for me in 1936. I have come to feel that there is an English parallel to the picture of Jesus in the Ramakrishna Mission Hall. I mean, of course, that it has increasingly seemed to me that instead of allowing the gospel to challenge the unexamined assumptions of our culture, we have coopted Jesus into our culture by giving him a minor role in what we call the private sector. The matter is very clear when we look at the layout of a news magazine like *Time* or *Newsweek*. We know that if we want to find any reference to Jesus we shall not find it in the section "World Affairs." It will be tucked away in the little slot between "drama" and "sports," among the optional activities for the private life. It does not challenge the assumptions that govern our understanding of public affairs.

Under the name of "modernization," Western culture has become increasingly dominant throughout the world, and Christian missions themselves have been powerful bearers of the process of modernization during the past two centuries. Missionaries have introduced Western education, science, and technology wherever they have gone, and they are still doing so. And yet we who belong by birth to this Western world know that our culture is in profound crisis. It is showing many signs of disintegration. The confident expectation of progress towards an ever-better world no longer exists. Educated Europeans have a deep feeling of guilt about our culture. There is a widespread belief that if we want real wisdom, we must go the East rather than to the Christian roots of our Western culture. The European literature of our time is filled with a sense of pessimism. The Chinese theologian Carver Yu, looking at Europe from the East, sums up our contemporary cultural scene as "technological optimism and literary despair."[1] What is our responsibility as bearers of the gospel, as missionaries, in this situation?

First, I suggest, *diagnosis*. Here I would like to make five points.

1. If we look at Western culture from the perspective of other, older cultures, its most obvious feature is that it is split into two parts: there is a public world of what are called "facts," and there is a private

---

1. Carver Yu, *Being and Relation: A Theological Critique of Western Dualism and Individualism* (N.p., 1987).

world of what are called "values." "Facts" are what everyone has to accept whether they like them or not; "values" are a matter of personal choice. "Facts" are what every child in school must learn and accept — for instance, that the development of the human person depends on the program encoded in the DNA molecule; "values," whether expressed in religious beliefs or otherwise, are matters for the Church and the home. Even as recently as a hundred years ago, every child in a school in Scotland learned as a fact that "man's chief end is to glorify God and enjoy him forever."[2] This was as much a fact as anything in biology or physics. Today such teaching is not permitted in the public schools. It is not part of the facts. We take pride in being a pluralistic society where many different creeds can flourish. We do not teach as public truth any particular belief about the *purpose* of human life. But this pluralism does not extend to the world of "facts." When there is disagreement about what are called "facts," we do not take it as an occasion for celebrating the glories of pluralism. No! We argue, we conduct experiments, we try to convince each other of error, and we do not rest until we reach agreement about the facts. In this public world of "facts," pluralism does not reign.

2. The root of this dichotomy between a public world of facts and a private world of values is to be found at that crucial turning point in European history, the turning point that led to the rise of modern science. At the risk of drastic oversimplification, one can say that the crucial decision was the decision to turn from asking questions about *purpose* to asking questions about *cause;* from final causes to efficient causes; from teleology to mechanism; from asking, "What purpose does this serve?" to asking, "How does it work?" Ancient Greek and medieval science asked about purpose; the new science asked about what makes things move. And, needless to say, the asking of that question has opened up enormous new vistas of both knowledge and power. But there is a price to pay. If one eliminates questions about purpose, then there is no way of finding a factual basis for values, no way of moving from the statement "This is" to "This is good." One can, for instance, undertake

2. From the Westminster Confession, 1644, but the phrase originates with John Calvin (1509–1564); see further Newbigin, *Foolishness to the Greeks*, 67; Newbigin, *The Gospel in a World of Religious Pluralism*, 15f.

an exhaustive analysis of a watch to show how it works at every level from its visible mechanism down to the operation of its molecular, atomic, and subatomic elements. In that sense one may discover "everything there is to know" about the watch. But the analysis would not enable one to discover the purpose for which all this mechanism is put together. And therefore there would be no factual way of distinguishing between a good watch and a bad one. If I say, "My watch has not lost ten seconds in two years," most people who were not philosophers would say, "Then it is a good watch." They would move easily from a statement of fact ("This watch has not lost ten seconds in two years") to a statement of value ("This is a good watch"). Most people would say that this was a good move. But this move is only possible if I know the *purpose* for which these pieces of metal were put together in this way. If, for example, it is for decorating my sitting-room, or for throwing at the cat, the conclusion "This is a good watch" does not follow. Only if I know the purpose can I say, "This is good." Knowing the causes that make the watch operate does not give me any ground for saying, "This is a good watch." If we eliminate questions of purpose, then "facts" are simple facts and we cannot call them good or bad; they are "value-free." And "value-free facts" are the currency in which our public world carries on its business.

3. One does not discover the purpose for which a watch exists by examining its parts. A person who had always lived in a society with no clocks or watches would not be able to discover a watch's purpose by the most exhaustive analysis and examination. He would have to ask the maker or someone else who already knew the purpose. It is impossible to discover the purpose (if any) for which the cosmos and human life exist by examining all the facts. The data for a valid induction do not exist — unless we are willing to wait until cosmic history has reached its terminus. At the dawn of the modern scientific age Lord Bacon advised his contemporaries to avoid speculation and to collect facts. By speculation he meant theological and philosophical theories about the purpose of human life. On these matters no certainty was possible. So they should concentrate on the facts that could be known with certainty.[3] The purpose of the entire frame of things

3. See further Newbigin, *Foolishness to the Greeks,* 79f. Francis Bacon devoted

could only be known if its author was willing to disclose it. In other words, it could only be known by revelation. And revelation has to be accepted in faith. It is a matter of personal decision, not public truth. So statements about human life being governed by the DNA molecule are facts, part of public truth. But statements about the purpose of human life being to glorify God and enjoy him forever are not facts; they are private opinion. Here is the fundamental split in our culture.

4. This split was enormously widened by the work of Descartes. Since Descartes, our culture has been dominated by the ideal of a kind of knowledge that cannot be doubted. Hannah Arendt has suggested that it was perhaps the invention of the telescope, showing that the stars and planets are not exactly as they appear to the naked eye, that gave birth to his passionate search for a kind of knowledge that could not be doubted, a kind of knowledge that involved no risk, no faith commitment.[4] The unquestionable and lucid certainties of mathematics were to provide the paradigm of real knowledge. In the English-speaking world this was powerfully reinforced by the work of John Locke (1632–1704), who defined belief as what we fall back on when we do not have knowledge. Thus "I believe" means "I do not know." Statements about God and his purpose are prefaced by the words "we believe," because we do not know. Statements in a textbook of physics require no such preface. They are simply statements of what is the case, as impersonal and inescapable as the statement that two plus two make four.[5] The developments of modern physics, and the work of philosophers and historians of science, have shown how misleading this is. All scientific knowledge rests upon faith commitments, upon beliefs that cannot be demonstrated by science itself. Faith is not a substitute for knowledge, but its starting point. Augustine was fond of saying, "I believe in order to understand." And Einstein in a classic sentence has said, "Insofar as the statements of

himself to science after being dismissed as Lord Chancellor by James I for alleged corruption in 1618. His need to establish his innocence presumably gave weight to his views on "facts."

4. Hannah Arendt, *The Human Condition* (New York: Harper, 1956), 257f.

5. Locke, *An Essay on Human Understanding.*

mathematics are certain, they make no contact with reality; insofar as they make contact with reality, they are not certain." The idea of a kind of knowledge that is totally impersonal, that involves no commitment on the part of the knower, is an illusion. But it dominates our culture.

5. It was obvious that in this cultural shift, the first casualty would be biblical authority. How can the Bible survive in this world of "value-free facts"? During the eighteenth century, at least in the English-speaking world, the defense of biblical authority took the form of a demonstration that its teaching was in accordance with "reason" as the Enlightenment understood it. But this defense rapidly crumbled during the eighteenth century. The result we now inherit in the twentieth century is a split within the Christian community that corresponds precisely to the split down the middle of our culture. On both sides the dichotomy between "facts" and "values" is accepted. On the one side are the fundamentalists, who assert the factual inerrancy of Scripture and who regard statements of Christian doctrine as factually correct propositions of the same kind as the statements of physics of astronomy (see, for example, the "creation science" advocated in the United States). On the other side are the liberals, who see theological statements as symbolic expressions of religious experiences that are essentially inward and personal. Theology is thus not concerned with factual statements about the world and about history. The Bible is to be read not as factual history but as the record of religious experience. Here, very plainly, is simply a reproduction in Christian terms of the fundamental split of Western culture. Both sides, fundamentalists and liberals equally, are operating within the assumptions of our culture. What is required is a far more radical challenge to those assumptions. How shall this be attempted?

Plainly the fundamental issue is epistemological: it is the question about how we can come to know the truth, how we can know what is real. What we have been looking at in this very hasty and superficial review of the development of thought in our culture is the breakdown of the connection between the objective and the subjective poles of our knowing. All knowing is an accomplishment of the knower; it requires and involves a personal commitment to the enterprise of trying to know and to understand. It has an essential subjective pole. But equally it has an objective pole. It "latches on" to some reality outside the knower. Otherwise it is not knowing at all. Its grasp may be limited and faulty, but nevertheless it is a grasping at something that is *there*, objectively. What has happened in our culture is a breakdown of the unity between these two, so that we have on the one hand a public world of so-called facts, which are supposed to be "objective facts," things that are there whether you believe them or not and that everyone has to learn to recognize and come to terms with, the world of public truth that forms the substance of the curriculum in the schools and universities. And, on the other hand, we have the world of "personal faith," which is subjective, a matter of individual choice. In this realm — as is often said — "Everyone needs to have a faith of his own." So long as the faith is sincere, we do not ask whether it is true; that would be an offense against pluralism. It is a matter of personal choice. And, needless to say, things affirmed in the creeds of the universal choice belong to the second category.

In his book entitled *The Closing of the American Mind,* the Jewish philosopher Allan Bloom sees a total relativism as the dominant feature of our culture. It is no longer possible to say that anything is "right" or "wrong." One does not speak this language any more. One speaks of "values," "lifestyles," and "authentic persons." Bloom traces this back to Nietzsche, who was (says Bloom) the first to recognize that the Cartesian method must in the end destroy every possibility of making firm affirmations of truth and falsehood, of right and wrong. The method of systematic doubt must ultimately make such affirmations impossible. The only thing that would be left is the will — the will to power. And, says Bloom, this talk of "values" is simply Nietzsche wrapped up in cotton wool. "Values" — as distinct from facts — are what some people *want.* They are a matter of the will, not of the truth. The only question is: "Whose will prevails?" The Hungarian physicist and philosopher Michael Polanyi has expressed this in a vivid metaphor.[6] He says that the last 250 years of European culture have been the most brilliant in human history, but their brilliance was created by the combustion of the heritage of a thousand

6. Polanyi, *Personal Knowledge,* 331. See Newbigin, *Foolishness to the Greeks,* 80.

105

years of Christian civilization in the oxygen of Greek rationalism; that the fuel is now exhausted; and that pumping in more oxygen cannot produce more light. In other words, we are at the end of the critical era.

Is it possible for us, living after and not before this era, to make firm affirmations of truth as truth? Is it possible to announce the gospel not as an option for private choice, but as public truth for all? Can we say with the apostle Paul, "I *know* whom I have believed" (2 Tim. 1:12)? Can we announce the gospel in the way that Polanyi approaches our problem, with a profound analysis of what is involved in the enterprise of knowing?

Most of the great discussions of epistemology in the past three centuries have approached the matter through the *visual* sense. And it is perhaps natural to do so, for it is obvious that our eyes can deceive us. Polanyi approaches the matter through the tactile sense. He takes the example of a surgeon using a probe to investigate a cavity into which it is not possible to look. A medical student using the probe for the first time will perhaps be conscious for a time of the pressure of the probe on the palm of his hand. As he grows in experience he will forget this. All his attention will be directed to what the tip of the probe is discovering in the invisible cavity. The probe becomes a kind of additional finger. It is an extension of his body. He *feels* what the tip of the probe is finding. He *indwells* the probe in a manner that is an extension of the way that I indwell my finger. He may be *tacitly* aware of the pressure on the palm of his hand, but *focally* he is attending to what the probe is "feeling" at its tip.

Polanyi takes this as a way of entry into the whole enterprise of knowing, of probing reality. Like the surgeon using the probe, we explore reality by *indwelling* a whole range of instruments — words, concepts, images, ideas. We have to learn to use them, and while we are learning we attend to the new words, the new concepts. But when we have become familiar with their use, we no longer attend to them. We are *tacitly* aware of them, but *focally* aware of the reality they enable us to probe. We *indwell* them. When we are learning a language we have to attend, for a time, to the individual words and to the grammar and syntax of the language. When we are fluent in the language we no longer attend to these, though we may be tacitly aware of them.

We use them acritically. We focus our attention on the meaning they convey. At some point we may find that we are not truly conveying the meaning. We will then have to look *critically* at the words, and perhaps find new ones. But while we are trying to communicate our meaning, we use the words acritically. We cannot at the same moment take a critical attitude to the words *and* use them to convey meaning.

We learn to use our own mother tongue in this way at an early age. As we grow we are introduced to further tools through which we extend our probings into the world around us: books, maps, theorems, classifications of date, concepts by which a whole area of thought is encapsulated, dictionaries, computers, and much more. While we use these things we *indwell* them. They become an extension of our own powers. We use them acritically to probe the area of reality we are exploring. At times we may become dissatisfied with the probe, look critically at it, and perhaps try to fashion another. But all these tools are part of an entire cultural tradition into which we are inducted by our training at home and in school. The vastly greater part of this is simply taken for granted and not questioned. It usually takes the shock of some disaster, or of an encounter with a radically different tradition, to move us to a critical look at our own cultural tradition. And, in any case, we can never take this kind of critical look except by relying acritically on some *other* way of grasping things. The idea that we can have a critical approach to everything at the same time is, of course, absurd. It is strictly impossible to doubt anything except on the basis of something that we do not doubt, some set of beliefs that we hold acritically.

All knowing, therefore, involves the acritical acceptance of a language of concepts, of ideas and images, that we indwell and through which we seek to probe the world around us. This acritical acceptance is at first not a matter of choice. The language, the ideas, the images are those through which our minds have been formed. There is no stance from which we might look critically at them. In due course, if we lead a normal life of active intercourse with others, this "fiduciary framework" or faith-based outlook will be called into question by those who inhabit a different framework. From that point onwards, my personal choice is involved: I can step outside the framework and look at it critically from within another. And I can be so impressed by the clarity and the coherence of the view obtained from within that other framework that I am drawn into it. In other words, I am converted. I undergo what historians of science call a "paradigm shift." Or I may stay within the frame I have inherited, seeking to make use of new insights to revise and extend it. In any case, there is a personal commitment involved. There is a decision, which means the risk of being wrong. But this personal commitment is, as Polanyi says, "with universal intent." It is firmly anchored to the objective pole. It is made in the belief that this is the way to grasp reality more truly, not just that it is what I personally prefer. It is made in the faith that what is shown as truth is truth for all. And if it is indeed what I believe, it will prove itself so by opening the way to fresh discoveries and fresh coherences and fresh clarities.

I have used the word *conversion*. Simatoupong asked, "Can the West be converted?" That is the question I want to address. Can the Church offer, in the context of our culture, a new "fiduciary framework," a new way of grasping the totality of things that can replace, not the private religious worlds of individuals in our culture, but the public world into which all of us educated in a European language have, from childhood, been inducted and in which we have lived? For two and a half centuries theologians have labored to understand the Bible from within the "fiduciary framework" of Western culture as it has developed since the end of the seventeenth century. Is it possible, in an intellectually coherent way, to undertake the reverse operation? Can we involve the critical principle in the other direction? Can we find in the Bible and the Christian tradition a "fiduciary framework" from within which a critical examination of our culture can be undertaken?

As we begin to answer that question, it is proper to note at the outset that there are grounds in the present situation itself for some optimism in our approach. It is agreed that the modern scientific method, which has been the prime factor in shaping our public world view, has excluded *in limine* questions of purpose. Modern science does not ask and does not attempt to answer the question, "For what purpose do things and people exist?" This is a methodological decision that has opened the way for the enormously fruitful work of modern science. But this decision on method cannot be converted into a decision about ontology; science certainly cannot prove that there is no purpose in the nature of things. Indeed, such a conclusion would be self-defeating, since science is a highly purposeful activity. And since it is in principle impossible to discover the purpose for which a thing exists simply by analyzing the thing into several parts, it is agreed that the question of purpose is left unanswered by science, not answered in the negative. And finally, in these preliminary points, since *purpose* is a personal word, purpose can only be known through the self-disclosure of the person whose purpose it is. If the whole frame of things and the whole human story have a purpose, we can know it insofar as the one whose purpose it is discloses it. We are bound, in strict logic, to invoke the concept of revelation. And so, in the context of our present discussion, we have to talk about the Bible and about biblical authority. We have to ask, "Is it possible, within our present culture, to speak with intellectual coherence about biblical authority?"

At this point I would like to listen to two Asian voices. A Hindu friend of mine, a Brahmin scholar, who has made a deep study both of the Bible and of the sacred scriptures of India, has often said to me, "I cannot forgive you Christians for the way in which you have misrepresented the Bible. You have introduced it to us as though it were a book of religion — of which we have plenty in India already. It is not. It is, as I read it, a quite unique interpretation of universal history and therefore a unique interpretation of the human person as an actor in that history." The other voice is the Chinese theologian Carver Yu, whom I have already quoted. He traces what he sees as the malaise of European culture to the fact that from its earliest beginnings in Greek philosophy, it has tried to find the really real in the concept of *substance,* of that which exists in its own right, independent of anything else. He says that this is in fact a false trial. The really real is known only in *relationship.* To use the words of Bishop Zizioulos of the Greek Orthodox Church, "being is communion." This accords well with findings of contemporary physics. The long search of physics to find the ultimate, irreducible particles by which matter is constituted has ended in something quite unexpected: the discovery not of small indivisible particles, but of changing relationships between nonmaterial entities.

The Bible is an interpretation of universal history as the history of the divine enterprise of creating faithful relationships, covenant relationships between persons and peoples founded on the covenant faithfulness of God. It has the whole cosmos as its theme. It sets the human story within the context of the cosmic story. It has its center and turning point in the death and resurrection of him who is the Word of God, through whom all things came to be and are. It looks towards a consummation that is beyond history and yet gathers up all that has been wrought through history.

All telling of history is, of course, selective. No history is written except on the basis of judgments about what is significant. No "facts of history" exist except insofar as what happened was judged important. The recorded facts will vary according to the judgment of what is significant, and that in turn depends upon what the "point" of the story is. Normally we do not see the point of a story until the end. But we are not in a position to see the end of the cosmic story. The Christian faith is the faith that the point of the story has been disclosed: the "end" has been revealed in the middle. The point of the story is not the triumph of human technology over nature, nor the cyclical rise and fall of civilizations. There is one human family and it has *one* center, Jesus Christ, and *one* history, the history of the making of faithful relationships with its Maker. To accept that means to live as part of a potentially universal community, looking towards a consummation whose character has been revealed in Jesus Christ, and of which we have already a foretaste in his risen Body.

How is this version of the human and cosmic story to be related to the version of the human story as it is told in our culture? That is the crucial question. To be human is to be part of a story, and to understand one's self is to understand the story. Our culture has preserved the biblical story for expressing in symbolic terms a way of looking at the life of the individual person and his hope of some kind of future beyond death. The biblical story has not been allowed to challenge the dominant version of the human story. "World history" is taught in our schools and universities without reference to the Bible, unless the Bible story appears as one small item in a larger picture. We have been trained, in other words, to look at the Bible version of the story from within another fiduciary framework. We include it in a syllabus for the comparative story of religions. As far as questioning the dominant framework, it is as harmless as a stuffed tiger in a museum.

I have quoted two voices from Asia. Let me ask you to listen to a voice from Latin America. The important thing, says one of the Latin American theologians of liberation, is not to understand the text, but to understand the world through the text. We can study the text from within the fiduciary framework of our culture, using all its well-sharpened critical tools to dissect it into its smallest fragments (which is how I learned it). In that method we may try to understand the text, but the text can no more question us than the stuffed tiger in the museum can frighten us. There is another possibility, as the Latin American theologian suggests. It is to interrogate the world from within the text. It is, to revert to Polanyi's language, to *indwell* the story as it is told in the Bible so that we are not looking *at* it, but looking *through* it to understand our world. That is what Christians did before they were trained in the critical method. It is how millions of Christians still use the Bible. It is how it is used in Liberation Theology — even if one has to make some criticism of that.[7] *We* are the Israelites who escaped from Egypt, crossed the Red Sea, wandered in the desert, were guided by the pillar of cloud and fire. *We* are still part of that same story acritically and are therefore given a stance from which we can exercise a *critical* understanding of contemporary culture. The matter at issue is not whether we are critical or uncritical; it is the question of which fiduciary framework we use when we exercise our critical powers, for no criticism is possible except from within a fiduciary framework that we indwell acritically.

To take this position means, of course, to be a minority in our culture. It means questioning the things that no one ever questions — like the Christian missionary in India questioning the laws of *karma* and *samsura*. And it means, I believe, being enabled to find a more rational way of understanding and coping with our world than the one offered in our contemporary culture. This culture is enormously productive of means but unable to speak about ends, fertile in finding

7. For Newbigin on liberation theology, see *The Gospel in a World of Religious Pluralism*, 149.

new ways to do things but incapable of answering the question "What things are worth doing?" It is not, let me insist, a matter of appealing to "revelation" against "reason." This absurd opposition is, I am, sorry to say, a commonplace English discussion. Reason is not a separate source of knowledge. It is the power by which we seek coherence in the data of experience, and it operates, can only operate, within a complex of language, concepts, symbols, images that make up the "fiduciary framework." No move towards understanding reality is possible except by the use of reason; the question is "Within what fiduciary framework is reason operating?" And when we offer a different fiduciary framework, an alternative to the one that is dominant in our culture, we are calling for *conversion,* for a radical shift in perspective. We need the boldness of the foreign missionary who dares to challenge the accepted framework, even though the words he uses must inevitably sound absurd to those who dwell in that framework.

In the contemporary crisis of Western culture there is a widespread failure of nerve. There is a widespread tendency to retreat from the whole splendid adventure of Western culture and to look elsewhere — especially to the East — for something different. That is a terrible mistake. We cannot run away from our responsibilities. It is we in the West who have developed this culture that is penetrating the whole world under the name of modernization. It is we Christians who have failed to challenge its fundamental assumptions, who have allowed the gospel to be coopted into it instead of challenging it. It is upon us that there now rests the formidable responsibility for a task that is both intellectual and practical: to recover a concept of knowledge that will heal the split in our culture between science and faith, between the public world and the private; and to embody in our congregations a style of life that expresses in practice the purpose for which God has created all things: to glorify him and enjoy him forever.

10

The Enduring Validity of Cross-Cultural Mission

It is a great honor to be invited to share in this event, an event that is significant for all of us, whatever part of the world we come from, who are committed to the Christian world mission. My first duty is to recognize the dedicated and imaginative leadership that has made the Overseas Ministries Study Center a source of strength for the Christian mission in all its many forms of outreach, and that has now prompted this very significant move to New Haven and the launching of the center on a new stage of its life.

Perhaps my only real qualification for being invited to address you is that I happen to come from overseas. I do not mean by that to endorse what was once described as the missionary mythology of saltwater, the idea that crossing a stretch of saltwater was the necessary condition for being a missionary. When I am asked to state my employment I usually answer "missionary" and can do that without endorsing the saltwater myth, but it is not unimportant that the first word in the title of this center is the word "Overseas."

After sixty-five years in Ventnor, New Jersey, the Overseas Ministries Study Center relocated to New Haven, Connecticut, in September 1987. Bishop Lesslie Newbigin gave this address at the service of dedication and inauguration of the new center on 5 October 1987. Reprinted by the kind permission of Dr. Gerald Anderson.

When the family of William Howard Doane founded the center in 1922, it was for those who were then called — without embarrassment — "foreign missionaries" and who needed a period of rest from their labors in foreign parts. The center has followed a general trend in replacing the words *foreign missionaries* with *overseas ministries.* I do not quarrel with that, though I do sometimes reflect upon the significance of the change. It was made, I suppose, because the old term was felt to have a hint of arrogance about it. It suggested images of the old pith helmet and the white man's burden. We are very eager to be disinfected of that old but clinging aroma. A missionary in training told me the other day that what he was getting was "hair-shirt missiology," so eager were his mentors to repent of the sins of our missionary predecessors.

We speak now of "overseas ministries" or — more comprehensively — of cross-cultural mission and ministry. It is to the study of the issues involved in these cross-cultural ministries that this center is dedicated. I want to affirm my conviction of the great importance of such studies, and therefore of this center, for the life of the Church. Whatever may or may not have been the sins of our missionary predecessors (and of course it is much more relaxing to repent of one's parents' sins than of one's own), the commission to disciple all the nations stands at the center of the Church's mandate. A church that forgets this, or marginalizes it, forfeits the right to the titles "catholic" and "apostolic." If there was a danger of arrogance in the call for the evangelization of the world in that generation, there is a greater danger of timidity and compromise when we lower our sights and allow the gospel to be domesticated within our culture, and the churches to become merely the domestic chaplains to the nation. I am not impressed by those who thank God that we are not like the missionaries of the nineteenth century — which the beloved Yale historian Kenneth Scott Latourette called "the Great Century" — the century that made it possible for us to talk today of the world Church. Of course it is true that there were elements of arrogance in the missionaries of that century, but that was because in the preceding centuries Christianity had become so domesticated within Western culture that when we carried the gospel overseas it sometimes looked like part of our colonial baggage.

The truth is that the gospel escapes domestication, retains its proper strangeness, its power to question us, only when we are faithful to its universal, supranational, supracultural nature — faithful not just in words but in action, not just in theological statement but in missionary practice in taking the gospel across the cultural frontiers. The affirmation that Jesus is *Lumen Gentium,* the light of the nations, is in danger of being mere words unless its value is being tested in actual encounters of the gospel with all the nations, so that the gospel comes back to us in the idiom of other cultures with power to question our understanding of it. In this sense the foreign missionary is an enduring necessity in the life of the universal Church, but of course, the missionary journeys have to be multidirectional and not — as in the former period — only from west to east and from north to south. I speak with some feeling because it is my privilege to work in Birmingham alongside a missionary sent to us by the Church of North India, and I know that England needs the witness of a Christian from India at least as much as India needs missionaries from the West.

A center like this, where the issues of cross-cultural mission are being explored, has an importance greater than for what have traditionally been called "foreign missions." Its presence here, alongside the great centers of learning and teaching that are now its neighbors, will be a reminder of the universality of the gospel, of the enduring validity of the call to make disciples of all nations. And that reminder is needed, for there are many voices in our culture that question the universality and the validity of that call. The contemporary embarrassment about the missionary movement of the previous century is not, as we like to think, evidence that we have become more humble. It is, I fear, much more clearly evidence of a shift in belief. It is evidence that we are less ready to affirm the uniqueness, the centrality, the decisiveness of Jesus Christ as universal Lord and Savior, the Way by following whom the world is to find its true goal, the Truth by which every other claim to truth is to be tested, the Life in whom alone life in its fullness is to be found.

Since the publication of the lecture by C. P. Snow with the title "The Two Cultures and the Scientific Revolution," the phrase that he coined has become very common, at least in my own country. We speak of the two cultures, and the phrase corresponds to a familiar reality. Our university campuses are divided into the faculties of science on the one hand and arts and humanities on the other. Theology, of course, belongs to the latter category. Theology is not about objective facts; for that you enroll as a student of science. Theology, like the rest of the matters studied in the other half of the university, is about things in which our subjectivity is involved — about *values*, where personal choice is of the essence of the matter. The physicist-priest W. G. Pollard, in commenting on this, says that these two cultures are not really comparable entities. The scientific culture is in the prime of its power — vigorous, coherent, convinced that it is dealing with reality and gaining a more and more full understanding of it. In the world of science there are, of course, differences of opinion, disputes, controversies, and rival schools of thought. But all these are understood to be about what is really the case, so that one expects to convince one's opponent of his error. One works on the assumption that eventually agreement will be reached. One does not accept pluralism (the coexistence of mutually contradictory accounts of what is the case) as a good thing. It is something to be overcome.

By contrast, says Pollard, the other culture is not a coherent culture at all. What goes on in the faculties of arts and humanities is the fragmented remains of what was once a coherent culture but is so no more. Here one abandons the hope of finding truth on which all will agree. Here pluralism is accepted as normal. What remains is not a culture comparable with the scientific culture. It is, in Pollard's words, "an ever-changing variety of remnants of what was once a universal culture in the Western world." And it is to this that theology has been relegated. Statements about the universal scope of Christ's saving work are not taken to be statements of objective fact, of what is actually the case. They are statements in story form of certain kinds of religious experience. They may be properly included in a syllabus for the comparative study of religions. Or they may be contributed to a dialogue in which different types of religious experience are shared, but they are not to be announced as factual truth, truth absolutely and for all.

It was not always so. Pollard speaks of the remnants of what was once a universal culture, though it was geographically limited to the Western world. Theological statements about Christ and his nature and work were part of a coherent understanding of reality, of how

116

things really are. This was itself the result of sustained intellectual effort of a rigor comparable to what we now see in the scientific culture. Dr. Frances Young, in her recent inaugural lecture as professor of theology in the University of Birmingham, reminded her academic audience of the immense intellectual energies that went into the effort of the early church fathers to formulate the truth of the gospel in the thought world of the age they lived in. That age was, like ours, one of relativism and syncretism in religious matters. Its intellectual atmosphere is tartly described in a famous phrase of Gibbon: "All religions were for the people equally true, for the philosophers equally false, and for the government equally useful." Professor Young contrasts the intellectual vigor with which the great theologians of the early centuries resisted this easygoing and seductive relativism with the contemporary drift toward utilitarianism and relativism. The latter she describes as "the modern version of the fall of Sophia, a breakdown of confidence in human powers of knowing, a failure of nerve easily compounded by disillusionment with the exploitative *hybris* of modern science and technology."

Allan Bloom, in his much-discussed book *The Closing of the American Mind,* has traced the origins of this breakdown. At least for me it was both illuminating and alarming to see the shadowy figure of Nietzsche behind what seemed to be our innocent and even laudable preference for talking about "values," "commitments," and "lifestyles" rather than for talking about right and wrong, truth and error. Bloom says Nietzsche was the first to recognize that on the basis of modern critical thought, it is strictly impossible to speak of truth and error, of right and wrong, and Nietzsche drew the conclusion that the only thing left is the will to power. This nihilism has, says Bloom, been domesticated in our culture in the soft-sounding language of "values." We ask of a statement, not "Is it true?" but "Are you sincere?" We speak not of right behavior but of authenticity. But nihilism will not permanently accept this comfortable domestication. Moral chaos must be the end of this road. And it will not be checked by appeals to tradition, to natural law, or to older "values." Only the revelation of God in Jesus Christ, only the living Word of the Creator can bring light out of darkness, order out of chaos.

Western culture was once a coherent whole with Christian vision at its center. It has disintegrated. If we seek now, as we must, a coherent vision for the human race as a whole, it cannot be on the basis of a tired relativism that gives up the struggle for truth. Nor can it be by pretending that the scientific half of our Western culture can provide coherence for the life of the world. We are at present busy exporting our science and technology to every corner of the world in the name of "development" and "modernization." But we also know that if all of the six billion of the world's people succeeded in achieving the kind of "development" we have achieved, the planet would become uninhabitable. There is an absurd irony in the fact that we are busy exporting our scientific culture to every corner of the world without any compunction about arrogance, but we think that humility requires us to refrain from offering to the rest of the world the vision of its true goal, which is given in the gospel of Jesus Christ. Relativism in the sphere of religion — the belief that religious experience is not a matter in which objective truth is involved but one in which "everyone should have a faith of one's own" — is not a recipe for human unity but exactly the opposite. To be human is to be a part of a story, and to be fully human as God intends is to be part of the true story and to understand its beginning and its ending. The true story is one of which the central clues are given in the Bible, and the hinge of the story on which all its meaning turns is the incarnation, death, and resurrection of Jesus Christ. That is the message we are entrusted with, and we owe it to all people to share it. If this is denied, if it is said that every people must have its own story, then human unity is an illusion and we can forget it.

I do not believe it is an illusion. I believe the word of Jesus when he said that in being lifted up on the cross he would draw all people to himself. I believe it because the cross is the place where the sin that divides us from one another is dealt with and put away. But I believe that the truth is credible only when the witness borne to it is marked not by the peculiarities of one culture, but by the rich variety of all human cultures. We learn to understand what it means to say that Jesus is the King and Head of the whole human race only as we learn to hear that confession from the many races that make up the human family. In the end we shall know Jesus as he really is, when every tongue shall confess him in all the accents of human culture. That is why this center for the study of the issues raised in cross-cultural ministry is important for us all.

We already have, in the ecumenical fellowship of churches, a first foretaste of that many-tongued witness. We owe the existence of this worldwide family to the missionary faithfulness of our forebears. Today and henceforth all missionary witness must be, and must be seen to be, part of the witness of this worldwide, many-cultured fellowship. Every culturally conditioned expression of the Christian witness must be under the critique of this ecumenical witness. The one Christ is known as he is confessed in many cultures. But we must reject the relativism that is sometimes wrongly called "the larger ecumenism." I am not referring to the fact, for which I thank God, that we are now much more open to people of other faiths, willing to learn from them, to share with them, to learn to live together in our one planet. I am referring to the fact that it is sometimes suggested that as the churches have come together to form one fellowship across their doctrinal differences, so — by a natural extension — the great world religions must move toward a fellowship of world faiths, and that this latter movement would be a natural extension of the former.

In fact, such a move would not be an enlargement but a reversal of the ecumenical movement. That movement was not born out of a lazy relativism. It was born through the missionary experience of the nineteenth century, when Christians, divided by centuries of European history, found themselves a tiny minority in the midst of the great ancient religious systems of Asia. In this new situation perspectives changed. The issue "Christ or no-Christ" loomed so large that the issues dividing Christians from one another seemed small. They did not disappear. The long theological wrestlings of Faith and Order are witness to the seriousness with which they were treated. But, real though they were, they were relativized by a new realization of the absolute supremacy of Jesus Christ. The separate Christian confessions would never have accepted membership in the World Council of Churches without its firm christological basis — Jesus Christ, God and Savior — a phrase later put into its trinitarian and biblical frame. It was only because the absoluteness of Jesus' lordship was acknowledged that the confessional positions could be relativized.

What is proposed in the so-called larger ecumenism is the reverse of this. It is a proposal to relativize the name of Jesus in favor of some other absolute. We have to ask: What is that absolute in relation to which the name of Jesus is relativized? Is it "religion in general"? Then where — in the medley of beliefs and practices that flourish under the name of religion — is the criterion of truth? Let it be brought out for scrutiny. Or is it, perhaps, "human unity"? But if so, unity on whose terms? André Dumas has correctly pointed out that all proposals for human unity that do not explicitly state the center around which unity is conceived to happen have as their hidden center the interests of the proposer. We have a familiar word for this. "Imperialism" is the word we normally use to designate programs for human unity originated by others than ourselves. The center that God has provided for the unity of the human race is the place where all human imperialisms are humbled, where God is made nothing in order that we might be made one. It is an illusion to suppose that we can find something more absolute than what God has done in Jesus Christ. It is an illusion to suppose that we can find something larger, greater, more inclusive than Jesus Christ. It is a disastrous error to set universalism against the concrete particularity of what God has done for the whole creation in Jesus Christ. It is only through the specificity of a particular historic revelation that we can be bound together in common history, for particularity is the stuff of history, and we shall not find meaning for our lives by trying to escape from history.

But we rightly bear witness to the universal scope of that particular history, the history that is the theme of our Scriptures, as we listen to the response of every human culture in every tongue and idiom to the self-revelation of God in Jesus Christ. The promise that the Holy Spirit will lead the Church into the fullness of the truth is set in the context of the missionary commission. So the insights given in the exercise of cross-cultural mission are essential to the fulfillment of that promise. That is why the work of this center is of importance not only to those who will be its students and its residents, but for all of us, for our growth into the fullness of the truth, for our learning with *all* the saints the length and breadth and depth and height of the love of God. To the One who by the power at work in us is able to do far more abundantly than all we can ask or think, to that One be glory in the work of this center, in the Church, and in Christ Jesus forever.

11

Mission in the World Today

A s the Father sent me, so I send you." With these words the risen Christ sent his chosen disciples out into the world, a movement launched into the public life of the world to continue what he had begun to proclaim, and to embody the reality of God's reign, God's fatherly rule over all things and all peoples. And with a gesture he reminded them of the central sign of the presence of that reign: he showed them his hands and his side. The body of the risen Lord is recognizable by the scars of the Passion, and his disciples will be corporately recognizable as his body when they bear the same scars. They are to proclaim and to embody — in foretaste but in real foretaste — the reality of that kingly rule that was crucially revealed in a cross and in the resurrection of the crucified one. The company thus launched into the life of all history this secret that is now an open secret, of a rule revealed to chosen witnesses now in the bearing of a cross and to be finally manifest to all in the return of the risen Lord to reign. History, cosmic history, now has a shape, a form that can be grasped: the central clue is the crucified Lord, and the horizon for all action in history is the advent of the One who is to come.

With this clue, and in the joyful expectation of this advent, the Church expanded in every direction — an explosion of joy that could not be contained but whose fallout, not lethal but life-giving, spread

An address given to the New College Missionary Society, New College, Edinburgh, as honorary president, 12 November 1987.

east and west and north and south. With our culture-bound minds we tend to think only of the expansion westwards. Church history seldom ventures eastwards beyond Antioch. For me, a journey through Afghanistan, Iran, and Turkey in 1974 was a vivid reminder of the fact that Christianity spread eastwards into those lands very early. However, without question the most dramatic explosion of the Christian energy was the one that occurred in the nineteenth and early part of the twentieth century, what Latourette calls "The Great Century," that carried the gospel into almost every part of the world and made possible what William Temple called "the great new fact of our time," namely the fact that the Christian Church is now a truly global society.[1]

The odd thing is that, while most Anglo-Saxons are very happy about the great new fact, they are embarrassed about the thing that made it possible — namely, the missions of the preceding century. Even when we read the reports prepared for the Edinburgh Conference of 1910, representing as they did the most informed and sensitive missionary thinking of the time, we feel uncomfortable with their conviction that "Christian Civilization" held the key to the future of the world. A missionary in training told me the other day that he was getting "hair-shirt missiology" — so eager were his teachers to confess the sins of our missionary predecessors. Of course it is much more pleasant and relaxing to confess the sins of one's ancestors than to be made aware of one's own. Yet, equally of course, we cannot deny that there was arrogance and a degree of insensitivity mixed up with the splendid courage and enthusiasm that summoned a generation of students to the evangelization of the world in this generation and that sent thousands of them to a lifetime of missionary service.

How do we explain the shift of perception? Is it just that, by the grace of God, the WASPs (White Anglo-Saxon Protestants) have acquired a new and uncharacteristic humility? I wish it were so, but I doubt it. I think the evidence shows that it is not an excess of humility but a shift of belief. We detect arrogance in the proposal to take the Christian message to every nation and proclaim it as the truth, but

---

1. K. S. Latourette, *The Great Century*, vols. 4–6 of *A History of the Expansion of Christianity* (Exeter, U.K.: Paternoster Press, 1970); Iremonger, *William Temple*, 387.

we are not embarrassed about taking Western science, technology, and political institutions into every part of the world under the name of "world development." That is not arrogance; it is the benevolent exercise of sharing our blessings with others who need them. We do so because we are sure that modern science gives us the truth about what is actually the case. To communicate it is not arrogance — it is simply our duty. But we see the preaching of the gospel as something different. It is not communicating knowledge of what is actually the case but rather the attempt to persuade other people to share our beliefs and our values — which is arrogance.

At a conference of clergy in which I shared recently, I was illustrating a point by referring to the experience of preaching in an Indian village. I was rebuked by a Roman Catholic priest, who told me I had no business to be preaching in an Indian village: I should have been sitting down and asking them to tell me what they believed. There is indeed a very right and proper place for that, and missionaries have been very much to the fore in listening to and interpreting the beliefs of other peoples. But that right and proper activity does not invalidate the other. We are not dealing with an excess of humility but with a shift in belief, in the public belief system that Peter Berger calls the "plausibility structure" of our culture.[2] Teaching physics is not arrogance: it is communicating knowledge of what is the case. Preaching the gospel is seen as arrogance because it is imposing my beliefs on others. It is not arrogance to tell others what we know; it is arrogance to try to persuade others of what we believe. Knowledge is one thing; belief is another.

I have recently been studying the legal arguments and judgments in a whole series of cases that have been going through the U.S. courts about what may or may not be taught in the schools. They offer a fascinating insight into our contemporary cultural predicament. The Louisiana State Legislature passed an act called the "Balanced Treat-

2. Peter Berger, *The Heretical Imperative: Contemporary Possibilities of Religious Affirmation* (Garden City, N.Y., 1979), 90–91, 148. Newbigin says he defines "plausibility structure" as a "social structure of ideas and practices that create the conditions determining what beliefs are plausible within the society in question"; *Foolishness to the Greeks,* 10–17.

ment Act" providing that "creation science" and "evolution science" should be taught together in the state schools. The children should be given both Darwin and the Bible and left to make up their own minds. The Supreme Court struck this down in a fifty-page majority judgment. The judgment makes no comment at all on the question of the truth or otherwise of Darwin and the Bible, on whether either or both of them give a reliable account of what is the case. The only issue to be settled was whether "creation science" is religion or science. If science, it may be taught; if religion, not. The question of truth does not arise.

Perhaps taking their cue from this argument, a group of Christians in Kentucky have taken their school board to court on the charge of teaching religion in the public schools and thus violating the First Amendment. The religion in question is "secular humanism." They argue that the school textbooks teach a certain view of what is the case, a view they call secular humanism. They call Paul Tillich as their witness to prove that whatever is one's ultimate concern is one's religion; that by carefully eliminating all references to God, or Christ, or Christian faith from the textbooks, the writers have shown their ultimate concern, which is their religion. The judge has found in favor of the plaintiffs. We shall see what happens when the case reaches the Supreme Court. In any case the legal arguments on both sides open up the profound dichotomy in our culture. Both science and religion profess to give a true account of what is the case: one is part of public truth, which every citizen must know and accept; the other is private opinion, which we have no right to impose on others.

I shall return at the end to a brief look at the sources of this dichotomy, but meanwhile its relevance to the issue of missions is obvious. It is a familiar and oft-repeated point that when Christendom was a compact geographical entity with minimum outside contacts, the Christian belief system could be accepted as public truth. The Shorter Catechism could be taught in the schools as part of what we ought to know. But now that we live in the global village with Muslims, Hindus, Sikhs, and Buddhists as our immediate neighbors, the situation is radically different. We find that many of them are as good as or better, certainly more devout, than most Christians are. What right do we have to try to convert them to our way of thinking?

(One might comment, if there were time, on the very odd idea that the truth of the Christian gospel stands or fails by the question whether Christians are better than other people; I refrain from doing so.)

At this point there comes into view what is sometimes called "the larger ecumenism." The argument goes like this: Christians have learned in the past seventy-five years to moderate their exclusive claims. Protestants and Catholics, Presbyterians and Episcopalians no longer pretend to have the absolute truth. They are learning to live as colleagues instead of rivals for people's allegiance. The time has come, it is said, to carry this movement further and apply it to the world religions. We should give up the idea of an exclusive Christian claim and acknowledge that we are all colleagues in the search for truth.

This rests on a complete misunderstanding of the ecumenical movement. Here in Edinburgh, if anywhere, we can never forget that the modern ecumenical movement was a child of foreign missions. It was because missionaries, especially in Asia, found themselves for the first time facing the stark contrast between Christ and no-Christ that they were led to relativize their own confessional positions in comparison with the absolute claim of Christ. The movement was not a carry-over of general relativism. The World Council of Churches could never have come into existence without its firm christological basis — "Jesus Christ, God and Savior." This was the absolute that relativized the claims of denominations, just as Paul's evocation of Christ and him crucified relativized the competing claims of the Corinthian factions.

The so-called "larger ecumenism" is not an extension of this but a reversal of it. It proposes to relativize the name of Jesus, and we therefore have to ask the sharp question: What is the absolute that relativizes the name of Jesus? Is it the absolute need for human unity? Then we have to ask: Unity on whose terms? As André Dumas has pointed out, every proposal for human unity that does not explicitly state the center around which such unity is conceived to be gathered always has the interest of the promoter as its hidden center. The history of the world is full of programs for human unity: we call them imperialism — at least when other people are their promoters. The

125

Christian Church offers Jesus Christ and him crucified as the one who makes human unity possible because he is the one through whom we are reconciled to God and to one another.

But perhaps the absolute is the universal religious experience of humankind? Then we have to ask two questions. First, why religion among all the things human beings are concerned with? The Bible certainly suggests what my friend D. T. Niles was fond of saying, that God is not chiefly interested in religion. But, second, where in all the medley of conflicting religious ideas is the criterion of truth? One does not have to read many pages of a book on the comparative study of religions to find out where the author's criterion is to be found — whether it is acknowledged or not. Few are as frank as Paul Knitter, who makes it quite clear in his book *None Other Name?* that his criterion is simply the *Zeitgeist:* we have to adjust our beliefs to what is generally acceptable to modern people.[3] Most Christian writers make it clear that they draw their criteria from Christ. This is true even for such a pluralist as John Hick. Although he asks us to move by means of a Copernican revolution from the idea that Christ is central to the idea that God is central, it is clear to any reader that his vision of God is drawn from the Gospels. But if we confine our attention to those who explicitly take Jesus as their criterion, the question remains: If God is as he is revealed in Jesus, must he not will the salvation of all? And since the vast majority of humankind have lived and died without ever hearing the name of Jesus, must God not have some other way of saving men and women? If he doesn't, is he not cruel and arbitrary? If he does, why missions?

There is, of course, a vast literature in which this matter is argued. What is striking — among all the disagreements — is the matter on which nearly all are agreed. With a few exceptions, which I shall mention later, all the discussions assume that the one question is: "Can the good non-Christian be saved?" In a recent discussion Gavin D'Costa divides writers on the subject into three groups: pluralists, typified by John Hick, who speak of many ways of salvation; exclusivists, typified by Hendrik Kraemer, who affirm only one way

3. Paul Knitter, *None Other Name? A Critical Survey of Christian Attitudes to the World Religions* (London: SCM, 1985).

— through Jesus Christ; and inclusivists, typified by Karl Rahner, who affirm that salvation is only through Christ but that the saving effects of his work extend beyond the boundaries of those who acknowledge him. I find myself in D'Costa's book bracketed with Kraemer, where I am delighted to be. I would want to be an exclusivist along with Kraemer in believing that God's work in Christ is (to use Kraemer's favorite phrase) *sui generis;* that there is nothing that can be put into the same category as the incarnation, ministry, death, and resurrection of Jesus. Kraemer affirmed this with passion and I would wish to do so too. But one should note that Kraemer never, as far as I know, said that all non-Christians were doomed eternally.[4]

Whence comes the misunderstanding? Surely by insisting only on one question—namely the question of the salvation of the individual soul after death. This is a proper question, but not in isolation. The Bible, in contrast to the Indian religions, does not speak of human life in these terms. It speaks of human life as part of a story, a story that is part of the whole story of the cosmos from creation to consummation. It is therefore, from a biblical point of view, equally important to ask about the meaning of the story as a whole, to ask where the clue to its meaning is, the clue by which all our lives as participants in the story are to be directed. I said that there were exceptions to the general rule that writers concentrate on the question of the destiny of the individual soul. I was thinking of my friend M. M .T. Thomas, with whom I have had many arguments and still have, but who seems to me to be asking the right question when he persistently sets this discussion in the context of larger political and cultural concerns and asks, What faith enables us to make sense of the public history of nations and of the world? I do not say that that is the only question, but that it is a necessary question. In the context of the Bible as a whole, we cannot rightly interpret the work of Christ as exclusively concerned with the destiny of individual souls after

4. Gavin D'Costa, *Theology and Religious Pluralism* (Oxford: Oxford University Press, 1986), 64, 66. "The first, adopted by Kraemer and Newbigin, simply states that we cannot know how those who do know Christ are saved, and must leave this to 'the wise mercy of God' and 'the mysterious workings of God's Spirit.'" Curiously, D'Costa severely criticizes Kraemer but ends up commending Newbigin.

death and apart from God's purpose for history as a whole. Otherwise how could we account for the fact that Paul, who certainly affirms the absolute centrality and finality of the work of Christ, also affirms that the Jews who have rejected Christ will be saved in the end?

As I read it, the Bible is not a set of separate stories of individual souls; it is the story of the cosmos, of the human family within the cosmos, and of every human soul within the story of the human family. Because it is a story and not philosophy or theosophy, particularity is its very stuff. The question that lies at the heart of the debate we are considering is the question about the relation of particularity to universality. How can God's universal love be tied down to a particular set of events in history, events in Palestine and not in Japan or India or Africa? That is the scandal, the stumbling block that those who question the propriety of missions stumble upon. Why should God not speak his own word to every soul and to every culture? But that is to do violence to the nature of human being as the Bible reveals it. We have to put the counterquestion: Is human being a set of separate stories, or are we — in some sense — part of one story? If the former, then we give up the hope of one world. If the latter, then we have to ask for the meaning of the story as a whole, and that means that we do not try to escape from the concrete particularities of history.

As we well know — or at least as we here in Presbyterian Scotland ought to know — the heart of the biblical story is in God's choosing, God's election of one people among all the peoples, and finally of one man among all people, to be the bearer of the secret of his saving purpose for all. It is a secret because it contradicts human ideas about world dominion. A man nailed to a cross does not look like the one to unify the world. But it is an open secret because it has been entrusted to a community chosen for the purpose of being witnesses. And their witness is a witness to the resurrection of the crucified, to the fact that the final victory of God's love lies beyond death and beyond the dissolution of the cosmos.

Those so chosen are not the good, the privileged, the exclusive beneficiaries of God's love. They are not those chosen for salvation as against the rest. The terrible warnings in the New Testament, much more severe than anything in the Old Testament, are directed to those who are within the company of the chosen. It is not the brambles that grow around the vine that are threatened with fire; it is the branches of the vine itself that do not bear fruit. One might almost reverse the Cyprian's old proverb and say, "Outside the Church no damnation." The secret is entrusted to the Church, and that is an awe-inspiring responsibility. But the final judgment is in the hands of God, and the elect are not given an advance copy of the judgment. There are many sayings of our Lord — not least the parable of the sheep and the goats — that suggest that there will be great surprise when it is published.

What, then, is the point of missions, if the non-Christian may be saved and the Christian may be lost? Have you thought what a Pelagian ring that question has? We want to be able to show that we accomplish something, produce results; that we have rescued some perishing souls. I don't read the New Testament that way. I think that the deepest motive for mission is simply the desire to be with Jesus where he is, on the frontier between the reign of God and the usurped dominion of the devil. We want his prayer to be answered: where I am there shall my servant be. We long that he shall see of the travail of his soul and be satisfied. That, I deeply believe, is the true motive.

The crucial question is one of truth. What is the true account of the story of which we are part? The reason for our embarrassment about missions is not an excess of humility. It is one expression of the pervasive relativism that dominates our culture. I have been reading the book called *The Closing of the American Mind* by Allan Bloom. It is a devastating analysis of the current academic science, dominated — as he sees it — by a total relativism. The central part of his large book traces the sources of the present situation through the last three centuries. Most of the threads, according to Bloom, go back to Nietzsche, who was the first to realize with terrible clarity that the movement of critical thought since the Enlightenment would make it finally impossible to say of anything: "This is true," or of any course of conduct, "That is right." Instead we have to speak of "values," "life-styles," "orientations," and so forth, because when the possibility of affirming truth is lost, the only thing left is the will — the will to power. The present debate about "values" in education illustrates his thesis. "Values" do not arise from a perception of what is the truth about the world, about the human story. They are an affair of the will. They are not an account of what is the case; they are what some people want because without them life is uncomfortable. And so we do not teach as a matter of fact, of how things actually are, that man's chief end is to glorify God and to enjoy him forever. We try to inculcate "values" — which is a totally different exercise, and rests on nothing except the will of those for whom it would be convenient if young people had those values.

If we believe that the Christian revelation gives us an interpretation of the human story that is true, then we will not be embarrassed about missions. But what about foreign missions? Are they not redundant now that the Church is planted in almost every nation? I do not think so. I think that cross-cultural mission is an enduring necessity, but in a context different from that of the nineteenth century. If the gospel is the clue to the meaning of the whole human story, then the bearer of that gospel must be the one ecumenical fellowship of churches embracing all cultures. But, and this is the crucial point, the gospel must never become domesticated within one culture. We know, or we ought to know, that this is a continuing danger. Missiologists have sometimes raised the cry of syncretism when they have seen churches in Asia or Africa trying to express the gospel in their own cultural forms. The most obvious examples of syncretism, however, are to be found in our Western churches, which have worked so hard to tailor the gospel to fit the so-called requirements of modern thought. Every church is tempted to do this in its own culture, tempted to become the domestic chaplain to the nation instead of being the troublesome, prophetic, missionary voice to the nation — challenging all syncretistic entanglements. Cross-cultural missions are needed even in places where the Church is already established — perhaps too established. They are the means by which the ecumenical family of churches can help each national church to maintain its distinctness and the authenticity as the bearer, not of that culture's self-image, but of the gospel of the crucified and risen Lord. I speak with knowledge, because I have as my colleague in the place where I work a missionary sent to us by the Church of North India, a Sikh convert, who is able to sharply challenge a great deal that we take for granted in our English Christianity.

We need cross-cultural missions to bear witness to that which is beyond every national and local culture, the story that is the real story of the human race in God's purpose. We bear witness to it because we believe that it is not just a symbolic way of expressing our values but the truth about human nature and destiny. Of course we know that this truth is contested. We do not pretend that it is public truth in the sense of not being contested. But we proclaim it as public truth in the sense that it is the truth by which all other claims to truth will finally be judged. The judgment is still ahead, and we are warned not to be judges in advance of that final judgment. We are witnesses — witnesses not of our religious experiences, but of Jesus, his incarnation, ministry, death, and resurrection. We cannot keep silent about this, because it is truth that concerns every human being. It is the truth about the human story. And so it must be told to every human being. That obligation remains till the end of time.

12

Reflections on the History of Missions

I have been asked in this paper to reflect upon the recent history of missions and to connect these reflections to the issues to be discussed at the Commission on World Mission and Evangelism consultation in San Antonio next month. As I have reflected, two phrases have often been in my mind. One is a phrase from the address of that great and beloved missionary Walter Freytag at the Ghana Assembly of the International Missionary Council (IMC) in 1957 in which he spoke of the "lost directness" of missions.[1] That is a very poignant phrase. I know what it is to go to a village where people have never heard the name Jesus and to tell them the Good News of God's love. There is a directness, a simplicity, and a joy in that exercise, something that has always given to the missionary enterprise its *élan*, its spiritual thrust. Now, when there is no longer any simple division of the world into Christian and heathen lands, that directness is easily lost. What is the spiritual thrust behind missions now?

The second phrase comes from a great English missionary, Bishop Stephen Neill. "When everything is mission," said Neill, "then nothing is mission." To put it sharply, does a world missionary conference have to deal with everything that is on the Church's agenda,

---

1. Orchard, *Report of the Meeting of the IMC.*

or does it have a specific task on which it must concentrate to the exclusion of other necessary tasks? If so, what is that task?

These two phrases encapsulate for me much of the debate with which my own life as a missionary has been occupied. Sixty years ago, as a Cambridge student, I signed the famous SVMU Pledge: It is my purpose, if God permit, to become a foreign missionary. I am still trying to work out what that commitment means.[2]

The early world missionary conferences had no problem of "lost directness." The conferences held in London in 1888, New York in 1900, and Edinburgh in 1910 did not think it necessary to write a message. Everyone knew what the message was. Edinburgh devoted splendid scholarly resources to exploring the best ways of communicating the message to people of each of the world's religions. No sharp line was drawn between the Christian message and the civilizing work of missions. It was still possible to speak of Christianity and civilization in one breath.

The conference in Jerusalem of 1928 no longer spoke in terms of Christian and heathen lands. It saw secularism as the looming danger everywhere. At moments some delegates were tempted to see the other religions as possible allies in the defeat of secularism.[3] It spoke with vigor of the role of missions in bringing about a new socioeconomic order.[4]

2. Officially it was not a pledge but a declaration. In 1919 the formula was changed on the insistence of Miss Hewat of Edinburgh University, because missionaries had such a negative image for students, to "It is my purpose, if God permit, to devote my life to missionary service abroad." This is probably the form to which Newbigin gave his signature. For the history of the SVMU and the pledge, see Denton Lutz, *The Evangelisation of the World in This Generation* (Hamburg: University of Hamburg, 1968); E. M. Jackson, *Red Tape and the Gospel* (Selly Oak: SOC, 1980), 41–60.

3. This was due to the influence of the Quaker Rufus Jones, who was also on the Laymen's Commission, and is to be found in some of the papers by American representatives. There was considerable debate as to what secularism was. Here Paton's contribution was significant. W. Paton, ed., *The Christian Message in Relation to Non-Christian Systems of Thought and Life*, vol. 1 of *The Jerusalem Meeting of the IMC* (London: Oxford University Press, 1928); E. Schlunk, ed., *Von den Höhen des Ölberges (Die Tagung des erweiterten Internationalen Missionsrates, Jerusalem 1928)* (Stuttgart: Missions Verlag, 1928).

4. It also created a Department of Social and Industrial Research with J. Merle Davies as its first director. See vol. 4 of the IMC Tambaram Series of reports.

And it did what none of its predecessors had done: it wrote a message. The message was so skillfully drafted by William Temple that it covered over deep disagreements about what the Christian message was. ("Our message is Jesus Christ.") These disagreements surfaced almost immediately.[5] There was the American Laymen's Report on Foreign Missions (1932), which looked for a convergence of the world's religions in working for the creation of a new social order. There was the work of J. H. Oldham and his colleagues, which led up to the Oxford 1937 Conference on Church, Community and State — an effort to confront the new paganism and racism of Europe.[6] And there were Hendrik Kraemer and his disciples with their affirmation of the uniqueness of the gospel and its discontinuity with all religions. At Tambaram (1938) it was Kraemer's thesis that set the agenda, but the debate was not concluded there — it rumbled on for the next twenty-five years.[7] Tambaram shifted the agenda in at least three ways. It saw the great danger not in secularism but in the new totalitarian ideologies that were sweeping Europe. It saw the necessity that churches should be missionary and that missions should be church based. And it made a passionate plea, voiced by the younger churches, for church unity. Tambaram, seen in retrospect during the dark days of war, was the beacon light that gave Christians everywhere the assurance that Christendom is now a family that truly encircles the globe. It made the ecumenical movement a reality for millions of people. It enabled Temple in his enthronement sermon as Archbishop of Canterbury to speak of "the great new fact of our time."

Whitby, Ontario (1947), was suffused with postwar optimism and

5. See the minority report of the Continental delegates, written by Hendrik Kraemer, and the account of the debate in Paton, *The Christian Message,* 478f. For a German view of the Jerusalem meeting, see M. Underhill, review of *Von den Höhen des Ölberges* by E. Schlunk, *International Review of Missions (IRM)* 18 (1929).

6. See the impressive preparatory work and the statements condemning racism, the first of their kind in the conference reports: J. H. Oldham, ed., *The Churches Survey Their Task: The Report of the Conference at Oxford on Church, Community and State, July 1937, London* (London: George Allen & Unwin, 1937). W. A. Visser 't Hooft and J. H. Oldham, *The Church and Its Function in Society,* vol. 1 of the *Church, Community and State* series (London, 1937).

7. Hendrik Kraemer, *The Christian Message in a Non-Christian World,* 1st ed. (London: Edinburgh House Press, 1938).

spoke of great evangelistic advance. But Willingen (1952) spoke of missions under the cross and even of the end of missions as we had known them. The conference had been called explicitly to clarify the nature of the missionary obligation of the Church, which had become a matter of acute perplexity. At the end, Norman Goodall, who had been responsible for organizing it, said that it had failed in its purpose. It was certainly not a failure, for it gave rise to many new initiatives, including the development of the worldwide chain of study centers sponsored by the IMC. But the debate on the missionary message ended in deadlock, and the report of the commission was not accepted by the full conference. The commission had been challenged, chiefly by Hans Hoekendijk of Holland and Paul Lehmann of the United States, to break out of the Church-centered missiology of Tambaram and to speak of God's work outside the boundaries of the Church, in scientific discovery, in political and social movements, and in the lives of ordinary people. It was a premonitory sounding of the theme that was to dominate the missiology of the next decade, the theme of God at work in the world outside of the Church. The Willingen conference also spoke of the Christian hope in eschatological terms, and this was the theme of the message prepared for the Second Assembly of the World Council of Churches at Evanston (WCC) (1954), but the assembly rejected it.[8]

The theme sounded tentatively at Willingen came out loud and clear at the Strasburg conference of the World Student Christian Federation on the Life and Mission of the Church (1960). Hoedendijck's message was the one that dominated the conference and was to dominate the whole decade. It was the decade in which the secular was acclaimed as the supreme manifestation of the gospel, the decade of Harvey Cox's *Secular City,* Paul van Buren's *Secular Interpretation of the Gospel,* and Arendt van Leeuwen's *Christianity in World History.* Action for civil rights became the paradigmatic form of mission. The missionary section at the Uppsala Assembly (1968) reflected this in its definition of mission as humanization, and its designation of the churches themselves as mission fields.[9]

8. On Newbigin's struggle to get it accepted, see Newbigin, *Unfinished Agenda,* 2nd ed., 123–126, 140.

9. See Newbigin's controversy with M. M. Thomas over this in "Baptism, the

The WCC's Commission on World Mission and Evangelism held a conference in Bangkok (1973) that marked a clear shift in perspective. Here the title was "Salvation Today" and the question was, "What does salvation mean for me now?" Questions of culture moved into the center. There was passionate affirmation of the need to find forms of Christian life that belong authentically to one's own culture and are not copies of another. There were angry voices from the third world and an embarrassed silence on the part of the representatives of the old mission-sending churches. For me personally Bangkok is memorable because of a sentence spoken (not publicly but under his breath) by General Simatoupong of Indonesia. I heard him say, "Of course the number one question is: Can the West be converted?"

The Fifth Assembly at Nairobi (1975) was far more positive than these earlier meetings in its affirmation of the need for explicit confession of Christ. It responded to the question of Bangkok by saying that Christ does not make copies but always originals. But a new element at Nairobi was the report of the section dealing with interfaith relationships. This report provided sharp questioning and was not accepted. It seemed to suggest that there were two alternative forms of human unity, one with its center in Christ and one otherwise. This proposal seemed clearly to call in question the basis of the WCC. I was not at Vancouver (1983), but I understand that something similar took place there. At a meeting in Madras (1988) called to celebrate the fiftieth anniversary of the Tambaram conference, strong voices were heard that appeared to deny the centrality of Jesus Christ and to suggest other models for human unity. In the earlier debates about mission, passionate as they were, there was never any question of the centrality of Jesus Christ. I do not think that the WCC can continue to play any significant role in the world missionary task if it does not adhere firmly to its basis. This is not one of the issues on the agenda

Church and Koinonia: Three Letters and a Comment," *Religion and Society* 19, no. 1:69–90. An exchange of letters between Lesslie Newbigin and M. M. Thomas, with a comment by Alfred Krass, republished in M. M. Thomas, *Some Theological Dialogues* (Madras: CLS, 1977); "Salvation, the New Humanity and Cultural-Communal Solidarity," *National Christian Council Review*, 3 March 1973; Newbigin, *The Gospel in a World of Religious Pluralism*, 211–221.

of San Antonio, but it will certainly have to be faced. But the San Antonio meeting has the immense advantage of being able to build on the remarkable Ecumenical Affirmation on Mission and Evangelism approved by the WCC's Central Committee in 1982. This splendid statement is a worthy outcome of these years of debate and (sometimes) confusion, and should set the parameters for ecumenical missionary thinking for many years to come.

Before going on to look at the issues chosen for discussion at San Antonio I would like to reflect a little on the history I have tried to summarize. This may help sharpen the issues as we look ahead.

Looking over the debates about the *content* of the Christian mission during these decades, one can see that there have been three overlapping phases. In the first phase the main thrust was towards the articulation of the Christian message vis-à-vis the world's religions. This was the major concern during the fifty years up to and including the debates that centered around Kraemer's thesis. A second phase saw the dominance of questions about the gospel and culture. Perhaps this was made possible by the development of the Theological Education Fund (TEF), which in its second mandate coined the new word *contextualization* (an invention of Dr. Shoki Coe from Taiwan) and stimulated theological colleges all over the third world to give more attention to the question "How does the gospel come alive in the various non-Western cultures?"[10] This question was very prominent, as I have said, at Bangkok and at Nairobi, and it continues to be a very important preoccupation in missionary thinking. Conservative evangelical missionaries have been particularly active in this regard. In a third phase, however, the emphasis has shifted toward the attempt to clarify the Christian message in relation to situations of injustice and oppression. This, of course, owes much to the development of the liberation theologies of Latin America, and it was in the center of attention at the Melbourne Commission on World Mission and Evangelism conference of 1980.

If one reflects upon this whole history from the point of view

10. The TEF was a division of the International Missionary Council set up to encourage the development of appropriate theological education in the third world, providing books, money, and so forth.

of the Church as one global community, the first comment to be made is one so obvious that it is often overlooked. All of these discussions have been conducted in one or more of the languages of Europe — English, German, Dutch, Spanish, Portuguese. Those who have taken part in them from the countries of the so-called third world are the intellectual elite of these countries. They have had a high degree of assimilation into the worldview embodied in these languages through periods of study in universities that use these languages. The use of these languages means that one's thinking is inevitably shaped by the worldview that dominates the intellectual life of Europe and its cultural extension, a worldview shaped partly by the Christian tradition at the root of European culture, but even more by the assumptions of the European Enlightenment. If I may illustrate my point in a personal way, I could refer to the experience of discussing these matters in a meeting at the United Theological College, Bangalore, and in a village congregation, the former in English and the latter in Tamil. The two discussions took quite different shapes, but it was the Bangalore discussion that was fed into the ecumenical consensus, not the other one. The point becomes clear if one looks at each of the three phases of the missionary discussions of the past century that I have just outlined. To discuss "religions" as though they were a separate department of human affairs alongside other human concerns is typical of our post-Enlightenment privatization of religion, but it may not be the right framework for understanding the realities we are dealing with. Similarly the discussion about missions and culture presupposes the same privatization. What does it mean to speak of "culture" apart from the whole business of human living? Why has there not been a similar discussion about missions and personal behavior? And the discussion of missions and the options for the poor, as led by the liberation theologians of Latin America, has been explicitly based on a Marxist analysis of the human situation — another form of post-Enlightenment thought.

What has been lacking in the long debate has been the attempt to examine all these presuppositions from the standpoint of the gospel. This is where the remark of General Simatoupong seems to me to be so relevant. He said that the most important question for the Christian world mission was, "Can the West be converted?" The main bearers of cross-cultural mission in the past 400 years have been also the bearers of European culture, and — at least during the past 250 years — this culture has been largely shaped by the beliefs of the Enlightenment. Also, much of European Christianity has been fundamentally syncretistic in that it has sought to accommodate the gospel to the supposed requirements of "modern thought" rather than exposing the mistaken assumptions of modern thought in the light of the gospel. For these reasons, the long debates that I have been briefly summarizing have failed to raise the more fundamental questions about what constitutes rationality. The 1928 Jerusalem conference did direct attention to the challenge posed by secularism to the Christian faith, but the questions were not radical enough and were not followed up. In the 1930s and 1940s the churches had to give all their energies to the battle against the new Western paganisms. And when the question of secularism came back into focus, supremely in the 1960s, secularization was seen as the fruit of the gospel, and the advance of Western secular ideas into the old ontocratic societies was hailed as the contemporary form of the Christian mission. Man had come of age, and to be a Christian was to live *etsi Deus non daretur* (as if there were no God).[11]

It is in this ideological context that we must assess the contemporary proposals for religious pluralism. Modern Western culture, as has often been said, is now two cultures: there is on the one hand the world of science, of public truth, which is to be taught in all the schools, a world of facts about which statements are either true or false. There is on the other hand a world of beliefs and values, which are not matters of public truth but of personal choice. Everyone is entitled to his or her own beliefs and values. One does not ask whether the beliefs are true or false: to do so is arrogance. One asks only whether they are sincerely held. In the public schools it is proper to teach children about the various beliefs and values of different human cultures, but it is not proper to teach that one of these is true and the

---

11. This phrase originated in one of Dietrich Bonhoeffer's final letters, and was widely misunderstood. The whole phrase was "To live before God as if there was no God," describing the nature of the witness he was compelled to give in prison, and not any lack of prayerful faith in him. "Man come of age" was a concept Bonhoeffer borrowed from Feuerbach, who challenged him in his final year.

others are false. The contemporary beliefs about the biological origin of human beings are taught as truth. But it is no longer permitted to teach as truth that human beings are made to glorify God and enjoy him forever.[12]

The American writer Allan Bloom, in his best-selling book *The Closing of the American Mind,* has pointed out that this language of values is derived via Max Weber from Nietzsche. Nietzsche saw that the development of post-Enlightenment critical thought would make truth statements impossible. What would remain would be the will, the will to power. "Values" are a matter of will; they are what you desire for yourself or for others. Facts are what you have to accept, whether you like them or not. Within this worldview it is obvious that statements about the unique lordship of Jesus are not to be understood as factual statements. They are ways of expressing one's personally chosen values. As Wesley Ariarajah has written, they are to be understood on the analogy of the little girl who tells her father, "You are the best daddy in the world." It is not be taken as a factually true statement; it is an expression of love, of value.

It is at this point that the furor created by the publication of Salman Rushdie's book *The Satanic Verses* is so significant. To Muslims, whose belief in the existence of God is not a matter of personally chosen values but the supreme fact, blasphemy is a terrible crime. For Western intellectuals, who have long ago ceased to believe that God really exists, the uproar is incomprehensible. Since the nation-state took the place of God in European thinking as the supreme disposer of health, wealth, and happiness, treason against the state is treated as the supreme crime, for which even democratic societies will award the death penalty. But blasphemy against God has no significance except that it offends the feelings of a few people who believe in him. As one watches the succession of Western intellectuals appearing on the TV screen to defend freedom of expression, they look more and more like schoolchildren who do not understand that it is dangerous to play with high explosives.

I think it is perhaps the new challenge from Islam that will compel us Christians to look much more critically — in the light of

12. From the Westminster Confession, 1644, VIII/2.

the gospel, not of the Qur'an — at the things we have taken for granted. I think when we do this we shall notice one thing that all the debates I have discussed have in common. It is that all of them have been terribly Pelagian. (As you know, Pelagius is the only first-class theologian that the British Isles have so far produced, so I should be an authority.) Let me say what I mean by this accusation. As I reflect on these debates, whether they are about how individual souls are to be saved, how truly humane Christian communities are to be fostered in all the cultures of the world, or how injustice and oppression may be removed, they have always seemed to be essentially about *our* program. Our activity was in the center of the picture. But as I read the New Testament I get a very different picture. There the center of the picture is God and his amazing grace, God and his mighty works of redemption in the Old and New Testaments, God in his faithfulness to what he has promised. In this perspective, mission is not a program so much as an overflow of grace. So the central question is not "How shall I or others be saved?" or "How shall this problem of cultural alienation or political oppression be solved?" but rather "How shall this glorious God be glorified?" Jesus warned his disciples that it was not for them to know the times and seasons that God had fixed by his own authority (Acts 1:6–8). He warns us against every tendency to see mission as our program. He promises that we shall receive power when the Holy Spirit is given, because the Spirit is the foretaste of the kingdom, the pledge that Jesus does reign even though his reign is hidden for a time so the world may have time to repent. The Church's mission is not primarily our program: it is the manifestation of the reality of the present, though hidden, reign of Jesus through the presence and power of the Holy Spirit. It is a kind of doxology, a glorifying of God in the midst of a world that turns its back on him.

It is interesting that the present decade sees two world missionary conferences with themes drawn from the Lord's prayer: the theme of Melbourne (1980) was "Your kingdom come"; that of San Antonio this year is "Your will be done." It would be wonderful if we had a conference in the 1990s with the theme, "Hallowed be your name."

And this brings me to some reflections, in the light of this discussion, on the four themes chosen for the San Antonio conference.

141

1. *Turning to the Living God.* This phrase comes, of course, from Paul's first letter to the Thessalonians: "You turned from idols to serve a living and true God." There are idols, false gods; and there is one living and true God. Radical choices have to be made. I think we have sometimes underestimated how radical this turning, this *metanoia,* has to be. It is often spoken of in merely moralistic terms — turning away from sins — and this usually means the things our society recognizes as sins. But what is called for is more radical. It is, as Paul says to the Romans, a transforming of the mind, so that one is not conformed to the ways in which our culture thinks. I have been much impressed recently by the work of the philosopher Alasdair MacIntyre, formerly the great atheist scourge of Christian believers, and now returned to the Christian faith. In his book *Whose Justice? Which Rationality?*[13] he develops at great length the thesis that all rationality is socially embodied, expressed in a language that is itself shaped by the specific historical experience of the community that uses that language. The idea (dominant in our culture) that there exists a supracultural rationality that can stand in judgment over all the culturally conditioned forms of rational discourse is an illusion. Christians are those people whose rationality is shaped by their indwelling the story of the Bible as it is lived out in contemporary society in the life of the Church. From within this indwelling, they see the world through the lenses provided by the story of the Bible with its center in the incarnation, ministry, death, and resurrection of Jesus. This view is challenged by another view that finds the clue to the human story in the growth and development of human mastery over nature, the development of science, technology, and democratic political institutions. The question is which view provides in the long run the more coherent and effective way of understanding and coping with the whole of human experience, including the important experience of evil, pain, and death. Christians since the Enlightenment have been busy trying to show that the Christian view is reasonable, and "reason" in this exercise has been defined in terms of the rationality of this other socially embodied tradition. But reason is not an autonomous authority. It is a function of a socially embodied tradition of experience. Turning

13. Alasdair MacIntyre, *Whose Justice? Which Rationality?* (London, 1988).

from idols to the living God means moving from one socially embodied tradition of rational discourse to another. It means, therefore, a more radical break with and critique of the reigning plausibility structures than has usually been recognized. It means becoming dissenters from the dominant assumptions of the world around us, no less here in western Europe than in Asia or Africa.

2. *Participating in Suffering and Struggle.* Turning from idols to serve the living God means following Jesus, and that means taking up the cross. It is right, therefore, to make this the next move. We are not authorized to proclaim the Kingdom except in the way that Jesus did; that is why, when Jesus sent his disciples out to continue his mission, he showed them his hands and side. To be with Jesus means to be with him in challenging the powers of evil in the power of his Kingdom, and in bearing the cost. I have two marginal comments to make in the light of recent ecumenical discussion of this theme. First, it seems to me that St. Paul sees the Christian as one who is already liberated and not as one who struggles for liberation. Struggle is not a New Testament word, but suffering is. We have been set free from slavery, Paul tells us, to be children of God, and the mark of our status as children of God is that we suffer with Jesus in order to be glorified with him. "Carry with us in our body the dying of Jesus so that the life of Jesus may be manifest in our body" (2 Cor. 4:9). Christian discipleship has this paradoxical character: right in the midst of suffering, we are more than conquerors through him who loved us. That, it seems to me, is what gives its distinctive quality to Christian participation in the suffering of the oppressed, the alienated, and the marginalized.

Second, there are many situations, alas, in which the Christian struggle has to be directed against those who hold power. There is a tendency to universalize this and to see the Church as always and necessarily a protest group. The Church after Constantine is condemned for using the Christian faith as a legitimization of power instead of a protest against power. But one has to ask, then, where legitimacy is to be found for the exercise of power, for power is a reality and no one can pretend to be exempt from its use. Very specifically, where does the legitimacy of the power of governments come from? To distance the Church totally (or to pretend to distance it) from the exercise of power is to surrender to Manicheism. Missions in the nineteenth century operated from positions of power. We are now acutely aware of the distortions that produces. Yet numerical growth of the Church today comes from the witness of those who are without power. It is, as so often, the suffering churches that are the effective witnesses. But all Christians have some power and some Christians have much power. We need guidance about the use of power in responsibility to the living God, as well as about protest against the irresponsible use of power.

3. *The Earth Is the Lord's.* The ecological problem, which is now such an urgent and daunting one, hardly surfaced at all during the missionary debates up to the beginning of this decade. It is only now, and suddenly, that we have become aware of the possibility of ecological disaster. This is one of the points at which we are becoming aware of the radical error at the heart of the dominant Western thinking of the past 250 years. In the development of our science and technology we have, as Jürgen Moltmann says, treated God's creation as if it were a bit of unclaimed property that we could use at our pleasure. This is a point at which the fundamental atheism of our culture has been most apparent. Yet in our rightful reaction against this, I think we must guard against another danger. Among those who have become aware of this radical defect in our European tradition, at least since the Enlightenment, there is an understandable tendency to look to the East, to Asia, for wisdom. One can understand this and sympathize. But a shift from atheism to pantheism will not bring us to reality. The dynamism Europe has introduced into world history cannot simply be switched off, nor can traditional societies be permanently embalmed in aromatic spices — however much the Western tourist industry might desire it. The integrity of creation is not something static. God has imparted what seem to be purposeful drives in the created world and certainly in human beings who are part of the creation. The only way to seek the integrity of creation is in a recovery of the sense of responsibility to the Creator and in a recognition that we have to answer before his judgment seat for the way we have exercised the stewardship he entrusted to us. One can understand the appeal of movements like the New Age as a reaction against the errors of our post-Enlightenment ideology, but they lack the one thing

essential: an acknowledgment of God as the supreme reality, the living God who has committed himself in boundless love to his creation, and to whom we owe an allegiance that takes precedence over all else. The transition from atheism to pantheism is not difficult. There is not a great deal of difference between saying "God is everything" and saying "There is no God." But how shall those who have assumed for centuries that the world can be understood, developed, exploited with reference to the hypothesis of God, how shall these be converted and turned to the living God? That, as Simatoupong said, is the number one question for the world mission: Can the West be converted? That leads us to the fourth topic of San Antonio: Communities Renewed in Mission.

4. *Western Communities Renewed in Mission.* During the period when the missions of the Western churches were at their strongest, the agencies of mission were not local congregations but supra-congregational agencies — whether voluntary societies or denominational boards. These were the agencies that created the IMC and have supported the Commission on World Mission and Evangelism. The integration of the IMC with the WCC, along with the corresponding moves in the various nations, was an effort to relate church and mission — a necessary effort. But it did not really touch the local congregation. Congregations were invited to support the work of missionary agencies with prayer and money; they were not themselves the primary missionary agencies. During the early 1960s when I was working in Geneva, I was involved in initiating the study of structures for missionary congregations. In my own mind this had arisen from the experience of putting into practice the missionary principles of Roland Allen in an Indian rural situation.[14] By departing from the traditional idea of the ministry of Word and sacrament, and turning responsibility over to ordinary village laborers and farmers and shopkeepers, we had been able to see a very rapid spontaneous expansion of the church. I was convinced that this had lessons for the churches everywhere. However, the program on missionary structures got carried away in the secularizing tide of the 1960s and ended up with the slogan "The world sets the agenda." I

14. Roland Allen, *Missionary Principles,* reprint (London: Lutterworth, 1964).

think that was a dead end.[15] But I remain convinced about the centrality of the local congregation. Where the Church is growing today, it is through the witness of small local groups, base communities, house-churches, and ordinary congregations. The experience of working for nine years as the pastor of an inner-city congregation in an English city convinces me that nothing can make the reality of the living God credible except a company of people who believe it and live by it. Apart from this, mission, whether conceived as evangelism or as social action, becomes a mere program, a campaign. I think that the only thing that can make the gospel credible, the only thing that makes it possible to believe that the ultimate authority over the whole universe resides in a man nailed to a cross, is a company of people who live in the biblical story so that they know it as their own story and as the clue to the whole human story. I have seen this especially in the black churches in Birmingham. They are among the oppressed people of our society. But their life is marked by a remarkable joy and hope. "We were slaves and the Lord redeemed us out of Egypt. We saw the Red Sea divide and we crossed over and the armies of Egypt were drowned. We were led through the desert by a pillar of cloud and fire. We were fed with manna in the desert. We were there when they crucified the Lord, and we met him when he came from the tomb. This is our story and it is the true story. We relive it as we read and ponder it week after week, and as we share the broken body and the shed blood of the Lord and so share his risen life." This is the reality, antecedent to any program, any campaign. It is the given reality. And it challenges people to ask — as they asked on the day of Pentecost — "What is going on?" And *that* is the question from which the real missionary dialogue begins. I believe that the only hermeneutic of the gospel is a local congregation that believes it and lives by it. I think, therefore,

15. This slogan has probably been more misunderstood than any other devised by the WCC. It originated at the Central Committee in 1970 and articulated the need felt by M. M. Thomas and others for the church to respond to the plight of Vietnam, Biafra, and so on. See Colin Morris, *Include Me Out* (London, 1968). Practical response took the shape of the Programme to Combat Racism, the Ecumenical Loan Fund, and so forth.

that nothing is more central to the world mission of the Church than the renewal of the life of local congregations. But they must be congregations who really believe in and live by the story that is the clue to the whole human and cosmic story, the story that has its center in the incarnation, ministry, death, and resurrection of the Lord Jesus Christ. I hope that the great gift of San Antonio to the world mission of the Church will be that it encourages local communities to believe in and live by the gospel and so to become the ministers of Christ to their neighbors.

13

Evangelism in the Context of Secularization

One must begin with some examination of the concept of secularization. Many sociologists now agree that the idea that has been dominant during the past half-century — namely, that the progress of modern science and technology must increasingly eliminate religious belief — has proved to be false. The present century has in fact witnessed a marked growth in religiosity in Europe. It is true that this has not been expressed in Christian terms. But in the forms of many new religious movements, in the enthusiasm for Eastern types of religious belief and practice, in the revival of various ancient forms of pagan religion, and in the enormous popularity of astrology among European peoples, there is a luxuriant growth of religion in what is called the secular society. Moreover, in those parts of Europe where people have lived for forty years or more under the control of the Marxist ideology with its claim to replace religion completely by a "scientific" doctrine of human nature and history, the Christian churches have shown a power of survival and renewal much more impressive than what has been seen in the areas that called themselves the "free world."

And there is a further point to be made. Leaving aside movements that are recognizably religious in the sense that they affirm

---

This article first appeared in Dutch in *Kerk en Theologie*, October 1990.

realities not available for investigation by the methods of empirical science, it is clear that there are, even in the most secularized societies, forces that have a religious character in the sense that they have the status of dogma and command total trust. In the great debates about secularization in the decade of the 1960s, when many Christians (such as Arendt van Leeuwen) welcomed the process of secularization as a form of liberation made possible by the Christian gospel, it seemed to be taken for granted that secularization created a space free of all ideological or religious control. In this space, human beings (and Christians among them) would find the freedom to exercise their own rational and moral powers without coercion from any dominant belief system. The secular society was hailed as the free society. Writers such as Harvey Cox in the United States and Denis Munby in England encouraged the Christians of their day to welcome the process of secularization as a proper fruit of the Christian message and a further stage in human emancipation.

But a candid look at the societies that call themselves "secular" must surely dispel such illusions. Dogma does not vanish when the name is dropped. It is impossible to pretend that children in the state schools of Europe are not being taught to accept certain beliefs about human origins, human history, all shaped by certain assumptions. The loud complaints of Muslim parents that I hear in England are directed against precisely the claim that what their children are being taught to believe are simply "the facts," while everyone must know that they are in reality beliefs that a Muslim must reject. They quite rightly see that their children are being taught (not in the classes on "religious education" but in the classes on science, history, literature, and sociology) to believe that human life can be satisfactorily understood and managed without any reference to God. They protest against the arrogance that assumes that things taught in school are simply "the facts," while religious beliefs are merely private opinion.

The apostles of secularization in the 1960s seemed to believe that human societies can flourish without any shared beliefs. But this is obviously not so. The societies we know in Europe share the belief that what human beings need to know in order to manage their lives is the body of assured knowledge that is available through the methods of science. Perhaps those critics are right to see Descartes as the key figure. The attempt to find a kind of certitude that left no room for doubt, and the discovery of that certitude in the existence of the thinking self *(cogito ergo sum)*, constitute the deliberate choice of a position that *is* open to doubt. Why should we imagine that human beings should have available to them a basis for certitude other than the one provided by a trustful dependence on the Author of our being? Descartes' starting point already begs that question. But the secular societies that have developed in Europe since the seventeenth century share the common belief that reliable knowledge about human nature, and therefore about how human life is to be managed, is to be found not by reliance upon divine revelation and grace but by reliance upon the methods of empirical science. This, broadly speaking, is the dogma that controls public life, as distinct from the private opinions that individuals are free to hold.

But the dogma does not measure up the realities of human nature. If there is no answer to the question "But why did this happen to me?" people will turn to astrology. If there is no answer to the question "What is human life really for? What is the purpose of human life and of the whole creation?" people will seek to fill the void with the search for instant pleasure in drugs, in sex, in mindless violence through which one can express the sense of meaninglessness. We have to be endlessly entertained and we have to have idols to fill the empty space from which the living God has been removed. In the end, the society we have is not a secular society but a pagan society, a society in which men and women are giving their allegiance to no-gods. The rational part of us puts its trust in the findings of science but is left with no answer to the question of ultimate meaning. The way is open for the irrational part of us to develop a pantheon of idols.

The "secular" society is not a neutral area into which we can project the Christian message. It is an area already occupied by other gods. We have a battle on our hands. We are dealing with principalities and powers. What, then, is evangelism in this context?

To our "secular" contemporaries the answer to this question is quite simple. The Christian Church is a voluntary association of people who wish to promote certain "values" for themselves and for society. These "values," like all others, are matters of personal choice.

They are not matters of "fact" that everyone has to accept. It follows that the success of these "values" depends on the number of people who support them. There is a diminishing number of people who identify themselves with the Christian churches. The churches are therefore in danger of collapsing. Evangelism is an effort by the churches to avert this collapse and to recruit more adherents to their cause. It is even possible that this way of understanding evangelism may be in the minds of some church members. It then becomes impossible to conceal the element of anxiety that infects the enterprise. It becomes very important that *we* should succeed. The shadow of Pelagius hangs over the enterprise. In contrast to this way of seeing things, it is a striking fact that nowhere in the letters of St. Paul does the apostle lay upon the Church the duty of evangelism. The gospel is such a tremendous reality that he cannot possibly keep silent about it. "Woe is me if I do not preach the gospel" (1 Cor. 9:16). He seems to take it for granted that the same will be true for his readers. He is not slow to warn, persuade, rebuke his friends; it is a matter of life or death for him that they should be utterly faithful to Christ. But he never lays upon them the duty to go out and evangelize. Why should this be so?

The first evangelism in the New Testament is the announcement by Jesus that the Kingdom of God is at hand. This, if one may put it so, is not ecclesiastical news but world news. It is not about "values" but about "facts." It is, strictly speaking, news, and it requires an immediate response in action. There is immediate excitement. People flock to hear. But it seems as if God's reign was not what we expected. There is both enthusiasm and rejection. In the end there is betrayal, condemnation, and death. God's reign has not appeared after all. There is despair and suicide. But what seemed to be the end is the new beginning. The tomb is empty, Jesus is risen, death is conquered, God does reign after all. There is an explosion of joy, news that cannot be kept secret. Everyone must hear it. A new creation has begun. One does not have to be summoned to the "task" of evanglism. If these things are really true, they have to be told. That, I suppose, is why St. Paul did not have to remind his readers about the duty of evangelism.

But can this have any relevance to the ordinary comfortable, respectable Christian congregation in the suburbs of a contemporary

European city? There is, let us admit, a big gulf between them. We have largely domesticated the gospel within our culture. We have quietly accepted, for practical purposes, the dogma that controls public life. We have accepted as the "real" history the story that is told in the school classrooms about the history of "civilization," which means the interpretation of the human story from the point of view of *this* moment and *this* place in the whole story. We have allowed the Bible to be inserted into this history as a very minor strand in the whole human story, one element in the history of religions, which is itself only one element in the whole fabric of human history. We have not had the boldness that, for example, our black-led churches in Birmingham show, to recognize the story that the Bible tells as the real story, the true story, the story that explains who we really are, where we come from and where we are going. If we were faithful to our best traditions, if we took the Bible seriously over the years by the constant reading of it, expounding it, meditating on it, then we would see the story that is told in the schools as a story that misses the real point. What is the real point of the human story, in which my life is only a small part? It is not in the achievement, somewhere in the distant future, of a perfect human civilization. It is not in the achievement of my personal ambition, after which I decline into senility. The point of the whole story has been made once and for all in the events that the New Testament tells. If we believe that, then we live by a different story from the one that is told in our society. And the difference will become clear and will provoke questions. I have taken the example of St. Paul to suggest that we may be missing an essential point if we speak about evangelism as a duty. One could also point to the striking fact that almost all of the evangelistic sermons that are recorded in the Acts of the Apostles are responses to questions asked, rather than discourses given on the initiative of the speaker. It would seem that if the Church is faithfully living the true story, the evangelistic dialogue will be initiated not by the Church but by the one who senses the presence of a new reality and wants to inquire about its secret.

How will the presence of the new reality become known? I suggest by three things: by a certain kind of shared life, by actions, and by words that interpret the actions. The first and fundamental one is a certain kind of shared life. At the heart of that life will be praise. St. Luke tells us that the first response of the first disciples to the resurrection of Jesus was that "they returned to Jerusalem with great joy and were continually in the Temple, praising God" (Luke 24:51). A community of people that, in the midst of all the pain and sorrow and wickedness of the world, is continually praising God is the first obvious result of living by another story than the one the world lives by. In our own century we have the witness of the churches in the USSR, who for three generations were denied the opportunity of any kind of outward witness by word or action, but who sustained through those years a life of praise, reflecting in their worship the glory of the triune God. It was that reality, the presence of something that by its very existence called into question the official story by which the nation was required to live, that drew men and women to faith in Christ through the darkest years of tyranny.

We know that the worship of a Christian congregation can become a dead and formal thing, having the outward form but lacking the inward joy of adoration. When that has happened, our duty is to pray for the reviving work of the Holy Spirit to kindle into flame the embers that are always there. We know that this prayer has been answered many times in ways beyond expectation. And where there is a praising community, there also will be a caring community with love to spare for others. Such a community is the primary hermeneutic of the gospel. All the statistical evidence goes to show that those within our secularized societies who are being drawn out of unbelief to faith in Christ say that they were drawn through the friendship of a local congregation. There is, of course, a kind of "loving" that is selfish — merely the desire to have more members for the congregation. This kind of "love" is quickly recognized. But a congregation that has at its heart a joyful worship of the living God and a constantly renewed sense of the sheer grace and kindness of God will be a congregation from which true love flows out to the neighbors, a love that seeks their good whether or not they come to church.

Second, the presence of a new reality will be made known by the acts that originate from it. Jesus' announcement of the gospel, that the Kingdom of God is at hand, was immediately implemented by actions of healing and deliverance. These actions are portrayed as

153

simple evidence that the power of God, his kindly rule over all powers, is present. They are acts of sheer compassion. A victim of leprosy, sensing the presence of this reality, says, "If you will you can make me clean." Jesus replies: "I will; be clean," touches him and heals him (Mark 1:40–41). There are no conditions attached. Nothing is said about faith and repentance. It is the love of God in action. The reign of God has come near.

When the Christian congregation is filled with the Spirit and lives the true story, such actions will flow from it. Primarily they will be the actions of the members in their several vocations every day. While there are also actions that a congregation or a wider church body may undertake, these are secondary. The primary action of the Church in the world is the action of its members in their daily work. A congregation may have no social action program and may yet be acting more effectively in secular society than a congregation with a big program of social action.

What is important in these actions — whether the personal actions of individual members or the corporate programs of a congregation — is that they spring out of the new life in Christ. It can be otherwise. They can be designed to attract new members, or to justify the congregation in the eyes of society by its good works. The Gospels make it clear that Jesus resolutely refused to make for himself a public reputation as a healer and a worker of miracles. His mighty works were indeed signs of the presence of the Kingdom, but when he was asked for a sign, he refused. When a multitude of people who had gathered around him were hungry, he fed them. But when they pursued him, he sternly told them that they must seek for the bread that does not perish with the eating (John 6:25). A program of church action may arise not from sheer compassion but from an ideological commitment to some vision of society shaped by the story that the world tells and not by the story that the Bible tells. The Church then becomes one among a number of agencies for promoting justice and peace, rather than the sign and foretaste of the new reality where alone justice and peace embrace, the sign pointing to the crucified and risen Jesus in whom alone we can receive both God's justice and God's peace.

Third, then, the presence of the new reality will be attested to by words. The Church has to speak, to announce the new reality, to preach. Here we have to reject two false positions. On the one hand there is the view that "actions speak louder than words," the view that the Church will win people's allegiance to the gospel by good lives and good works and that preaching is unacceptable and unnecessary. The word *mission* is used to describe a range of activities in which explicit naming of the name of Jesus has no place. On this two things may be said. The first is that Jesus himself preached and instructed his disciples to preach. Not, as we have seen, that each act of healing or deliverance was accompanied by a sermon. Not at all. But the acts of healing and deliverance were not self-explanatory. They might even be the work of the devil (Mark 3:21ff.). And when Jesus sent out the Twelve with the authority to heal and deliver, he also told them to preach. It is clear that the preaching is an explanation of the mighty works, and that the mighty works are evidence that the preaching is true. They are not separable (Mark 6:7). Second, therefore, we have to say that the preaching of the Church carries no weight if it does not come from a community in which the truth of what is preached is being validated (even though always imperfectly) in the life of the community. But the life of even the most saintly community does not by itself tell the story, the story in which the name of Jesus has the central place.

If these general affirmations are true, I would suggest that in thinking of evangelism in a secular society, and — in particular — in thinking of the reevangelization of Europe, the following five points may be helpful.

1. Evangelism is not the effort of Christians to increase the size and importance of the Church. It is sharing the Good News that God reigns — good news for those who believe, bad news for those who reject. Evangelism must be rescued from a Pelagian anxiety, as though *we* were responsible for converting the world. God reigns and his reign is revealed and effective in the incarnation, ministry, death, and resurrection of Jesus. As we grow into a deeper understanding of this fact, as we learn more and more to live by the other story, we become more confident in sharing this reality with those who have not yet seen it.

2. The clue to evangelism in a secular society must be the local

congregation. There are many other things of which one could speak —mass evangelism of the Billy Graham type, Christian literature, radio and television, study and training courses, and so on. These are auxiliary. Many of them can be very valuable. But they are auxiliary to the primary center of evangelism, which is the local congregation. The congregation should live by the true story and center their life in the continual remembering and relating of the true story, in meditating on it and expounding it in its relation to contemporary events so that contemporary events are truly understood, and in sharing in the sacrament by which we are incorporated into the dying and rising of Jesus so that we are at the very heart of the true story. The congregation that does this becomes the place where the new reality is present with its heart in the praise and adoration of God and in the sharing of the love of God among the members and in the wider society. And here, of course, an immense amount depends upon the leadership given through preaching, pastoral encouragement, and public action by those called to ministry in the congregations.

3. It will be a major part of the work of such congregations to train and enable members to act as agents of the Kingdom in the various sectors of public life where they work. This kind of "frontier" work is very difficult, and although many promising starts have been made during the years since the last war, there is still much to do. It must become a part of ordinary congregational life that members are enabled to think through and discuss the ways in which their Christian faith impinges on their daily life in their secular work. Here is the place where the real interface between the Church and the world, between the new creation and the old, takes place. Here is where there ought to be a discernible difference in behavior between those who live by the old story and those who live by the story the Bible tells. It ought at many points to lead to differences in behavior, to dissent from current practice, to questioning. And this, of course, will be the place where the counterquestions arise. The Christian will be asked, "Why do you do this? Why do you behave like this?" Here is where the true evangelistic dialogue begins. At present it is very rare to find this kind of situation because the churches have so largely accepted relegation to the private sector, leaving the public sector to be controlled by the other story.

4. From this it follows that it will also be the task of the local congregation to equip members to enter into this dialogue, to explain the Christian story and its bearing on daily life. And of course the explanation will be not be complete without the invitation to become part of the community that lives by the other story and to learn there what it means to do so. Here is where the call to conversion comes, but it is not only a call addressed to the heart and the will, and not only concerned with personal and domestic life; it is also a call addressed to the mind, a call to a radically different way of seeing things, including all the things that make up daily life in the secular world.

5. If this approach is right, evangelism is not just the call to personal conversion, although it is that. It is not just a program for church growth, although it is that also. It is not just preaching, although it is that, and it is not just action for changing society, although it is that too. It is not a program for the reestablishment of the *Corpus Christianum* in Europe with the Church in the supreme position. Most certainly it is not that. But I believe it is possible to hope for and to work for something different — a Europe (a "common European home") that is a Christian society, not in the sense that it is ruled by the Church, and not in the sense that everyone is a Christian, but in another sense, which I would indicate as follows. It is possible to envision a society in which Christians have engaged so seriously over several decades with the consequences of the Enlightenment (good and bad) and with the kind of society that has developed at the end of the twentieth century that those who achieve the highest standards of excellence in all the sectors of public life — politics, industry, learning, and the arts — may be shaped in their public work by the Christian story. Then the worship of the triune God as he is made known to us in Jesus may again be the focus of ordinary life in our towns and villages.

Whether or not that is in the purpose of God for our continent, the main point is quite simple. We are entrusted with good news, the news that God reigns. That must be the starting point of all our thinking, and our evangelism will be an overflow of that joyful faith. Who knows, perhaps God has in store for our poor old secularized Europe a new birth of faith in the twenty-first century.

157

14

Mission in a Pluralist Society

No society is totally pluralist. In every society there is what Peter Berger calls a "plausibility structure"—a set of beliefs and practices that render some beliefs plausible and some implausible in that society.[1] Every society has certain agreed-upon ways of doing things, and certain assumptions that are normally not questioned— perhaps not even consciously held. And, thank God, no society can completely destroy human freedom. Modern totalitarian states in Europe and elsewhere have made, and are making, strenuous efforts to do so, but the human spirit still finds some place for the exercise of free choice, even if it is the choice of martyrdom. On the other hand there is no society in which freedom of choice is unlimited. It is well known that the Christian faith shows more vigor and expansive power in many societies that place severe limits on human freedom than in many societies—such as those of western Europe—that claim to be both pluralist and free.

Christianity was born into a religiously pluralist world, and in that sense pluralism does not present a new problem for the Church. But that world did not have as its "plausibility structure" the assump-

1. Berger, *The Heretical Imperative,* 90-91, 148. Berger's "plausibility structure" is discussed at length in Newbigin, *Foolishness to the Greeks,* 10; Newbigin, *Truth to Tell,* 53.

A contribution to the Festschrift for Lukas Vischer.

tions and practices that prevail in the free pluralist democracies of western Europe. In this situation, the Church does confront something new, something it has not yet learned to come to terms with. It is in the free democracies of western Europe that the Church has been in steepest decline for more than a century. The Church seems to cope with tyranny better than with freedom.

We have to confront the paradoxical relation between freedom and truth. In the "free" societies of western Europe it is axiomatic that free inquiry is the necessary condition for the attainment of truth. Truth, it is held, will be found only where there is freedom to question all assumptions, and therefore will only be found in a society that grants that freedom. Yet it is one of the marks of contemporary European thought that there is a profound skepticism about the possibility of knowing the truth. Indeed pluralism is celebrated as the proper social implication of the fact that truth is unknowable. This typical assertion of the liberal democratic society contrasts with the saying of Jesus: "If you continue in my word, you are truly my disciples and you will know the truth and the truth will make you free" (John 8:31f.). Is it freedom that enables us to find the truth, or is it the truth that enables us to find freedom? That saying of Jesus precipitated the most furious attack by his hearers, an attack that led straight into his further declaration that these hearers were not free as they supposed, but were the slaves of sin. They were not free to know the truth; only the truth could set them free.

When this claim is really understood, the response of the liberal Western intellectual is no less angry. The basic dogma of liberal society, which when questioned may also provoke extreme anger, is the dogma that the human reason and conscience have the freedom, and the capacity, to search out and know the truth. European societies have in general accepted the invitation of Descartes to seek indubitable certainties upon which could be founded a structure of knowledge formulated with the clarity of mathematics. But this Cartesian program, so far from resting on indubitable knowledge, concealed a vast and unproved assumption — namely, that the cosmos and human nature are such that it is possible for us to know the truth of things without dependence on any word from the Creator. When one thinks about it, it is an astounding assumption. But it is normally unquestioned in the "free" societies of western Europe. Free inquiry, unfettered by any dogma, is seen as the way to establish truth. If there be divine revelation, it must produce its credentials before the bar of free inquiry. The human person, apart from divine grace, has the freedom to know and also the right to know the truth. When this fundamental dogma of liberal society is questioned, there is the same anger as that which erupted at the words of Jesus I have quoted.

The Cartesian program created a dichotomy in the human quest for truth. It created on the one hand the idea that there is a world of objective facts that can be known without the involvement of any subjective commitment, and on the other hand the idea that what falls outside of this category is personal opinion and unreliable. It created a dichotomy between public doctrine and personal opinion. In respect of things falling into the second category one could only say "I believe"; in respect of the first category one would say, "I know," or rather — to eliminate the subjective element altogether — "it is the case." In respect of the first category, Western society is not pluralist. All educated people are expected to know "what is the case." The element in our liberal culture that occupies the scientific part of the university campus does not accept pluralism. Here there are, of course, differences of judgment about many matters, but these differences are not accepted as mere matters of taste or personal preference. They are the occasion for vigorous debate, experiment, testing, and argument. Scientists who differ do not say to each other, "That may be true for you but it is not true for me." In the other part of the campus, the part occupied by the arts and humanities, it is different. Here pluralism reigns. The words *true* and *false* are out of place. Here the talk is of "experience." And here, of course, is where, at least in British universities, theology is located. Here we do not talk about "what is the case," but about "experience," about "values," about what is personally "meaningful" to oneself. Here, even in the theological faculty, we no longer say "God spoke to Moses," but rather "Moses had a religious experience." We do not say "Jesus rose from the dead and the tomb was left empty," but rather "The disciples had a series of religious experiences." And here, therefore, pluralism reigns.

Thus the two poles of our knowing — the objective and the subjective — have fallen apart. In truth, of course, all knowing has both a subjective and an objective pole. It is subjective in the sense that there is a knower, who is a subject, and the range and accuracy of his knowledge will depend on factors personal to himself—his diligence, his honesty, his imaginative power, and of course the cultural tradition by which his mind has been formed. But there is also the objective pole, that which the knower seeks to know, that for which he gropes and struggles, that which alone can give him the satisfaction of saying, "Now I know." This falling apart of the poles is the disaster that threatens our culture with disintegration. It has created on the one hand the illusion that there is a world that can be known without the knower accepting any personal responsibility for his knowing, and on the other hand the skepticism that concludes that everything falling outside this kind of knowledge is merely personal opinion. And it is inevitable that this skepticism begins to infect the more confident half of our culture, the scientific part, so that we reach the stage at which any claim to know the truth is regarded as merely a disguised assertion of power. Inevitably also such a world becomes a meaningless world because the self is alone in a wide sea where there are no fixed points from which one could take bearings. Of course, whatever the literary theorists and the philosophers may say, most people most of the time will live their lives on the assumption that there is a real world about which one can be either well informed or else mistaken, a world about which one may make statements that are true or false. People will also continue to use this knowledge to manipulate the world with ever-increasing ingenuity to serve the purposes they choose to embrace. But when it comes to the question, "What purposes are in fact appropriate for a human being to choose?" there can be no answer. It is a matter of personal opinion. The truth about human nature and destiny is not a matter of knowledge; it is just a matter of belief. And belief is seen as what we have to depend on when knowledge is not available.

Yet, as Augustine said (in his famous *Credo ut intellegam*), we believe in order to understand. All knowing of a reality beyond the self is a venture of faith for which we have to take responsibility. Responsibility is a personal category, and all knowing is personal, because it is persons who know, or seek to know, or claim to know. The Cartesian program of impersonal knowledge, seeking a basis for indubitable certainty within the human mind itself and without dependence upon grace, has led to skepticism about the whole possibility of knowing the truth. And if truth is ultimately unknowable, we are left only with the will — the will to power. And so instead of speaking about "true" and "false," we talk about "values." "Values," as we understand them, are not "facts." They are a matter of personal choice. They are an expression of what we want, of the will. The pluralist society thus becomes a battleground for conflicting wills. We do not seek to convince one another of the truth of what we believe, because truth is unknowable. We can only fight for space to practice our chosen values.

What is the mission of the Church in a society that is pluralist in this sense?

The first thing to be said is negative. The mission of the Church in this kind of society is not to promote "values." This is the role society tends to cast us in. In my own country at least, the Church is widely regarded as a "good cause" that deserves some support, even if one does not accept its dogma. And it is easy for the Church to accept this role casting, for we are all part of the wider society. It seems to me that there are two dangers in this situation. The first is that we try to justify ourselves by our good works. The churches are engaged in a wide variety of social services. This is, of course, right and proper. But it can lead to a blunting of the sharpness of the challenge that the Church's dogma offers to the prevailing dogma of society. If it is not clear that the Church is affirming and offering as public truth a belief about the nature and destiny of human life that is sharply at odds with the assumptions of society, the "good works" will lose their proper character as signs of the presence of another regime, another jurisdiction.

The second danger is that our understanding of evangelism is distorted. If the Church is a "good cause" standing for certain "values," then the important thing is to increase the number of people who support these "values." Evangelism, against a background of declining numbers, begins to look like a rather desperate effort to support this "good cause." It becomes tinged with anxiety. It loses its character as the announcement of good news, as the proclamation of truth, saving truth, truth that is true and decisive even if those who acknowledge it are a small minority.

In seeking to commend the Christian faith as public truth, we have to consider how it is to be communicated in ways that can be effective in the pluralist culture of which we are a part. A missionary going from his native culture to communicate the gospel to people living in another culture has to steer a path between two opposite dangers. By asserting the radical newness of the Good News he may fail to communicate at all; his message remains incomprehensible. Or, in the effort to be understood, he may so adjust his presentation to the culture of those he addresses that it fails to challenge that culture and is simply absorbed into it. The gospel is comfortably domesticated within the culture. A foreign missionary must learn the language if he is to communicate at all, and that means that he must use words and phrases and concepts that have been wholly shaped by the receptor culture. The words he uses will not mean exactly what he intends them to mean until the gospel has been accepted and the life of the Church has begun to develop, and the old (pagan) words begin to be filled with new meaning. Crucial to this process is the translation of the Bible. It is when the Bible is available in the language of the people that the old pagan words become filled with new meaning because they are used in a new context. They become part of a new and different story, and therefore of a new and different way of understanding the whole human situation. I am thinking of my own experience among the Tamil churches in South India. It is obvious that Christians use such words as *God, sin,* and *grace* with a meaning different from the meanings that the same Tamil words have for Hindu neighbors. A former colleague of mine pointed out that the biblical verse "Jesus Christ came into the world to save sinners" has for a Tamil Hindu the meaning "Jesus Christ came into the world to provide free food and lodging for dropouts." It has the meaning that is has for Christians only because it is understood from the story of the Bible as a whole. The Hindu will come to understand them in this sense only by becoming part of the community that shapes its life by the story the Bible tells. If the Bible story ceases to have the decisive place, then the words will revert to their old meaning.

The foreign missionary, going from one culture to another, is unable to escape these issues. If we think of a missionary approach to Western pluralist society, the problem is much more difficult. The culture we have to address has grown out of originally Christian roots. Although most of the philosophers and other writers who were the leaders of the movement of Enlightenment in the eighteenth century were quite consciously setting out to attack and destroy the Christian belief system, the churches have to a large extent conceded the ground those leaders claimed. The main intellectual effort of Christian thinkers has been to establish the "reasonableness" of Christianity. The effort has been to show that Christian belief — with some adjustments — could be accommodated within the belief system of the "modern" world. "Religion" could be and must be kept "within the limits of reason." The churches (or at least the non-Roman churches) largely surrendered control of education into the hands of governments who were primarily concerned to train young people in the science and technology that would equip their nations to compete in the world markets. Christian teaching became a marginal part of public education or was excluded altogether. The intellectual framework of public life, which had been shaped by the biblical story, was now shaped by a quite different story — namely the stories of the rise to greatness of the various nation-states of Europe and, later, the story of the rise of civilization. European Christians, like other citizens, are formed intellectually from the earliest stages of their education within this understanding of the human story. It is very hard for them to question it. The missionary problem here is not one of communication. We already know the language because it is our own language and we use words every day with the meaning that our culture gives them. The problem is domestication. We are so much a part of our culture that it is hard to question it. We largely accept the "plausibility structure" and try to adjust our beliefs to fit it.

Why, then, does the Bible not function in our culture in the way that I have described its functioning in — for example — the culture of the Tamil people? I suggest that part of the answer lies in the fact that both "fundamentalists" and "liberals" have read the Bible through the spectacles provided by post-Enlightenment culture. Because that culture has created a dichotomy between "facts" and "values," the former being matters of impersonal knowledge, known without the possibility of doubt, and the latter being matters of personal experience and choice, it has perhaps been natural that the Bible should be interpreted in one or the other of these two ways. Both parties to this lamentable dispute about the Bible are children of the Enlightenment. For the fundamentalist, the Bible is a collection of indubitable facts of the same kind as those which scientific textbooks claim to provide. Where they differ, the Bible is right and science is wrong. The character of the Bible as a summons to the adventure of faith, calling for interpretation in different circumstances, requiring the exercise of fallible human judgment at every stage through the original writing and the many translations to the contemporary reader — in fact, all the subjective elements in the formation and reception of the Bible — are played down. By contrast the liberal sees the Bible as a record of "religious experience," with all the variety that this implies. The emphasis is not on the Bible as a canonical whole, but on the many different threads of human experience that have gone into the making of it. The Bible represents simply an element in the story of human culture. It cannot confront and address human culture. If the dialogue between fundamentalists and modern culture is a dialogue of the deaf, with the liberals there is no dialogue at all, only a variety of voices within one human society.

It seems to me that the gospel can only be communicated to our pluralist society by communities that take the Bible as the fundamental framework of their thinking, as the way they understand the world and the human story. To live in this way is not to pretend to know the whole truth or to be possessed of indubitable knowledge. All knowing (and it cannot be repeated too often) is a venture for which we must take responsibility, knowing that we can be wrong. To live in the world of the Bible, with all the tensions that are within the Bible story, to take it as the framework within which we try to understand and find our way through the perplexities of living now, is to be embarked on a journey with the confidence that we have a reliable clue for our exploration — not that we know the whole truth.

In my experience the great difficulty we face in commending this way to others is the persistence of the Cartesian illusion that there is available to us a kind of knowledge that cannot be doubted. When one seeks to commend the Christian faith to people in our society, one is met by the question "But can you prove that it is true?" It is obvious that if one were to offer some "proof," something supposedly more certain than the Christian story, something by which that story could be "proved" to be the truth, there would have to be further search for the proof that the alleged certainty was certain. One would be embarked on an infinite regress. What has to be challenged is the assumption that there exists some basis for knowledge that is more reliable than God's revelation in Jesus Christ and in the whole story of which his story is the crucial part. And when it becomes clear that there is no such indubitable certainty, the easy move is a relapse into skepticism. All claims to know the truth are discounted. If we cannot have the whole truth so guaranteed that we need accept no responsibility and take no risks, then we will abandon the search for truth altogether. This is the final failure of nerve, and it is already manifest in the kind of pluralism that regards all ultimate beliefs as equally acceptable and equally unreliable. It is a sign of approaching death.

The Church is called to bear witness to the gospel not only as truth for the personal life but as public truth. It goes without saying that in our pluralist society Christianity is tolerated as a personal opinion, and Christians are free to associate together for the expression of their belief. But Christianity is not tolerated as a factor in the argument about public truth. I have already referred to the role of the schools — the primary factor in the dissemination of public truth. There was a time when the Christian faith provided the overall framework within which children were intellectually formed. This is no longer so. Even where provision is made for "religious education," this is marginal, and — at least in contemporary Britain — it is concerned with the world religions, among which Christianity is only one among equals. But the important point — as Muslim parents in Britain are saying with increasing anger — is that the curriculum as a whole is based on the assumption that the world can be understood and can be satisfactorily managed without reference to the hypothesis of God. It is not that education is neutral. There is no possible neutrality. As the result of their schooling children come to believe some things and not others. They do not leave school with minds unshaped by any creed. Their minds are indeed shaped by a very definite creed, but it is not the one Christians repeat in church.

One could multiply illustrations of the point I am seeking to make about public doctrine. A psychiatrist, a sincere and practicing

Christian, was asked whether in her dealings with patients she made reference to her Christian faith. She replied that this would of course be unprofessional conduct and therefore forbidden. Asked if her psychiatric training was a help in her life in church, she answered that it was. The church was an arena where she was free to be a psychiatrist, but the profession was not an arena where she was free to be a Christian.

There are economists who are sincere Christians and who (in a Christian milieu) will discuss the bearing of the Christian faith upon the theory and practice of economics. They would not have the same freedom to make the Christian doctrines about economic behavior part of their public teaching. Birmingham University is shortly to appoint a lecturer in Muslim economics— financed from Muslim sources. I have not heard that any university has appointed a lecturer in Christian economics, or that any Christian agency has offered the funds for such an appointment. There are sincere Christians in the British Parliament. It would be very unusual to hear a theological argument used in a parliamentary debate on an issue of economics or social welfare.

When a Christian writer puts forward arguments such as those of the preceding section, it is often assumed that what is being proposed is some sort of theocracy, a return to the "Christendom" synthesis in which the Church could employ the coercive power of the state. Such a return is of course impossible, and would be undesirable even if it were possible. It is of the very essence of the gospel that it calls for a freely given personal response. We touch here again on the paradox of freedom. According to the word of Jesus in the passage quoted earlier, we are not naturally free. Freedom is Christ's gift because he is the truth. But God gives us freedom to refuse the gift of freedom. Yet the freedom is still his gift, for we have nothing that is not his gift. Perhaps the crucial word is another from St. John's Gospel: "No one can come to me unless the Father who sent me draws him" (John 6:44). The fact that the cross stands as the central Christian symbol must forever forbid the identification of the gospel with political power. The Church's witness to the gospel must always be made in the knowledge that the manifest reign of God can only be at the end when he brings all things to final judgment, that for the present age the reign of God must be veiled in the weakness and foolishness of his Church, and that it is God alone who can reveal to people his presence within this veil. Here is the crucial difference between Christianity and Islam.

We do not have to choose, however, between two alternatives — between a Christian theocracy on the one hand and, on the other, a society in which Christianity is merely an option for private opinion. There is another possibility. At this point it seems essential to distinguish between two kinds of pluralism. I would like to call them "agnostic pluralism" and "committed pluralism." By the former I mean a situation in which it is assumed that ultimate truth is unknowable and that there are therefore no criteria by which different beliefs and different patterns of behavior may be judged. In this situation one belief is as good as another and one lifestyle is as good as another. No judgments are to be made, for there are no given criteria, no truth by which error could be recognized. There is to be no discrimination between better and worse. All beliefs and all lifestyles are to be equally respected. To make judgments is, on this view, an exercise of power and is therefore oppressive and demeaning to human dignity. The "normal" replaces the "normative." What is acceptable depends upon statistics. If a majority of people do this or believe that, then this is "normal" and no higher norm is available.

As an example of "committed pluralism" I would like to take the scientific community — what Michael Polanyi used to call "the republic of science."[2] The scientific community is pluralist in the sense that it is not controlled or directed from one center. Scientists are free to pursue their own investigations and to develop their own lines of research. They are free to differ from one another and to argue with one another. There are indeed "orthodoxies," but these are developed in the course of the cooperative work of scientists, not imposed from a commanding center. This kind of pluralism is very different from the "agnostic pluralism" I have described. It is different

2. Michael Polanyi, *Knowing and Being,* discussed in Newbigin, *Gospel in a World of Religious Pluralism,* 43f. VIII/6. For criticism of "the republic of science," see R. J. Brownhill, "Freedom and Authority: The Political Philosophy of Michael Polanyi," *Journal of the British Society of Phenomenology* 8, no. 3 (October 1977).

because there is a commitment to search for the truth, a commitment that implies the belief that the truth can be known— not fully and completely, but in part and with increasing depth and range and coherence. It is therefore not an anarchic pluralism, but a directed and committed one. It follows that the freedom to explore is exercised with recognition and respect for the limits established by the work of previous scientists. Some things have been learned and are accepted as true. They provide the guidance for what is still to be discovered. Scientists therefore rely upon and work within a very strong tradition. Because they believe that truth can be explored and to some extent known, and because some things have been learned and can be accepted as true, the scientist works within the tradition of what has already been established. Once again, because it is believed that truth may be known and because there is a commitment to seek to know more, where different scientists come up with different opinions, they are not simply left as the personal preferences of these different scientists. Because truth is at stake, the differences become a matter of argument. Experiment, testing, and further argument continue until one of the two views prevails or else some fresh way of seeing things enables the two views to be reconciled.

Granted that there are important differences between the data scientists work with and the data theologians work with. But these do not justify the huge discrepancy between the way scientists pursue their quest for knowledge and the way differences of religious belief are handled. After all, science is simply a very far-reaching development of the ordinary common sense we use to try to deal with the world. Our effort to know, to understand the world we live in and our situation within it, cannot be totally bifurcated into one area where truth is knowable and another where it is not. The universe is in some sense one, and the human knower is one person, not two. The idea that there is no third way between an agnostic pluralism and a despotic theocracy is another by-product of the split between a false objectivism and a false subjectivism. It is surely possible to envision, and therefore also obligatory to work for, a society that is pluralist in the sense that the scientific community is pluralist, a society that believes in the possibility of knowing the truth about human nature and destiny and that is committed to seeking further understanding. Within such a society the Christian Church would be free and would be in duty bound to put forth its belief with the fullest confidence into the public argument about all human affairs. It would *not* be "unprofessional conduct" to profess the Christian faith in the school classroom, or the university lecture room, or the psychiatrist's consulting room. There would always be room for other views, but they too would have to sustain their part in the public debate.

One of the conditions for the Church's faithful participation in such a pluralist society would be that the Church would have the same kind of respect for its tradition as the scientific community has for its scientific tradition. It must no longer encourage those who are "radical" only in the sense that they have lost their roots and are drifting with the current of contemporary fashion. While recognizing that all traditions are open to correction and development, it must ensure that those who undertake these tasks have first had a thorough apprenticeship in the tradition. I realize that this will be attacked as a recipe for authoritarianism, but I shall not be unduly worried by the attack. To question and criticize specific exercises of authority is a necessary duty, but to reject all authority is folly. Of course if truth is in principle unknowable, then any claim to speak the truth will be denounced as a mere attempt to exercise power. Science has become the most dynamic element in our culture because the scientific community has continued to believe that truth is knowable and that, insofar as it is known, it has authority. Science thrusts powerfully forward because it has strong traditions. The relatively anemic state of theological studies has arisen because we have so largely accepted the division of human knowing into two areas — one where knowledge is supposed to be objective, impersonal, and valid for all human beings of whatever culture or temperament, and another where all is subjective, dependent upon personal and cultural factors — and because we have allowed theology to be located in the second of these two wrongly demarcated areas.

I have argued that a claim that the Christian faith must be affirmed as a public truth does not mean a demand for a return to "Christendom" or to some kind of theocracy. It does not mean that the coercive power of the state and its institutions should be at the service of the Church. I have taken the example of the scientific community as one whose findings are emphatically part of public doctrine, not private opinion, but that does not seek the coercive power of the state in its support. But it will be immediately obvious that, in our society, as in any human society, there is no escape from the exercise of power. Governments take the advice of scientists in making laws about the conditions under which food is produced and sold, drugs are marketed, and houses are built. Moreover — and this is much more important — insofar as governments control the educational system they exercise a very powerful control over what the majority of people think and believe. There was a time when entrance to the universities of Oxford and Cambridge was conditional on professing the faith of the Nicene creed. The removal of that requirement was hailed as a great liberation. But, of course, it was not that all credal tests were removed. In effect another creed replaced the Nicene — the set of beliefs about the world and about human life that were inculcated in the curriculum of the schools. No one can now enter the universities without having mastered and internalized those beliefs.

The question about the use of the power of the state in matters of ultimate belief is being raised in an acute form in Britain at this time. There has already been strong dissatisfaction among Muslim parents who claim that the present school curriculum is systematically indoctrinating their children with beliefs that they regard as false. The reference is not at all to what goes on under the title of "religious education." The reference is to the curriculum as a whole that, to put the matter briefly, leads their children to live in a world from which God has been banished. Under the name of "assimilation" they are being prepared to be part of an atheist society. This smoldering resentment has been fanned into flames by the publication of Salman Rushdie's *The Satanic Verses,* and by the failure of the British courts to condemn this as blasphemy. To Muslims, blasphemy is the most serious of all possible crimes. To the vast majority of British people it is not a crime at all. If it has any importance it is merely that it may offend the sensitivities of a minority of Christians, Christians being themselves a minority of the population. For most British people the most serious crime is treason against the state, because the state has long ago replaced God as the ultimate authority. Words that threaten

171

to undermine the state are punishable — and of course the business of spies and traitors is with words. But words that mock the authority of God are not punishable. To Muslims this seems wrong.

Certainly in a society that has effectively banished the Christian faith from its public doctrine, blasphemy laws could not be enforced. And laws that cannot be enforced are bad laws. But it is difficult to see how a society that acknowledges nothing as sacred can long remain a coherent society. If I may refer again to the example of the scientific community, it is clear that within this community, truthfulness in dealing with the fact is a matter of sacred obligation. A scientist who knowingly tampers with evidence would be excluded. Other communities have points of ultimate commitment, issues that are matters for expulsion. If these points were made a matter of mockery within the community in question, it would disintegrate. When Western Christendom fell apart in the seventeenth century and Europe's intellectual leaders turned to another vision of the human story, Europeans were driven to see the human story in terms of the stories of their several nations. The nation became the focus of ultimate commitment. And, as we know from bitter experience, the nation — even the best — is not a fit object for ultimate commitment. Can European society endure if nothing is sacred?

The Pope has called for the reevangelization of Europe. There has been a wide response to the call. What will a response require? What will be the nature of the Christian mission in and to this pluralist society, in which the last remains of total state control are being dismantled? Certainly it cannot mean an attempt to restore the hegemony of the Church over public life. Nor can it only mean the multiplication of the number of believers, although it must certainly not mean less than that. There certainly can be no reevangelization of Europe without the conversion of a great many Europeans to the Christian faith. But what will be the implications of such conversion? What, if one may use an ugly phrase, will be its behavioral content? It cannot be confined to the part of behavior that concerns personal and domestic affairs. It will have to include a questioning of the whole "plausibility structure" that governs the public life of the European democratic societies. And this is a formidable task that will call for both an immense intellectual effort and much courage.

What we are looking for is not a new "Christendom," but a society in which those whose thought and practice set the tone and direction of the different sectors of public life include a large number of Christian men and women who have thought through the implications of the Christian faith for those areas of the life of society. This requires, I think, the following:

1. Something that I can only call a recovery of nerve in the Church as a whole. The Church has been too eager to adapt its teaching to the creed of modernity and not energetic enough in challenging that creed. Plausibility structures are strong, and to those dwelling in them they seem eternal. And yet if one stands outside the structure for a moment, its fragility becomes apparent. What, for example, could be more absurd than the idea that the whole universe has come into existence by a series of accidents, and that it functions like a machine — constructed by nobody for no purpose? These absurdities are taught and accepted as public truth. The Christian faith, taken as a whole, gives an infinitely more rational account of the universe and of our experience in it than does the contemporary creed. Perhaps we are at a point in history similar to that in which the fathers of the Church did their great work in the first four centuries. They were part of a world that had lost the belief that truth was knowable. They were locked in the dualisms of matter and spirit (the "sensible" and the "intelligible"), and of human freedom and determinism ("virtue" and "fortune"). Through their profound reflection on and living out of what had been given in the incarnation of the Son of God, they were able to offer a new model for understanding the total human situation — the Trinitarian model — that provided the starting point for a whole new flowering of human culture.

But for anything similar to happen in our own day, we need courage. Specifically we need the courage to know that all knowing involves risk, and to hold as true what can be doubted and what a majority of our contemporaries do doubt — to hold it as true not just for ourselves but for all. As in every claim to know something, the claim is made by a subject. It is saved from mere subjectivity by the fact that we make it public, proclaim it and test it out in all the situations and all the cultures of the human story. In that sense the mission of the Church is not only a proclamation of the gospel, but

173

also an exegesis of the gospel, because it is by testing it out in every situation that we learn what it involves. We only know what it means to say, "Jesus is Lord" when we have embarked on the enterprise of obedience to him in all the infinite various contexts that make up the tapestry of human life.

2. That leads into the second requirement, which concerns the equipping of Christians to bring their secular employments under the obedience of Christ. This is a matter in which there are hardly any accredited teachers and we all need to be learners. I know this is nothing new. It has often been said (in Britain most notably by J. H. Oldham[3]), but little has been done. There is urgent need for the Church to give higher priority to the formation of groups of Christian men and women in particular sectors of public life. These would include education, industry, commerce, politics, drama, the arts, natural and social sciences, and historical studies. The groups would explore ways in which a Christian perspective can be developed in these areas, and ways in which this perspective can challenge and redirect contemporary practice. The object of the exercise, of course, would not just be to bring the participants to some greater clarity, but also to equip them to bring a Christian contribution to current practice by their speaking, writing, and action. The very fact that this has been so often said with so little result is evidence of the difficulty of the task. This is reason not for giving it up but for giving it more attention. And I wonder whether our relative failure in this matter has something to do with the timidity I referred to in the preceding paragraph. Such efforts by individual Christians in their secular work can be very lonely and difficult. They need the backing of a Church that is confident in its faith.

One could legitimately hope that efforts in this direction could

---

3. J. H. Oldham (1874–1967), after being forced to return from missionary service in India in 1901, became secretary to the Edinburgh WMC, created the *International Review of Missions* (1912), defended German missions in wartime, and then through his work for the Life and Work Movement (as he did less and less for the International Missionary Council) became one of the architects of the World Council of Churches. However, his main interest as a layman was Christian witness in the corridors of power and the professions. The biography on him that was started by Kathleen Bliss is being completed by Keith Clements.

lead to a situation in which leadership in many fields of public life is being given by those who are committed Christians and who are seeking to discover what Christian obedience means in these areas. Such leadership would help to convert society as a whole from an agnostic and anarchic pluralism to a committed and truth-seeking pluralism. And if the word *leadership* provokes the charge of "elitism," I am — once again — not seriously alarmed. To be elite (elect) is to be chosen for a task and to be responsible to the one who has chosen you. Elitism has become a bad word because those who should have seen their calling as one for responsibility have seen it as one for privilege. Such self-serving elites have brought just condemnation. But no society can be healthy without responsible leadership. To evade the calling to leadership out of fear of the charge of elitism is unworthy.

3. But the Church is much more than its leaders. Perhaps one of the weaknesses of former "frontier" activities such as I sketched in the preceding section was that they did not take seriously enough the ordinary life of the local congregation. It is easy to talk about "the Church" but to ignore or despise the ordinary local congregation, which can often be so slow moving and so inward looking. Yet this is where the Church actually exists, and it is futile to replace this concrete reality with an ethereal entity that is not visible in flesh and blood. It is in the local congregation of believing Christians that the courage is to be nurtured that will enable us to challenge our culture with the gospel. It is a well-established fact, at least in Britain, that the great majority of those who come to faith in Christ come through the witness of a local congregation. Here, in the midst of a world of illusions, is the place where truth is spoken and celebrated, where God is praised and thanked, and where God's grace is given and received to be poured out in care for the neighborhood. Here is where we learn to live in the story that the Bible tells, to affirm it as our own story, and to see our contemporary world in the light of the true story. Here is where we can learn (and this calls for study in local groups) to question the assumptions that are taken for granted in the world outside, where we can develop a certain godly skepticism regarding the things that are praised and celebrated in our societies. The local congregation is the only effective hermeneutic of the gospel. Europe

175

was originally evangelized from the top down. Kings were converted and their peoples followed. If it is to be reevangelized, it will be from the bottom up. The thousands of local congregations throughout Europe need to be reaffirmed, encouraged, and enabled to be the centers from which a new way of seeing the world can dawn on a society that has lost the belief that truth can be known.

15

Mission Agenda

I am grateful for the invitation to be associated with the celebration of this centenary, especially at a time when the enterprise of foreign missions is widely regarded even by Christians as something that belongs to the past, and by others as a matter for ridicule or for downright condemnation. It is no exaggeration to say that among the general public, at least in England, the reigning stereotype of the foreign missionary is of an arrogant intruder who talks but does not listen, a destroyer of precious cultures, a stooge of the imperialists. Shortly after my return from India in 1974 I was informed by a clergyman in Birmingham that he regarded foreign missions as simply the theological form of racism. But there is also irony in the situation, for there is much celebration of the fact that there are flourishing churches in Asia and Africa and the Pacific Islands, that Christianity now encircles the world, that we can rejoice in what William Temple, in his enthronement sermon at Canterbury during the darkest days of the war (1942), called "the great new fact of our time" — the fact that for the first time in its long history the Church embraces the whole globe.[1] There is irony because while we celebrate the fact, we

1. Iremonger, *William Temple,* 387.

A paper delivered in Dublin, November 1992, during the celebrations to mark the centenary of the Dublin University Mission.

177

are apologetic about the activities that brought it about. A recent and much admired history of nineteenth-century English Christianity makes no mention of foreign missions. Yet it is certain that any church historian writing a hundred years from now will see the global expansion of Christianity in the nineteenth and early twentieth centuries as one of the most remarkable chapters in the whole long story.

Those who founded the Dublin University Mission a hundred years ago belonged to that adventurous student generation that adopted as their slogan "The Evangelization of the World in This Generation." It was an amazingly daring watchword.[2] They did not mean, of course, the *conversion* of the world in their generation. They looked to bringing about a situation in which the whole world would be within earshot of the gospel. As we look back now, we can see that — if not in one generation, at least in one century — they came amazingly close to reaching their target. We do well to celebrate their vision and their daring.

But the irony goes deeper than the perception of missions and missionaries. In spite of the enormous and unprecedented explosion of the world's population in the past hundred years, the proportion of the world's people who confess Jesus as Lord remains roughly what it was one hundred years ago. But there has been a vast shift in the center of gravity. While churches in what we call the third world grow rapidly, sometimes spectacularly, the churches in the old Christendom decline or are on the defensive. Christians coming to Europe from Asia and Africa are amazed and shocked to find Christians in the old Christendom so apologetic about their faith, so timid, so anxious to assure everyone that they do not want to impose their faith on anyone else. This was what struck me the most forcibly when I returned from India to England. Indian Christians are a small minor-

2. The watchword dominated student evangelism in Britain from 1895 to 1904, but then encountered such fierce theological objections from Indian students who said it was imperialistic, and from J. H. Oldham, F. Lenwood, and Scottish students, that it was dropped after the 1908 Quadrennial. An echo of it can be heard in Archbishop Randall Davidson's speech closing the WMC in Edinburgh in 1910; John R. Mott, *The Evangelisation of the World in This Generation* (New York: Harper, 1900); Tissington Tatlow, *The History of the Student Christian Movement* (London: SCM, 1933), 109–112, 119–134, 314f.

ity of the population, but they are quite unembarrassed about commending their faith to their friends, and the church continues to grow. In England I found a great anxiety lest it might appear that Christians had something to tell other people that they did not already know. It was the world that should teach the Church, not vice versa. *Intra Ecclesiam nulla salus est.* Even the great missionary societies that had been, under God, the bearers of the gospel to every corner of the world were now anxious to speak only of interchange, of global sharing, and of course this is right. Mission can never again be seen as a one-way traffic from north to south. It is the shared business and the shared joy of the whole global family. Its heart is and must always be evangelism — the telling of the story that is the true story of God's dealing with the world, the only story by which people and nations can find and fulfill God's purpose for them.

And this telling of the story has to continue not only within each human culture, but cross-culturally. Foreign missions cannot be sent into retirement just because the Church is present in all parts of the world. Foreign missions are an abiding part of the responsibility of the Church everywhere, and for a reason that needs to be clearly stated. In missionary circles we have talked much about the problem of inculturation, but not enough about the problem of domestication. In every society that has received the gospel, there is a strong tendency to domesticate the gospel within the thought-forms of that society in such a way that it ceases to challenge the assumptions that govern the society's life and becomes simply part of the culture. The tension that must exist in every society between the gospel and the culture is slackened. Or, to put it in another way, the gospel is heard only as grace and not as judgment, as affirmation and not as challenge. If this domestication is to be avoided, every society needs the witness of those who confess Christ in the idiom of another culture. By the same token, the integrity of our confession of Jesus as cosmic Lord requires that we test this confession in every human situation, in relation to every human claim, and in every human culture. As the late Dr. Visser 't Hooft wrote, "Missions are the test of faith."

This brief reference to the problem of domestication will serve, I think, to introduce an examination of the factors that have led us into the situation I have described, where European Christians have lost their confidence in the validity of the foreign missionary enterprise. It can be described as the convergence of two movements of thought.

First, we need to bear in mind that the great missionary expansion of Christianity in the last two hundred years went along with and was intimately bound up with global expansion of European political, economic, and cultural power, which was itself an outcome of the profound shift in European consciousness that those who shared in it called "Enlightenment." *Enlightenment* is a conversion word. It is the word used of the decisive spiritual experience of the Buddha. And the intellectual leadership of Europe did go through a profound conversion. They saw themselves and their history in a new light. It was no longer the Bible that interpreted the human story and therefore provided the locus of truth. Rather truth was to be found by the exercise of the autonomous reason. Its ideal form was provided by mathematics. Newton's cosmology had provided the new paradigm of truth, what Lessing called the eternal truths of reason that are independent of any particular history. These truths were accessible to every rational human being and could therefore form the ground for human unity. The long period of the Christianization of Europe was now seen as the dark ages or, at best, the middle ages between two periods when reason reigned — the ancient classical world and the present.

It was in the power of this vision that European nations began to carry their beliefs, their science and technology, their commerce, their political institutions — in short, their civilization — to the ends of the earth. And Christian missionaries were part of this expansion. They were confident that Christianity and civilization went together. Unlike some earlier missionaries (Robert de Nobili, Ziegenbalg, William Carey) and certainly unlike St. Paul, they saw it as an intrinsic part of their task to start schools, hospitals, agencies of what we now call "development," in which peoples were invited to accept European ideas and institutions along with the gospel. They did not see human society as multicultural. The use of the word *culture* in the plural belongs only to this century. There were not many cultures; there was, if you like, one ladder called "civilization," and people were on different rungs of the ladder: they were either more or less civilized.

The use of the word *culture* in its anthropological sense is also recent. Its first recorded use is in 1867, and it was then a translation of the German word *Kultur*. That German use, two decades or so before, was part of the romantic reaction against the rationalism of the Enlightenment. It was brought from its horticultural to its anthropological usage to convey the point that there is more in human life than can be measured on the grid of eighteenth-century rationalism: the traditions of a people, their art and music, their myths and folk-tales, their ways of doing things that are lost if everything has to go through the sieve of a mathematical rationality. So the concept of culture in its modern anthropological sense was born. And Europe was a sufficiently heterogeneous society to enable the rational and the romantic perceptions of human affairs to coexist in the nineteenth and early twentieth centuries.

What we have witnessed in the twentieth century is the replay on a much larger and more diverse stage of the reaction against Enlightenment rationalism. The impact of European ideas, science, technology, political systems, and economic and military power on the peoples of Asia, Africa, and the Pacific has produced a similar but much more powerful reaction in the name of culture. Just because European Christendom had allowed the gospel to be so thoroughly domesticated within the post-Enlightenment world of thought and practice, the reaction from what we call the third world has been directed against the whole European package, including its Christian elements. The situation is, in fact, full of still more ironies. The nations of the third world, released from imperial control, are seeking at the same time to affirm their cultural integrity over and against westernization and also to acquire the technology that has given the West its power. The slogan everywhere is "modernization," which is, of course, the replacement of traditional ways of thinking, organizing, and managing with ways developed in Europe. And with an even sharper irony, Christians in the West who have become embarrassed about sending evangelistic missionaries because this would be a form of cultural imperialism are enthusiastic about what is called development, which is precisely the export of European ideas and technology to the societies of Asia and Africa. This history alone would not suffice to explain the contemporary Western embarrassment about foreign missions if it had not been for another part of the story to which I now turn.

The second part of the story relates to internal developments within European Christendom. At the heart of the great burst of confidence in European civilization during the last two centuries was belief in the power of reason both to understand the human situation and to provide the techniques for production, control, and management of human affairs. Reason, in contrast to faith, was the avenue to reliable knowledge. Faith, in the classic definition of John Locke, was a persuasion that fell short of certainty. The roots of this go, of course, far back into European history, into the classical world of Greece and Rome, and into the medieval synthesis of Aristotelian and biblical thought. This synthesis made a sharp division between what can be certainly known by reason and what has to be accepted by faith on the authority of the Church. In the seminal work of Descartes there was offered the paradigm of certain knowledge achieved by developing clear and distinct ideas from indubitable grounds. The model was that of mathematics. Whatever lay outside of this paradigm was not certain knowledge, but a matter of faith. The way to certain knowledge was therefore by the critical principle: everything that cannot be shown to be certain is to be doubted. A Chinese Christian philosopher has contrasted this with the traditional Chinese view that the way to knowledge begins with awe, with opening the mind and soul to the vast mystery of existence.[3] But it is not too much to say that the critical principle has been seen during the past two hundred years as the great glory of European culture, the means by which it has achieved mastery in science, technology, and political organization.[4]

What has happened in the present century is what Nietzsche foresaw — namely, that the critical principle must necessarily, in the end, destroy itself. For if we make a critical examination of the critical principle itself, it is obvious that no critical activity is possible except on the basis of something that, at that moment, is *believed* to be true. All rational thought and speech necessarily rely on language, which itself embodies a way of understanding things that is developed

3. Yu, *Being and Relation.*
4. This is a recurrent theme of Newbigin's writings in the 1980s. See Newbigin, *Foolishness to the Greeks,* 13; Newbigin, *Gospel in a World of Religious Pluralism,* 10. Also see chapter 8 of this volume, "By What Authority?"

through a tradition, and on models and concepts that have similarly developed. One cannot make any statement at all without (for the moment at least) relying on these words, models, concepts. One can, of course, criticize these models, but only by an acritical acceptance of other models.

One cannot rationally doubt all one's beliefs at the same time. If the critical principle is accepted as the primary tool of knowledge, and not (as it should be) a necessary but secondary tool — if, in other words, we cannot know anything without believing something — then the method of Descartes must lead to the conclusion that Nietzsche drew, and that is now drawn daily in our society, which is going through a profound loss of faith in the possibility of knowing truth. That conclusion is that what is true for you may not be true for me. Truth statements are all culturally conditioned (which is true), and therefore none of them are reliable (which is false). We do not ask, "What is true?" but "What is meaningful for me?" The self becomes the only knowable reality, and even the self is elusive. "Who am I?" becomes a question that people in more stable societies never dream of formulating. Words no longer refer to a reality beyond the mind of the person who uses them. No one, in this scenario, has the right to say to someone else, "This is true, true not only for me but also for you." There is no absolute truth, true for all; each of us must create his or her own truth.

At this point the two stories that I have tried to tell converge. The powerful reaction of non-Western cultures against the arrogance and dominance of European power over the past two centuries hits us just at the moment when the intellectual core of that confidence is collapsing from within. It is not surprising that there is a profound loss of nerve, and that Christian missions are among the casualties. It is not surprising that many contemporary Christians (at least of my acquaintance) are eager to repent of the arrogance of their missionary grandfathers, and reluctant to use the confident language their forebears used about the evangelization of the world. I have taken part in a great many ecumenical missionary gatherings, and I have had the impression during the last twenty years or so that at these gatherings the only contribution many of the European participants could make was the repetition in one form or another of "*Nostra culpa; nostra maxima culpa.*" The West African scholar Lamin Sanneh of Yale has written incisively on what he called the Western guilt complex and its effects on the Christian mission.[5] It is good to repent of one's sins, and perhaps even of the sins of one's grandparents, but unabsolved guilt by itself is not creative. It only paralyzes. It is only as forgiven sinners that we can engage in mission, and part of the way to do that is to accept correction and rebuke from those who have been injured. But it is an unacceptable form of paternalism to think that we are responsible for all the wrong in the world.

What now, in this global perspective, is the agenda for mission? Let me put down a few markers that I think must guide us. The human agency of mission is the global Church that is now present, even if in numerical weakness, in every nation. And let us always remember that precisely where it is small and vulnerable, as for example in Afghanistan today, it is often the most vibrant, full of life and growing. If we are asked today, as some have asked, "What is your strategy for world evangelization?" the answer must be that it is to help and empower every local congregation of Christians to be a true and living part of the body of Christ, that is to say, to be the place where the reign of God, the kingship of God, is both embodied and proclaimed. And, as I have argued, this must mean also the sending and receiving of Christians to and from other places so that the local church is both saved from domestication and also enabled to learn, with all the saints, more of the length and breadth and height and depth of the love of God than it could learn if it was confined in its mission to its own locality. The global mission of the Church is from every place to every place.

The context of this global mission is what we must now call the global city, for we are now in a situation where the development of rapid travel and instant communication has bound us all together more and more tightly into a single economic and financial unit. Three years ago one could not have said this, for the world was divided between two power blocks based on rival ideologies, both

5. See Professor Lamin Sanneh's address to the Swanwick conference, "The Gospel as Public Truth," July 1992, in the conference papers available from the British and Foreign Bible Society, Stonehill Green, Swindon, SN5 7DG.

products of the Enlightenment. Today one of these ideologies is overwhelmingly dominant. It is locking even the smallest communities into a more and more tightly knit fabric of economic and financial relations. After the collapse of Marxist communism as a world power, the only effective challenge to this global system comes from Islam, which rejects both ideologies and seeks to create a world order based on the revealed will of God as interpreted by the prophet. As the capitalist free-market system runs into deeper crisis, I think that Islam will be, in the twenty-first century, perhaps the major contender for global power. Whether or not this proves to be so, we have to recognize that the process called "modernization" is continuing and accelerating throughout the world. In Europe this process has had the effect of neutering the Church, leaving it on the margins of society.

We rightly rejoice at the wonderful growth of the churches of the south and the east, at their vitality and infectious faith. But we would be deluding ourselves if we did not recognize that the same acids of modernity (to use Walter Lippmann's phrase of sixty years ago) are bound to have the same effects in the third world as they have had in Europe. Christians are not exempt from the process of modernization, and indeed missionary societies are devoting considerable resources to accelerating this process by enabling Christian leaders from all parts of the world to undergo the kind of training that is offered in European universities and colleges. While the grassroots memberships of these churches remain to a large extent part of their traditional culture, the leadership is increasingly shaped by the worldview that prevails in the West.

This globalization of human society has, very naturally and properly, led missionary societies to move away from the one-directional model of mission to a model that emphasizes sharing, listening, and dialogue. My own lifetime as a missionary has been in the context of this shift, and I have shared in it to the full. It would be perverse to want to go back to the earlier model. And yet I think there is a danger in the present model that often goes unrecognized. It is this: practically all of this interchange and dialogue takes place in one of the languages of Europe — English, German, or Spanish. It takes place among those who share the common background of an education in one of these languages. There is therefore a great danger that the assumptions that underlie the use of these European languages are not questioned. I can only speak from personal experience, but I know, for example, that there is a wide gap between the way interfaith conversation happens when it is conducted in Tamil among people who have never been through an English educational process, and the way it is conducted among those, Indian and European, who share the same kind of academic formation.

But this means that the most difficult and important missionary frontier is not crossed. If one is looking at the total situation of Christianity in the contemporary world, addressing European culture is the most urgent question, and for two reasons: first because it is modern, post-Enlightenment Western culture that, in the guise of "modernization," is replacing more traditional cultures all over the world, and second because, as we have seen, this culture has a unique power to erode and neutralize the Christian faith. It is the most powerful, the most pervasive and (with the possible exception of Islam) the most resistant to the gospel of all the cultures that compete for power in our global city. My concern, therefore, is that the contemporary emphasis on sharing and dialogue, right and proper as it is, may lead to an evasion of this most urgent and most difficult task — namely, the development of an effective missionary engagement with modernity.

The development of the intellectual and spiritual equipment for such an encounter must be an ecumenical task, calling for the wisdom and experience of Christians from all the cultures that now have their voice in the family of churches throughout the world, but I think that we in Europe who have been responsible for creating this phenomenon that we call modernity must accept a large measure of responsibility for the task. It is a matter for thankfulness that an international body of missiologists have committed themselves for a ten-year period to work together on the development of a missiology for Western culture.[6] During the past two or three decades missionaries, with the help of cultural anthropologists, have done much work in clarifying the issues involved in bringing the gospel to people of many cultures in what we have been calling the third world. No similar intellectual

6. Wilbur Shenk is coordinating this group.

effort has been devoted to the much more urgent and more difficult task of developing a missiology for what we have called the First World. It is beginning.

The final point I would make is that everything depends on a recovery of confidence in the gospel. I spoke earlier of the loss of nerve that is apparent in Western culture. It was Gilbert Murray, I believe, who said that Greek civilization collapsed through loss of nerve. I think the same danger faces the culture that we call modern scientific culture. It has prided itself on possessing the tools by which reliable knowledge can be had about our world and ourselves. This knowledge was ideally embodied in laws that had the precision, the certainty, and the timelessness of mathematical equations. This certainty was supposedly based on pure reason and did not depend on any tradition, or on the uncertain records of the past. In one of the most famous sayings of the age of reason, Lessing said that accidental happenings of history cannot prove eternal truths of reason. That effectively removed the Bible from its traditional place as the locus of reliable truth. What is happening now is that Lessing is being stood on his head. Beginning from Nietzsche, the postmodernists are telling us that the so-called eternal truths are simply products of particular histories. There are no absolute eternal truths, there are only stories — metanarratives that make rival claims to authority in human affairs. The European narrative is only one among many, and as the recent responses to the five hundredth anniversary of the painful discovery of Christopher Columbus by the peoples of the Americas have reminded us, this narrative is now widely contested.

Surely this reversal of Lessing's dictum is justified. There is no exercise of human reason that is not socially embodied, rooted in a tradition that is carried by a language. The gospel is not a statement of eternal truths in the style of mathematics; it is the story of what God has done. It is contested in the name of other stories. We have no suprahistorical standpoint from which we can demonstrate with any kind of infallibility that it, and not others, is the true story. Our role is more humble. We stand among all other human beings with their different stories to bear witness to what God has done. We do so because we have been laid hold of and commissioned to do so. Our telling of the story is an act of gratitude and faithfulness towards God.

Our telling of the story is authentic when, as the risen Jesus reminded his disciples, our corporate life is marked by the scars of the conflict with the powers of evil. "He showed them his hands and his side." It is not in our power to convert men and women to faith in Christ. That can only be the work of the Holy Spirit. But when we are faithfully following Jesus both in living the story and in telling it (and we must never put these over against each other), then the Church can become the place where the Holy Spirit does his work of conversion.

Because the Western Church has been so long and so deeply domesticated within Western culture, when this culture loses its nerve we are in danger of losing ours. We may rightly be apologetic about the arrogance that has sometimes marked Christian missions in the past, but we have no call to be apologetic about the gospel. If God indeed has done what in all our liturgies we affirm that he has done, then it is a most tremendous fact that must be told as public truth in every culture and in every generation. To think otherwise is implicitly to deny its truth. But our telling of it is corrupted when we think in terms of our success rather than in terms of the glory of God. Too much missionary talking has been fundamentally Pelagian, as if it were our enterprise. We tell the story as an act of love and gratitude to God, that our blessed Lord may see the travail of his soul and be satisfied. So I come back at the end to those thousands of local congregations, communities of worship where God is glorified and the love of God flows out in spontaneous service and witness to the community. Recent surveys in England about how people in contemporary society come to faith in Christ have shown that the overwhelming proportion come through the witness of a local congregation. And we can never forget that during the seventy years in which the churches in the Soviet Union were denied all possibilities of witness and service outside the walls of the church, it was the witness of authentic worship that drew to Christ men and women who had been shaped and formed from cradle to university by an atheist ideology. In those years there was little possibility for the Church to be domesticated in the culture. The contrast was too sharp. Perhaps we can learn from their experience how to live and tell the story in the midst of our modern, scientific, liberal, free-market culture in such a way that the story recovers its sharp cutting edge. If we can do that, we shall perhaps render the greatest service that we can to the total mission of Christ in this global city.

16

The Ecumenical Future and the WCC: A Missionary's Dream

The editor of this publication has invited me to join in a "dialogue of dreams and visions" about the future of the ecumenical movement and of the World Council of Churches (WCC). According to the prophet Joel, I should confine myself to dreams, leaving visions to my younger colleagues. I have a lot of diffidence about joining the dialogue, but I will tell my dream.

A Changed Context

Because I have been a missionary for most of my working life, and because I was involved in the merger of the International Missionary Council (IMC) with the WCC thirty years ago, I begin by asking, "How far have the concerns of these two bodies become one?" And, of course, if the answer is not a total affirmative, I am the first culprit. The IMC, formed after the Edinburgh conference of 1910, was born in a vision of the world won for Christ. Christendom was still a "home base" for the world mission of the Church, even though Christendom

Reprinted by kind permission of the editor of the *Ecumenical Review*. From vol. 42, no. 1, January 1991.

was full of old and new evils. The vision was that every people should hear the Good News of Jesus. It was ecumenical because it was missionary, because the whole world belonged to Jesus and must be reclaimed from the hostile powers that have usurped his domination. It was therefore primarily concerned with bringing those who did not know Jesus to know him.

One could say that the WCC was born in the death throes of "Christendom." The parent Life and Work and Faith and Order movements were dealing with people who were already Christians. But these Christians were slaughtering each other in bloody wars. They had failed to address the monstrous evils of their own societies. They were fragments and unable to speak and act together. Both parent movements, in their different ways, were movements for the reformation of the churches of the Western world. The churches of Asia and Africa were hardly present in their minds. They were not chiefly concerned with the question that was for the IMC the primary question: "How do people who are not Christians become Christians?" Evangelism was marginal. Even though many of the same people were involved in these movements and in the missionary movement, the fundamental thrusts were different.

The original basis of both movements was in the large churches of western Europe and North America, the bodies that we used to call "main-line" churches. These bodies have been in decline for most of this century, and the decline is now accelerating in North America, where they used to be strongest. Meanwhile there has been a rapid growth of conservative evangelical movements, sometimes embodied in large, wealthy, and powerful organizations (typically in North America) but also in a proliferation of small independent local groups gathered around charismatic leaders. The original base of the IMC/WCC has shrunk dramatically.

Meanwhile the whole *oikoumene,* the whole inhabited earth, has become locked together into a single economic-financial-technical unit in a way that would have been scarcely conceivable in 1910 or even in 1948. Until the recent collapse of the "command economies" of eastern Europe, this single economic-financial complex could only claim part of the world (euphemistically "the free world"). Now there seems nothing to prevent it from becoming global. With the new developments in information technology, the whole financial-economic system takes on more and more the aspect of an impersonal entity that human intentions may wreck but cannot control or direct. Peoples who have for millenia organized their lives on the basis of different beliefs are inexorably sucked into the operation of this global economic complex by a process known as "development." Resistance is usually ineffective.

The human aspect of this is the development of beliefs, attitudes, and skills that together enable people to enter into the process of "modernization." Modernization is the displacement of ancient cultures by the particular kind of human culture that has developed in Europe and its cultural offshoots in the course of the past three hundred years. Missionaries were among its earliest carriers. It has its deep roots in the old Christendom. Its birth and growth would have been impossible in any other milieu. But in its full development it has a unique power to disintegrate and dissolve ancient belief systems, including the belief system from which it originally sprang. Lippmann's often-quoted phrase "the acids of modernity" makes the point. Modernization is primarily an affair of the cities, which are also the centers of power. Rural areas remain more rooted in traditional culture. Perhaps the fundamental divide in our world is not between east and west, or between north and south, but between the city and the village.

While the old Christendom has been in decline, new and powerful centers of Christian culture have developed in other parts of the world. To an astonishing extent the call for "the evangelization of the world in this generation" has been honored — if not in one generation, at least in one century. The vigorous missionary outreach is now mainly from the churches of the "third world." Not only is the rapid growth of the churches in many areas the result of the evangelistic outreach of the local churches, but in the field of international and cross-cultural mission new and powerful thrusts are coming from such burgeoning churches as those of Korea. But in contrast, it is now typical to find in the old main-line churches an acute embarrassment about missions, partly the result of guilt about the wrongs of colonialism, partly a fundamental loss of nerve that manifests itself in all aspects of Western culture outside of its science and technology. The traditional main-line missionary societies are now mainly agencies of interchurch aid. The vast new missionary challenge — namely, that presented by modernization, is one that they find it hard to respond to because they are part of it.

Toward a Missionary Encounter with Modernity

How is the WCC to respond to these vast changes from the days of its conception and birth? How is it to represent, to focus, to inspire the witness of the universal Church to this new global situation? The great danger that faces an organization like the WCC is what the first general secretary of the British Council of Churches, Archie Craig, called "omnipotent mediocrity," the danger of trying to respond to every issue at the expense of decisive leadership on the crucial issues. What are the crucial issues for the WCC as we look forward to the third millennium of the Church's story?

The WCC's basis commits the member churches to seek to "fulfill their common calling" to the glory of the Triune God. That calling is to continue the mission of Jesus, according to his word: "As the Father sent me, so I send you." The WCC has to be a focus and inspiration of world mission. It must have at the heart of its life the passion that those who do not know Jesus as Savior and Lord may come to know him and to serve him. There are two things that I do *not* mean by saying this. I do not mean that evangelism should be treated as a priority in distinction from all those actions through which the Church has to embody the wrathful love of God in afflicting the comfortable and comforting the afflicted. The mission of Jesus was not only a verbal proclamation of good news but also the embodiment of good news in a life and death that were God's sovereign rule in action. The mission of the Church, modeled after that of Jesus, has to be both word and deed, the life of a community that already embodies a foretaste of God's Kingdom. Second, I do not mean giving primacy to what are called "unreached peoples," although that is also a proper and necessary part of the Church's mission. I am thinking more of those who have already been all too effectively reached by the forces of modernization, who are being locked into the global system that dominates the life of the world. I am asking that the WCC should be and should be seen to be an enabler of the Church's universal mission to make Christ known, loved, and obeyed throughout this entire global city of which we are all a part. And I am asking the WCC to recognize that it is not enough to address the *symptoms* of modernization — we have to address the causes, the underlying belief systems that sustain it. We need a theological clarification of the issues involved in a global missionary encounter with modernity.

As modernity extends its hold over all peoples, locking them more and more tightly into a single global economic-financial complex, two consequences are so obvious and so universal that they shout for attention. One is the polarization of the world into a rich part that grows richer and a poor part that grows poorer. This polarization takes place both within nations and between nations. It seems to be an intrinsic element in the development of the type of economic and financial system that has become global. The other consequence of the system is the destruction of the environment. It is now widely recognized that if "development" should advance to the point where all peoples shared the lifestyle of the most affluent, the planet would quickly become uninhabitable. It seems natural that these two issues, the issue of justice for the poor and the issue of responsibility for the environment, should be seen as the most urgent issues facing an organization that takes the whole world for its concern. It is not difficult to convince thinking people that these are the urgent issues, though it is more difficult to move them to action about them.

The danger, however, is that we attend to the visible phenomena and not to the less visible realities that underlie them. The culture that developed in western Europe from the eighteenth century onwards, and that now — under the name of modernization — is becoming the global culture that dominates the centers of power throughout the world, has within it a body of beliefs that shape and sustain its outward forms. It is this body of beliefs that has to be addressed as an essential part (not the whole) of the Church's response. But it is very difficult to address it for two reasons. One is that modernity pretends to have no creed. It pretends to stand for an "open" society in which all creeds are tolerated. It applies to itself the adjective *secular,* with the implication that it is neutral in respect to beliefs that come under the name "religion." In this way it conceals from its adherents the fact that it is itself based on a particular view of the human situation, a view that is open to question. It claims to be ready to question every dogma, but it reveals its own dogmatic basis when it is faced by a firm affirmation of another belief. The adjective *fundamentalist* is available to dismiss any confident affirmation of transcendent truth. At the heart of modernity is the assertion that human reason, apart from divine revelation, is capable of finding the truth and coping with the world. The contrary affirmation, namely that God has in fact revealed his nature and purpose, is tolerated as a private opinion, but not if it is offered as public truth to govern the public worlds of education, politics, business, culture.

The second reason it is difficult for the Church to face modernity is that the creed for modernity has made such deep inroads into the life and faith of the churches in the Western world where it had its origin. Those of us who, like the present writer, have been shaped from childhood by the assumptions of modernity have tended to adjust our Christian believing to the supposed requirements of modern thought rather than subjecting modernity to radical and skeptical questioning from the point of view of the gospel. And we have been eager to share our findings with the churches that live in more ancient and stable cultures. The result is that much of the leadership of the worldwide Church shares this syncretistic relationship to the creed of modernity. Two different creeds compete within us, and there is need for a very different and sometimes painful effort to recognize and face the half-hidden *credo*.

The Calling to Seek Justice

In one important respect I think the global situation the WCC faces is going to change drastically. During most of the present century the main global alternative to Christianity has been Marxism. Marxism seemed to offer a practical, this-worldly, hope of bringing into being the just society that Christians prayed for but seemed powerless to produce. Marxism was, like capitalism, a product of the European Enlightenment, and it claimed to be able to bring down to earth what

Christians looked for in heaven. The claim has proved false, as it was bound to do, but the claim of free-market capitalism to produce a free society is equally false. I think that in the twenty-first century the main global alternative to Christianity will be Islam. Islam is now, with a renewed confidence and with great material resources, making a global claim to offer a kind of society in which God is affirmed as sovereign and all human life, public and personal, is ruled by revealed law. This claim comes into head-on collision with the claim of modernity to provide an open society in which all creeds are tolerated but none except its own is allowed into the public domain. Islam will not accept relegation to the private sector as Christianity has — in many societies — so tamely done. Islam, like Marxism, seeks to identify ultimate truth with actual political power. The union of truth with power lies beyond death, and in that sense Christianity has to be otherworldly. The City of God cannot be built by human hands on earth — it is a gift from heaven. But the Muslim challenge will compel Christians to question the privatization of their faith and to challenge also the idea that public life is an arena from which the truth claims of the gospel are excluded.

I am not here talking about what are called "Christian values." "Values" are merely what some people choose, unless they are based in some reality that is independent of people's personal wishes. When a society begins to talk about values, this is probably a sign of approaching death. Values have no substance unless they are rooted in some reality, something that exists apart from the personal preferences of individuals. I am talking about the truth claims of the Christian gospel, about the affirmations that the Church must make about God, human life, and the created world, affirmations that are at present excluded from public doctrine in "modern" societies.

Christian involvement in issues of justice for the poor has been considerably influenced by Marxism. This influence is likely to decrease. There will be a new urgency in clarifying the Christian belief about the possibilities and the limits of human well-being on this side of death, about the relation between God's justification and human justice, and about the role of the local eucharistic community in every place as a foretaste and sign of God's justice, as well as an instrument of that justice. Marxism has not been able to deliver what it promised — a human society that overcame the evils of capitalism and created justice and freedom on earth. Capitalism has not delivered such a society. Adam Smith himself was clear that free markets would not work except in the presence of a certain moral framework, and when modern capitalism began to develop in the Western world in the eighteenth and nineteenth centuries, it very quickly became clear that free markets could not ensure a minimum of humane treatment for workers. The market had to be controlled in the interests of human good. The market is the best means available for continuously balancing supply and demand, but it cannot be the ultimate over human life. Everything depends upon the fundamental beliefs about human nature and destiny that permeate the society in which the market operates. There will always be a need for controls of the market. We certainly cannot seek the kind of theocratic society that Islam represents. But we can and must affirm that every local eucharistic community where we celebrate the acts through which we are enabled to participate in God's justice and God's mercy is a center from which we can radiate the kind of human behavior in which markets can operate for the common good. They can be places where people are delivered from the ideology of capitalism and can make markets human. To *multiply* such centers throughout the world must surely be the first priority for a world council of churches. In other words, the question "How can modern people be enabled to know Jesus and put their trust in him?" must become the very central issue on the agenda of the council.

The Calling to Care for Creation

In respect of the other great global issue — namely, the threat to our human environment — there has been no major alternative to Christianity because the issue has only come into full consciousness recently. Neither capitalism nor Marxism has shown any capacity or inclination to deal with it. A purely secular ethics, with no transcendental reference, finds it hard to give any valid reason for curbing our own desires for the sake of remote descendants who have no power to exert sanctions on us as our contemporaries do. Moreover, the natural science we depend on for our public doctrine assures us that the universe we live in is on a descending path to total entropy from which nothing can save it, as our own bodies are on a similar path to decay. If the human race is going to perish anyway, why not sooner rather than later? Where can the motive come from for caring for the planet?

It cannot come only from nostalgia for a lost security in the womb of nature. It is understandable that modern people feel this nostalgia. We have treated the natural world as something at our disposal. We have forced it to answer our questions and used the answers to manipulate nature in accordance with our whims. We have therefore become alienated from nature, and we feel the pangs of bereavement when we see "primitive" peoples who have escaped modernization. So it is understandable that there are New Age movements that invite us to turn back and become again part of nature, seeking to unite ourselves again with the cosmic forces in ways that bypass our arrogant rationality. Astrology and transcendental meditation become big industries, and long-forgotten pagan rites are celebrated again in Europe. But the New Age is a very ancient blind alley. Nature is not a source of ethics. There is no right and wrong in nature. Its governing realities are power and fertility. To make nature our ultimate is to be delivered to death. Nature's smile can be charming, but her teeth are cruel.

Why should we care for the planet if it is doomed in the end to decay and death? The answer must be because it is the planet that God has created to be cherished and husbanded by his human family as the theater of his glory; because God delights in it and has created human beings to share his delight; because in his incarnate Son Jesus Christ he has taken created nature upon himself to fulfill and glorify it; and because in the bodily resurrection of Jesus from the dead he has given us the pledge and proof of his purpose to bring a new creation out of the death and decay of the old. It is hard to see what other ground there can be for a real commitment to care for the created world even when this means the giving up of present advantage. We have little experience to help us here, for the ecological crisis is a new one. Until recently there seemed to be ample room on the surface of our planet for all its inhabitants, and room to dispose of all our waste. It is only now, in this generation, that we are forced to ask the question, "Why should I put the care of the creation above my own present advantage?" The answer to that question has to be so based in reality that it can halt the accelerating rush of modernity to carry to the limit the human power to exploit the natural world.

Conclusion

I have taken these two issues, justice for the poor and care for the creation, as the two most obvious issues thrown up by the global spread of the process of modernization. Modernization submerges ancient cultures and sweeps more and more people into a single process. The role of the Church must not be to simply address and seek to alleviate the symptoms — although it must certainly do this. But, more fundamentally, the Church has to bear witness to the truth that unmasks the illusions and falsehoods of modernity. And the WCC, leading and focusing this witness of the churches, must take this as its central task. Centrally, basically, primarily, the WCC must stand for the worldwide communication of the Good News of the human situation as it is embodied in Christ. It must be, and be seen to be, a leader for the churches in their global mission. This does not now mean primarily the kind of cross-cultural mission for which the IMC was the enabling agency. It must be the enabler and inspirer of the local eucharistic communities in every part of the globe to bear faithful witness to the truth as it is in Jesus.

For this to happen, there has to be a great effort of theological clarification to help all the churches to see what this mission involves. The present work of Faith and Order on clarifying the one faith that we confess is very important. And the WCC has one great resource that the IMC never had — the presence of the Orthodox. The modernity that now dominates the world had its origins in Western Christianity and largely in the Protestant part of it. It seems to me that the radical individualism that is so central to modernity has something to do with the fact that Western Christianity has not taken the doctrine of the Trinity as seriously as Orthodoxy has done. If the ultimate source of all being is the communion of three persons in one God, then human society cannot be what modernity conceives it to be. Now that the pressure of Marxism on the greatest of the Orthodox churches has been (to some extent) lifted, I hope that the missionary thinking and action of the WCC will gain new strength and coherence from the Orthodox witness.

There are a thousand issues that a world council of churches could legitimately take up, and hundreds that the WCC is pressed to take up. But there must be a focus. For the WCC as it looks beyond the seventh assembly and into the next century, I would plead that the focus must be this: to help the whole Church to bring the whole gospel to the whole world by helping each local eucharistic community to be faithful to that gospel.

17

Learning to Live in the Spirit in Our European Home

The year 1992 is the year of the Single European Market. But our hope for Europe, surely, is that it should not be just a marketplace. It must be a home. And it will not be a home unless it rediscovers what made it a spiritual and cultural reality — namely the Christian gospel. Without Christianity, Europe is merely a peninsula of Asia. How can we learn to live together in the power of the Spirit who is the Spirit of the Father and the Spirit of Jesus? It is very difficult.

We can get help from those who have experiences of other cultures. I listened recently to a cultural anthropologist who has worked mainly in India, but who has now turned his attention to our modern Western culture. He identified the unique character of this culture as follows: in "modern" Western culture the world is seen as divided into a public realm of "facts" that everybody "knows" and a private world of "values" that people may or may not believe in. The English writer C. P. Snow has written a book entitled *The Two Cultures* that expresses the same point. The division is visible on the campus of the university in the division between the science faculty and the faculties of arts and humanities. In the former we deal with "facts,"

Congress of the Arbeitsgemeinschaft Missionarischer Arbeit, EKD, Hannover 1992.

about which you can be right or wrong. Here everyone is expected to agree about the "facts"; they are not matters for personal opinion. In the other half of the campus it is different. I cannot tell you that your "values" are wrong; you are free to choose what values appeal to you.

This way of relating belief to knowledge operated in European thought through four hundred, perhaps seven hundred, years until it was challenged at that great intellectual turning point when the work of Aristotle became available in Latin. It is important to remember that Aristotle came into European thought through the work of Muslim theologians and philosophers. In the great ferment of thought that this set in motion, it fell to St. Thomas Aquinas to reformulate Christian teaching in the light of this new way of thinking. The result was a completely different way of relating faith and knowledge from that of Augustine. In the great work of St. Thomas we find in Book I rational proofs of the existence of God. Here is knowledge that is accessible to reason without the aid of faith or revelation. In Book IV we learn of those things that cannot be known by reason alone but that depend on faith — the Incarnation, the Trinity, the Atonement. This dichotomy between what are matters of knowledge and what are matters of faith has remained with Europe ever since and is (as we all know) operative today.

But the "knowledge" is insecure. Skeptical arguments can be mounted against the "proofs" for the existence of God. Moreover, with hindsight, we can see that the "God" whose existence was proved was not the Blessed Trinity. In fact this "God" looks remarkably like a synthesis of the Prime Mover of Aristotle with the Allah of the Qur'an. Why is it that when you say the word "God" in the ears of an average western European, he immediately thinks *not* of the Blessed Trinity but of a solitary monad only vaguely related to the name of Jesus?

I want to suggest that in our concern to communicate the gospel to our European home, we can regard the postmodernists as allies up to a certain point. It is the simple truth that all human beliefs about the world are rooted in particular histories. Human thought is not disembodied; it is part of human history. All of it is historically and culturally conditioned. There is no supracultural truth. But this does *not* mean that there is no such thing as truth. It does not mean that we abandon the claim to know the truth. Among all the stories that human beings tell about themselves and the world, there *could* be a true story. No logic requires us to deny this possibility. And this, of course, is what the Christian Church confesses. We believe and confess that there is a true story that gives the clue to the meaning of the whole human and cosmic story, because God has chosen a people to be the bearer of the meaning of the whole story. This is the story the Bible tells, with its center in the incarnation, ministry, death, and resurrection of Jesus Christ. Our task is to tell this story. To tell the story and live by the story is what it means to be the Christian Church.

But before I go on to develop the implications of this, we must pause to look at one problem. It is the deep division that exists among us about the authority of the Bible. I refer to the division between those who label each other as "fundamentalist" and "liberal." If you have followed my argument so far, you will readily see that this split is simply a surface manifestation of the deeper split in our culture between what we call "facts" and what we call "values." If the spectacles we wear (supplied freely to all through our educational system) cause us to see "facts" and "values" as two quite different things, then we shall ask, "Is the Bible a book of facts or a book about values?" It must be either one or the other. And so we have on the one hand those who treat the Bible as a book of certain and indisputable facts such as we imagine a textbook of physics to be. There is no room for human subjectivity, no room for the influence of human culture, no room for the human subject. And we have on the other hand those who see the Bible as part of the history of religious experience. It is all subjective. Human religious experience is infinitely various, and the Bible can only represent a very small sample of this vast variety. Parts of it may be "meaningful" for me; I can neglect the rest.

What both these points of view have in common is that they relieve me of personal responsibility. The true understanding of the Bible is that it tells the story of which my life is a part, the story of God's tireless, loving, wrathful, inexhaustible patience with the human family, and of our unbelief, blindness, disobedience. To accept this story as the truth of the human story (and so of my story) commits

203

me personally to a life of discernment and obedience in the new circumstances of each day. When I accept this as the true story and begin to live within the story that the Bible tells as my own story, then the Bible becomes the spectacles through which I see the world. I do not examine the Bible through the spectacles provided by our "modern" culture; I begin to see the world (the "modern" world) through the spectacles that the Bible provides.

Of course we live among people who tell other stories — the story of "civilization," with Columbus as a hero; the Marxist story; the Muslim story. We are all in the midst of the story and none of us has seen the end. Till then, we walk by faith, not by "indubitable knowledge." There is no other way for human beings to walk. We have no superior standpoint from which we could demonstrate that ours is the true story. But we can point to one feature of our story that is unique. All the other stories look to an end within history. They look to the intrahistorical triumph of their cause. They are therefore inherently imperialist. The Church has sometimes acted in precisely that imperialistic way, but that is to betray her gospel. What is unique about the Christian story is that its crucial turning point is the event of Calvary and Easter, when we learn that the triumph of God is an event beyond history that gives meaning to all history. This means that we can always be at the same time realistic and hopeful. We can face, as Amos and Jeremiah did, the most shattering disaster for the visible cause of God, and yet continue to act in confident hope because we know that the real victory has already been won.

Of course the story will always be treated with skepticism and disbelief. That has always been so. What can make it credible is the existence of communities of people, local congregations, who believe it, celebrate it, live by it, act on it in the world. And for that we need pastors who believe it, live by it, and allow the Bible to shape the way they see the world. And we need Christians who learn to see the world through the spectacles of the Bible. Here I would like to speak of my own experience. I more and more find the precious part of each day to be the thirty or forty minutes I spend each morning before breakfast with the Bible. All the rest of the day I am bombarded with the stories that the world is telling about itself. I am more and more skeptical about these stories. As I take time to immerse myself in the story that the Bible tells, my vision is cleared and I see things in another way. I see the day that lies ahead in its place in God's story. I can then go into the unpredictable happenings of the day knowing that I will not be lost. When Europe is filled with congregations of believing people who are learning to live by the true story, then Europe will indeed be not just a common market, but a common home.

Select Bibliography of Works by Lesslie Newbigin

Things Are Not Shaken: Glimpses of the Foreign Missions of the Church of Scotland in 1937. Unsigned. Edinburgh: Church of Scotland Foreign Mission Committee, 1938.

Living Epistles: Impressions of the Foreign Mission Work of the Church of Scotland in 1938. Unsigned. Edinburgh: Church of Scotland Foreign Mission Committee, 1939.

"The Kingdom of God and the Idea of Progress." Unpublished notes of four lectures given at the United Theological College, Bangalore. 1941.

"The Ordained Foreign Missionary in the Indian Church." *International Review of Missions (IRM)* 34 (1946):86–94.

The Reunion of the Church: A Defence of the South India Scheme. London: SCM Press, 1948. Republished in revised form 1960.

A South India Diary. London: SCM Press, 1951. Second revised edition 1960. Also published as *That All May Be One. A South Indian Diary: The Story of an Experiment in a Christian Unity.* New York: Association Press, 1952. Also published in Danish in 1953.

"The Christian Hope." In *Missions under the Cross: Addresses Delivered at the Enlarged Meeting of the International Missionary Council in Willingen, FRG, 1952,* edited by Norman Goodall. London: EHP, 1953.

The Household of God: Lectures on the Nature of the Church. London: SCM Press, 1953. Revised version 1964. American edition, New York: Friendship Press, 1954.

"The Present Christ and the Coming Christ." *Ecumenical Review* 16 (1954):118–123.

Sin and Salvation. London: SCM Press, 1956. CLS special edition, translated from the original Tamil.

"The Missionary Dimension of the Ecumenical Movement." *Ecumenical Review* 14 (1962):207–215. Reprinted in the *IRM* 70 (1981).

"Report of the Division of the World Mission and Evangelism to the Central Committee." *Ecumenical Review* 15 (1962):88–94.

The Relevance of Trinitarian Doctrine for Today's Mission. Commission on World Mission and Evangelism study pamphlet, London: EHP, 1963. American edition entitled *Trinitarian Faith and Today's Mission.* Richmond, Va.: John Knox Press, n.d.

Honest Religion for Secular Man. London: SCM Press and Philadelphia: Westminster Press, 1966. Published in Italian in 1968.

Christ Our Eternal Contemporary. Meditations given at CMC, Vellore, in July 1966. Madras: CLS, 1968.

The Finality of Christ. London: SCM Press and Richmond, Va.: John Knox Press, 1969.

"Which Way for Faith and Order?" In *What Unity Implies: Six Essays after Uppsala,* edited by Reinhard Groscurth. Geneva: World Council of Churches, 1969.

"Mission to Six Continents." In *The Ecumenical Advance: A History of the Ecumenical Movement,* vol. 2, *1948–68,* edited by Harold E. Fey. London: SPCK, 1970.

Journey into Joy. Addresses given at CMC, Vellore, April 1971. Madras: CLS, 1972. Republished, Grand Rapids, Mich.: Eerdmans, 1973.

The Good Shepherd: Meditations on Christian Ministry in Today's World. Madras: CLS, 1974. Republished in revised form in Leighton Buzzard: The Faith Press, 1977.

"What Is a Local Church, Truly United?" *Ecumenical Review* 29 (1977): 115–128.

The Open Secret: Sketches for a Missionary Theology. London: SPCK and Grand Rapids, Mich.: Eerdmans, 1978.

The Light Has Come: An Exposition of the Fourth Gospel. Grand Rapids, Mich.: Eerdmans, 1982.

The Other Side of 1984: Questions for the Churches. Geneva: World Council of Churches, 1983. Also in Dutch.

Unfinished Agenda. London: SPCK, 1985. (Autobiography)

Foolishness to the Greeks: The Gospel and Western Culture. London: SPCK and Grand Rapids, Mich.: Eerdmans, 1986.

The theological section of "Faith in the City of Birmingham. The Report of the Bishop of Birmingham's Commission." 1988.

"A Sermon Preached at the Thanksgiving Service for the Fiftieth Anniversary of the Tambaram Conference of the International Missionary Council." *IRM* 87 (July 1988).

The Gospel in a World of Religious Pluralism. London: SPCK, 1989.

Truth to Tell: The Gospel as Public Truth. London: SPCK, 1992.

Unfinished Agenda. Second edition. Edinburgh: St. Andrew Press, 1993.